American
GREATNESS

American
GREATNESS

HOW CONSERVATISM INC. MISSED *the* 2016 ELECTION
& WHAT *the* D.C. ESTABLISHMENT NEEDS *to* LEARN

CHRIS BUSKIRK
& SETH LEIBSOHN

WND Books

American Greatness

Published by WND Books, Washington, DC, WND Books is a registered trademark of WorldNetDaily.com, Inc. ("WND")

Book designed by Mark Karis

WND Books are available at special discounts for bulk purchases. WND Books also publishes books in electronic formats. For more information call (541) 474-1776, e-mail orders@wndbooks.com or visit www.wndbooks.com.

Hardcover ISBN: 978-1-944229-84-9
eBook ISBN: 978-1-944229-85-6

Library of Congress Cataloging-in-Publication Data Available Upon Request

Printed in the United States of America

17 18 19 20 21 22 LBM 9 8 7 6 5 4 3 2 1

For Gina and Sallie,
who make everything better.
First, last, and always.

Contents

Foreword

EIGHT YEARS OF A DEMOCRATIC PARTY WHITE HOUSE was eight years of Republican political sufferance. And a lot of Independents suffered, too. To say the Republican Party was resolute to recover the White House in 2016 would be an understatement. But it also engaged in overstatements, or overthinking: it had convinced itself it had one of the most talented benches in its modern history, just the right mix of candidates to vie for and select the one candidate best poised and talented to win the 2016 election.

For years, we had attended conferences, listened to speeches, watched Sunday morning shows with these Republicans of great promise, great spirit, great talent. One day an attendee at a conservative conference might hear a speech by Bobby Jindal and say "That's our guy for 2016." Another person might have heard Chris Christie and said "He's the only one with the fight to take it to the Democrats." Another: "Listen to how thoughtful and intellectual Jeb is, just what we need to show the country who we really are." Scott Walker was a hero not just to reform-minded governors but a national audience, especially for taking on the unions and prevailing like few others. Others would email around the speeches of a Marco Rubio or Ted Cruz, impressed by their verbal abilities and (depending on one's worldview) "purity."

They all ran for the presidency—as did others. There was the more libertarian Rand Paul, the highly impressive and unflappable Carly Fiorina, and the rock-solid Rick Santorum. Ohio's John Kasich entered the race, as did Mike Huckabee and, also, famous surgeon Ben Carson. But the one person who almost nobody thought could win, the one who had spoken at few Republican or conservative events over the past several years—or anytime, really—was a man known by many to hold some fairly liberal views and have little political acumen. He had never run a race before—ever. He had changed many of his positions over short periods of time. He seemed to have a thin skin when criticized. He was, by any account, the last person an expert would think of as a good candidate to run for the presidency of the United States as a Republican. But all the others lost to him, and lost big.

The American people and the voters in the Republican primaries wanted something else, something different from what the experts thought, something different from what the standard Republican thinking had been: strong on social issues, strong on national defense, strong on economic liberty and tax policy. Donald J. Trump was none of those things—or was he? What language was he speaking that the voters heard and the experts and other candidates did not? Was 2016 merely about illegal immigration? If so, several of the above-mentioned candidates were just as tough on it as Trump. Was it about the Supreme Court? Few doubted anyone would take the courts more seriously than Ted Cruz. Was it about the economy or health care? Who knew more about those issues than the others?

No, something else was at play. For years, conservative think tanks had engaged, as well as a few prominent Republican candidates, in what had been criticized as "the culture wars." Those "wars" were about a lot of different things, but one thing Republicans had learned to shy away from, or been instructed by the experts to shy away from, was talk about the culture: the way we live, the way we organize our families, our entertainment, our education systems; the way we talk about race and crime. And yet, somewhere along the way conservative activist Andrew Breitbart had seized on something former Senator Daniel Patrick Moynihan had said years before. And the voting base loved it.

Senator Moynihan had once pointed out, "The central conservative truth is that it is culture, not politics, that determines the success of a society."[1] Andrew Breitbart created a political and news site, Breitbart.com, on a version of that: "Politics is downstream from culture." And at the end of the day, or the end of the 2016 primary election season, it had become clear: a man more familiar with the culture than perhaps anyone in the country—a reality television star and creator, a marketer of lifestyles, a hotel builder, a casino owner—was someone who knew better than any political expert just what it was that moved people and what bothered them, what they liked and what they disliked. He, the political novice but cultural avatar, would become not only the standard bearer for the Republican Party, but the forty-fifth President of the United States.

Few analysts or experts saw this coming or saw it as even remotely possible. Most thought it impossible—first for Trump to win the primaries, and certainly for him to win in a general election against the strongest political machine and family the Democrats had ever had. Some saw it coming, though. They may not have been experts but they may very well have been the people the experts forgot about: voters. And a few others saw the possibility as well, most of them radio talk show hosts. Why them? Well, for the most part they were conservative but, more importantly, day in and day out they listen to people, they take calls and emails: lots of them. From where? The base.

And what is that base? They are truckers who drive across the country and listen to a lot of other experts on satellite and other talk radio stations. They are ranchers and farmers and nurses and doctors and small business owners and accountants and electricians—and some of them are the recently unemployed, too. They are the single best polling population in the country. They are the country. And they are the voters. And while cable and network news certainly talks to or at them, or some of them, it does not listen to them and actually interact with them every day. And neither do highly paid political consultants and pollsters. Easy test: how many holding this book can say they have ever even talked to a pollster?

A few of us did see the Trump possibility of victory, even in the dark days when Hillary Clinton was "winning" by double digits. On the national level, we were the hopeful few, but only few. Our group included mostly national radio talk show hosts, hosts like Sean Hannity, Laura Ingraham, and Mike Gallagher—and a few others at more local levels. Two of them are my friends and, in one case, former employee, Chris Buskirk and Seth Leibsohn. They unreservedly said Trump would win, and long before the primaries were wrapped up and before the Republican convention in Ohio. This is a book about what they saw and what we saw. But more important, this is a book about what the Republican primary voters and general electorate saw and heard when they saw and heard the now forty-fifth President of the United States: Donald J. Trump. While many Democrats, and not a few Republican consultants, are still scratching their heads, it is safe to say that to some of us at least, the coming Trump presidency was no surprise. This explains why.

—WILLIAM J. BENNETT

Acknowledgments

We could not have written or completed this book without the help and support of several friends and colleagues. In particular, we thank Jim Ryan and William Bennett for their early encouragement and always smart thoughts. Radio host Mike Gallagher deserves a special place in our—and America's—heart, for his heart and head and support over the course of his career but especially, for us, the past election cycle and since. Our colleagues at American Greatness Julie Ponzi and Ben Boychuk have been especially, well, special. Charles Kesler and Tevi Troy, thank you always for thinking through various thoughts and theses. Michael Anton, who put up with so much but did so much, is owed more than we can ever say. Jim and Sandy Buskirk and Marian Leibsohn thank you always for everything. Steve Twist, Debbie Moak, and Steve Moak are counselors and friends anybody would be fortunate to have, and we are honored they are ours. Finally, our team at WND, especially Geoffrey Stone and Michael Thompson, thank you!

1

THE AGONY OF VICTORY

HOW ALL THE "EXPERTS" GOT THE ELECTION WRONG

NO ONE WAS MORE SURPRISED BY DONALD TRUMP'S WIN than the experts. Watching CNN's coverage was an exercise in schadenfreude, the likes of which one is unlikely to know more than once in a lifetime. It was delicious for Trump supporters—all the people who who went to his rallies, who endured the naysayers and detractors in the media, and who eventually voted for him. And yet it was still supremely frustrating.

Where had these media experts been? How did they miss a national phenomenon of this magnitude? It was the equivalent of The Weather Channel missing Hurricane Katrina—but not just failing to see Katrina bearing down as the skies grew dark, the winds picked up, and the rain started to fall, but forecasting sunny skies and telling viewers to fire up the barbecues and enjoy a day at the beach.

They didn't see his primary victory coming despite the fact that

Donald Trump took the lead in the polls in August of 2015 and except for one blip in October never relinquished it. They didn't see Donald Trump beating Hillary Clinton despite the energy of his supporters or the size and number of his rallies. They didn't take into account the social media metrics that suggested that Donald Trump's support was broad, deep, and, above all, energized.

They didn't see the Trump tsunami coming because they didn't want to see it coming. Because they were conditioned and incentivized not to see it coming. Stephen K. Bannon, President Trump's chief strategist, put it this way in an interview with the *New York Times* less than a week after the inauguration: "The media here is the opposition party. They don't understand this country." He's right. Never has the disconnect between the elite media, comprised of the mainstream and legacy conservative media on the one side, and rank and file voters all around the country on the other, been more pronounced or more visible than during the 2016 election.

Something going on in America completely escaped the notice of the best and brightest who congregate in Washington, D.C., in Manhattan, and at conferences, cruises, and retreats with high-brow titles. Did they miss it intentionally or has the country's ruling class really grown so far apart from the country class it purports to rule? And, either way, how do you miss something so big in the face of such overwhelming evidence?

He who has ears to hear, let him hear.

It was the same on all of the television networks. Commentators projected a tangible sense that something totally unexpected and incomprehensibly foreign was happening. Wolf Blitzer would have found the scene easier to understand if aliens had landed and demanded that he take them to his leader. At least he would have been prepared for that by seeing movies like *Independence Day*. His only conundrum would have been which leader he take his new alien overlords to see: John Podesta, Robbie Mook, or directly to Herself: Hillary Clinton. But a Trump victory and the concomitant prospect of a Trump presidency? The elite mind boggled at the very notion. All around the country, Trump voters watching the elite media melt down on live television and on social media—at least those who were not dizzy with euphoria—thought to themselves, *This is what a nervous breakdown looks like*. And that added to the victory. Donald Trump had challenged the media, he'd called them out, he'd prodded and provoked them to the point of simultaneous hysteria and dread, and he'd won and won big.

The scene of palpable shock wasn't limited to CNN—it played out on every major media platform regardless of political orientation. MSNBC's Rachel Maddow was no more shocked or appalled than the *Weekly Standard*'s Bill Kristol or *National Review*'s Jonah Goldberg. And that is one of the most interesting aspects of the total systemic failure of the media-political-intellectual establishment that is focused on politics: It was not overtly ideological; the fault line did not appear along the usual Right-Left divide, at least not in the way we have understood it in this country for the last generation or so.

When was the last time that conservative journals like *National Review* and the *Weekly Standard* were in substantial agreement with the bastions of the Progressive Left like the *New Republic*, *Mother Jones*, and the *American Prospect* in a presidential election? The answer, of course, is never. Not once. That they should unite in 2016 tells us something about the current state of the country, our elites, and our politics.

Much the same could be said of the scholars who inhabit the think-tank universe. There were a few notable exceptions, but by and large the intellectuals aligned with the roughly conservative American Enterprise Institute and the libertarian Cato Institute were no more enthusiastic about Donald Trump's candidacy than their leftist neighbors at the Center for American Progress.

John Bolton, former U.S. ambassador to the United Nations, was a notable exception. He is a senior fellow of the American Enterprise Institute and was a Trump campaign advisor. But other than him, AEI's list of scholars and fellows was notable for the stridency of its anti-Trump beliefs. Their anti/never Trump cadre included the following:

Jonah Goldberg, a senior fellow of AEI, expressed a certain preference for Hillary Clinton when he wrote that America can't survive a Trump presidency, saying, "America can survive four years of Hillary Clinton, it can't survive a political system divided by Sanders-style socialists and Trump-style nationalists."[1]

James Pethokoukis took to writing anti-Trump hit pieces for left-wing outlets like *Vox*. Publius Decius Mus, the anonymous and probably the most influential essayist of the 2016 election, eviscerated Pethokoukis' misguided "Conservative Case Against Trump" in an essay he wrote for *American Greatness* as follows:

> Whenever you find an article that begins with the title, "The Conservative Case" for or against something, lock your door, check your wallet, and grab your gun. You know what's coming is an unadulterated sell-out of everything "conservatism" purports to hold dear.
>
> The words directly following the ellipses usually denote some obviously non-conservative thing, like "a $5 trillion budget" or "transgender bathrooms" or "4-foot-11, 80-pound female Navy SEALS." Do any liberals ever write "a liberal case" for something obviously conservative, such as the traditional two-parent family or constitutional originalism?
>
> No, this self-sabotaging practice is unique to the American Right, which perhaps helps explain why it's in such disarray.[2]

AEI is also home to anti-Trump Republicans like Michael Rubin[3], Michael Auslin[4] and ex-Bush deputy defense secretary Paul Wolfowitz. You will recall Wolfowitz as the former whipping boy of the conspiracy-minded Left who was strenuously defended during and after his tenure at the Defense Department by rank and file Republicans, to whom he refused to return the favor by at least remaining silent during the election. Wolfowitz told *Politico* in August 2016 that Donald Trump is a security risk to the United States and that he is so concerned about Donald Trump that he "might have to vote for Hillary Clinton even though I have big reservations about her."[5] Got that? Even though Hillary Clinton is bad,

Donald Trump is undoubtedly worse. So says one of the architects of the Bush administration's failed nation-building policy in Iraq.

Another Bush administration veteran and AEI fellow, James Glassman, who was the undersecretary of state for public diplomacy, backed Hillary Clinton during the election saying that she was "by far the superior candidate."[6]

It's enough to makes one's head swim. If the Bushies and all of the Republicans who reported to Washington from Central Casting with their bow ties and horn-rimmed glasses backed Clinton and, like Glassman, thought she was the better candidate, what have Republicans and Democrats been arguing about for the past thirty years? The only reasonable explanation is that from the perspective of DC insiders the only real argument was about whose turn it was to be in charge.

But outside of the Beltway, regular Americans knew and loved America. And they had learned well the lessons taught by conservatives of prior generations: respect for the Declaration and the Constitution, love of the country and her people, a reasoned devotion to and understanding of the basic principles of self-government. It turned out that the average Republican voter in Warren, Michigan, understood constitutional government better than the average conservative intellectual in Washington, D.C., and valued it more highly.

But why shouldn't the writers and intellectuals confidently oppose Donald Trump for president? No one they knew voted for Donald Trump. Sure, maybe there was a rogue uncle back in Ohio (which Trump won by eight points despite the more or less active opposition of John Kasich, the state's Republican governor) but he was always a crank anyway. Certainly no one whose opinion mattered was voting for Trump—none of the smart people who do the hiring and firing in Washington, who book you on TV, publish your think-pieces, give you book contracts or think-tank fellowships. No, none of them would vote for Donald Trump.

In fact, no matter where the pundits and writers and talkers went, they found collegial unanimity. Whether it be in Washington, D.C.,

Manhattan, Santa Monica, San Francisco, or Chicago. Even in deep-red Texas all of their friends, colleagues, and remotest contacts in Austin agreed: Trump is awful and could never become president. And what the heck, Hillary ain't so bad. Just ask the small army of former Bush officials who publicly endorsed her. Sure, there's the corruption from Whitewater to the Clinton Foundation to Tenneo, and there are the massive policy failures (Hillarycare anyone? How about Benghazi, the Russian reset, or the retreat from Iraq?), but the D.C. insiders thought: "She's one of us. We know her. And most of all, *she's not him!*"

Where some portion of rank-and-file Republican voters made the commonsense decision to support Trump because, they reasoned, he had to be better than the noxious Hillary Clinton (hadn't Conservatism Inc. been preaching that sermon for twenty-five years?), those same conservative luminaries drew exactly the opposite conclusion. They were willing to see Hillary Clinton in the White House—and with her would come Bill, John Podesta, Donna Brazile, Huma Abedin, and the rest of the travelling carnival known as Clinton, Inc., in a package deal—rather than elect the overwhelming nominee of their own party.

Some of the conservative writers argued that they weren't *for* Hillary; they were just against Trump. Some of them decided not to vote, some voted for the unknown congressional apparatchik Evan McMullin, and some, we can be sure, secretly pulled the lever for Hillary. But writers aren't generally very good at math, so when presented with a binary choice (that means a choice between two outcomes, for the writers out there), they did the only thing they knew how to do: They wrote essays and blog posts and did television interviews arguing that what every rational person knew to be self-evidently true—that either Hillary Clinton or Donald Trump would be the next president—wasn't a binary choice at all. They asserted that by an act of sheer will (or petulance if you prefer), they could suspend the laws of statistics if only they could write enough huffy, virtue-signaling essays.

No, they told us, there were other possibilities that would deny either candidate the 270 electoral college votes necessary to win and would throw the election to the House of Representatives, like the election of 1800. In their dreams the Republican majority in the House would deny the White House to their own party's nominee and give it to the unknown Evan McMullin or Mitt Romney or Paul Ryan or whoever the smart guys decided was better than the standard bearer elected by the people.

National Review's Jonah Goldberg was so strident in his opposition to Donald Trump that he was ready to ignore the voters altogether and hope for salvation by an electoral college gone rogue. He wrote, "Personally, I wouldn't mind if the Electoral College rejected them both and just picked McMullin out of conscience."[7] Apparently an outright rejection of the will of the people—also known as the consent of the governed—is what passes for conscience within institutional conservatism these days. Remember, these are the same folks constantly appealing to their conservative principles as a basis for their rejection of Donald Trump. But it didn't take them long to get from opposing a candidate to advocating an anti-democratic and, yes, anti-republican putsch to deny the will of voters in favor of enlightened will of the few. Apparently, 2016 was the year that became part of "principled conservatism?"

Ultimately, all of their plots and plans were based on the same version of reality and the sort of grasp of basic mathematics that relies upon winning the lottery to pay the mortgage. But the anti-Trump schemers exposed more than the self-evident truth that liberal arts majors can't count very well. Most Americans, even those on the Left, have understood for a long time that the mainstream media is effectively an arm of the Democrat Party. What most people didn't know is that the legacy conservative media had gone native. This election exposed that unfortunate reality.

Sure, they learned their talking points from Buckley and their policy positions from Reagan, but it turns out they were just as dismissive of voters and just as out of touch with the country as the leftists and progressives they had railed against for so many years. The Buckley quotes and the superstitious invocations of the name of Reagan were just a cover for a movement whose intellectual standard bearers and media defenders had largely accepted the premises of the Progressive Left.

Just as surprising, we found out that they didn't know as much about historical American conservatism or the American founding as we thought. And because you can't love what you do not know, we found out that they were far less attached to either than was expected of a political and intellectual movement that wraps itself in the symbols and language of unapologetic patriotism. But when faced with a presidential candidate who spoke confidently about the American nation and people first they ran, then they resisted, and finally they rebelled.

When Donald Trump talked about the forgotten working class and criticized a post-American global elite more comfortable in Shanghai than Sandusky, he gave voice to many people who had given their allegiance to the Republican Party but who hadn't gotten much in return. Seeing high-brow Republicans and conservatives support Hillary Clinton, against whom they had so much to say over the years, was the final insult.

Candidate Trump also spoke to more than a few people who had supported Democrats for decades—especially in places like Pennsylvania, Michigan, and Wisconsin, states Republicans haven't won for years but that gave Donald Trump the presidency. This offended checklist conservatives who believed nothing more than "unions bad." It also offended the free-trade absolutists who believe that any multilateral agreement with the words "free trade" in the title (a) really produces the kind of idealized free trade they learned about reading Hayek and Schumpeter and Friedman when they did that fellowship back in college and (b) that such agreements are good for everybody "in the aggregate."

"In the aggregate" is the caveat tacked onto all of these debates about the benefits of trade agreements because it means you can't be held accountable if all the American workers get fired and their jobs get exported. As long as global GDP rises as a result of the deal, who cares how we get there. But back at home the American citizens who voted for the people signing off on these trade deals still cling obstinately to the backward notion that the American government should be negotiating trade deals with the specific objective of benefitting this country and its people, not just in the pursuit of some high-minded ideals.

This is not to say that Donald Trump or the people who voted for him are opposed to free trade. Rather, they are realistic about the way the world works. They understand better than the intellectuals who have fetishized free trade that in any deal negotiated between countries there will be give and take. They understand this because unlike the people negotiating the deals or writing scholarly essays advocating them it is they—the residents of middle America—who will pay the price for any bad deals. They are the people who can't afford to take into account the aggregate effect on global GDP; they have to contend with the disaggregated effect, that is, the real-world consequences.

America has been a trading nation since the founding, and the American people want to continue that tradition. It has served us well. They just want some confidence that their government is looking out for their specific interests, that their representatives are representing them and not just a disembodied idea. They want the American government to hold American citizenship in as high a regard as do most Americans. They've been promised a lot over the years and the results have been . . . mixed. Now they want some good faith assurance about the basics—that American government exists primarily for the benefit of American citizens.

And while the conservative grandees didn't—and don't—like Donald Trump's approach to trade, which places the interests of American workers and American prosperity above the interests and prosperity of our trading partners and above devotion to abstract ideas, the application of which is considerably more complicated in the real world than in the classroom. "Free trade" is a means not an end. Conservatives have conflated the two believing that anything labelled "free trade" is an end in itself. But free trade is good for the United States—or any country—only when it increases the prosperity of the nation and its citizens. Likewise, they have been bitterly opposed to, even offended by, his approach to citizenship. Donald Trump, like nearly all of the first forty American presidents (Jimmy Carter, as usual, being the lone exception), takes a high view of American citizenship grounded in a high view of America and the natural rights described in the Declaration, which the Constitution was created to protect for its citizens.

Likewise, until the second half of the twentieth century, America's presidents and the Congress largely believed that their power was bound by the Constitution and that the laws they enacted should be enforced. In the post–Cold War era both parties grew drunk on the notion that America was the sole global superpower. And whether or not they believed it explicitly, they acted like we had reached the end of history and America's wealth and power obligated her to devalue her own interests and act as the global enforcer of justice and good—a sort of real-life Justice League. The only problem is that history doesn't end, and our capacity for justice and good works abroad are predicated on our maintenance of liberty and constitutional government at home. And maintaining self-government over the long haul remains one of mankind's unsolved riddles.

Still, the elites of both parties, like trust-fund babies who had no hand in earning the wealth that made their lives so pleasant, agreed with a wink and a nod that America was rich enough, her freedom secure enough, and her goodness pure enough to do away with such antiquated notions as borders, culture, and citizenship. To listen to the media and to the saccharine pleas of our elected officials, America is obligated to take all comers no matter what because of a poem written by a nineteenth-century socialist. Unfortunately, the words of that poem are better known and treated with higher regard than the fundamental governing documents of this country. Many have heard the famous words inscribed on the base of the Statue of Liberty:

> *Give me your tired, your poor,*
>
> *Your huddled masses yearning to breathe free,*
>
> *The wretched refuse of your teeming shore.*
>
> *Send these, the homeless, tempest-tost to me,*
>
> *I lift my lamp beside the golden door!*

But how many recall this from the U.S. Constitution:

We the people of the United States, in order to form a more perfect union, establish justice, insure domestic tranquility, provide for the common defense, promote the general welfare, and secure the blessings of liberty to ourselves and our posterity, do ordain and establish this Constitution for the United States of America.

If you work in media or in government there is a good chance you are more influenced by the former than the latter. The good news is that for the average voter the opposite is true. Most Americans continue to value their citizenship. It is mostly elites who have so little regard for American citizenship and who have conspired to nullify the nation's immigration laws. These same people were traumatized by Donald Trump's promise to enforce the nation's laws and build a wall to protect our border, much as Mexico has done to protect her own southern border from illegal immigrants.

When Donald Trump adopted immigration as his signature issue in August 2015 it marked a profound split. It was the moment his campaign truly caught fire, and it saw him break away from the pack and never look back. It also marked the moment when Donald Trump became public enemy number one for the media and political elite. Nothing so marked the divide between the country class and the ruling class.

When Donald Trump said he wanted to Make America Great Again, ordinary Americans were thrilled. Those of a certain age heard strains of Reagan's Morning in America theme from the 1984 campaign. And those of every age heard something they hadn't heard in far too long—a candidate for president who was confident and proud of America but concerned that those charged with minding the store had neglected their duties. Trump's bold confidence and vision for a reinvigorated America was welcome balm after eight years of Obama's apology tours, bows, and hectoring lectures.

The voters who backed Donald Trump were tired of Obama's apology tours and Clinton's nuanced corruption. They were tired of

Republicans' lip service to voters. So they exulted when they heard Donald Trump say that he would Make America Great Again. They heard, "we're all in this together" and "we can make this country better than ever if we're willing to unite as Americans." They heard that American citizenship means something and shouldn't be taken for granted or devalued by ignoring our laws, history, or culture.

But the elites were embarrassed. They did what many who are embarrassed do—they got angry and lashed out. Their anger clouded their judgment. What were just talking points from the primaries became gospel by spring. And the angrier they got the more Donald Trump, following Sun Tzu's maxim to irritate an angry enemy, kept winning.

But this didn't happen in a vacuum. It happened in a bubble. At least that's been the narrative. A bubble is "a situation isolated from reality and unlikely to last." The bubble has lasted longer than it should have, but in reality the space inhabited by the political-media-academic complex is more like a black hole. Once living matter enters it is lost forever—not even light can reach it.

Don't believe me? Let's see if you can tell if the following headlines came from conservative or Left/liberal media outlets:

WHY PRESIDENT TRUMP WOULD BE A BIGGER DISASTER THAN PRESIDENT CLINTON[8]

DONALD TRUMP IS CRAZY, AND SO IS THE GOP FOR EMBRACING HIM[9]

"NEW NATIONALISM" AMOUNTS TO GENERIC WHITE-IDENTITY POLITICS[10]

THE WHITE NATIONALIST PROPAGANDIST WHO WILL ADVISE PRESIDENT TRUMP[11]

THE END IS NIGH: DONALD TRUMP, HORSEMAN OF THE REPUBLICAN APOCALYPSE[12]

HERE'S WHY DONALD TRUMP'S LONG CON WORKS SO WELL[13]

THE ART OF THE CON[14]

THANK GOODNESS TRUMP IS A COMPULSIVE LIAR[15]

The answer is that they all come from self-described conservative media outlets—from such stalwarts as *National Review* and the *Weekly Standard*. They come from the places that the last few generations of Americans relied upon and trusted to be the keepers of the conservative flame. But for these institutions and their writers America became just an idea divorced from the real nation and its people. Politics became a game. Not only would they never feel the consequences of their bad policy ideas, they lived in a world where virtually no one they knew would either.

It is striking that the few conservative intellectuals and writers who backed Donald Trump were by and large the ones that were the farthest from Washington and New York. Many of them were associated with Hillsdale College, located in rural Michigan; the Claremont Institute in Los Angeles; and our own journal *American Greatness,* whose founders are in California and Arizona.

The response to the Trump candidacy and his supporters from the institutional Right was swift and vicious. It didn't take long before the chief exponents of Conservatism Inc.—that archipelago of magazines and think tanks that make up the infrastructure of professional conservatism and suck up vast sums of donor dollars—wanted to take names so that they could settle scores on some future night of the long knives. Witness, for example, Amanda Carpenter. The former speechwriter and communications director for Senator Ted Cruz was looking forward to taking out her outrage on the peasants who supported Donald Trump when she volunteered to maintain the master list of the guilty—so they could be dealt with later.

Writing in Mark Levin's *Conservative Review* Carpenter was looking for some payback against Trump supporters:

It's time to make a list.

A list of those so-called conservatives and Republicans endorsing Donald Trump, the megalomaniac who regularly threatens his opponents and the press, raves about making members of our military adopt ISIS-like tactics, has funded Obamacare and Gang of Eight Democrats, promises to forcibly relocate American companies to his liking, and has demonstrated again and again he intends to govern as a tyrannical King rather than a President.

Call it a boycott, call it a blackball, call it a blacklist, call it whatever you want. I'm done with these folks and other conservatives should be, too. Anyone who will defend a man condoning random acts of violence at his rallies has lost his morals; he will defend anything at all.

So, I'd like to remember who supported Trump so I never give any kind of credence to their judgment. "Never Trump" means never those who support him as well.[16]

She went on to list elected Republicans who had endorsed Trump. It's a good list to look at now that the election is over, to see who was out in front and bore the brunt of the Never-Trump backlash during the campaign.

In its infamous "Against Trump" issue, *National Review* led off with an anti-Trump takedown by radical leftist Samantha Bee's new best friend, Glenn Beck. In it the ideologically fluid Beck criticized Trump, saying that he represented a crisis for conservatism and that Trump would be easily beaten by Hillary Clinton. Beck was right about the crisis for conservatism, but not in the way he thought. The crisis is real and overdue. It is the crisis of a movement that was never really a movement—it was a coalition of sometimes very different political philosophies that united in the 1960s, '70s, and '80s to defeat the threat of expansionist Soviet communism.

But when the Cold War was won, the coalition of traditionalists, libertarians, realists, paleoconservatives, neoconservatives, and others lost the one big thing that kept them together: a common enemy. Since then the neoconservative wing of the coalition has succeeded in capturing most of the institutions that make up Conservatism Inc., but they never won the support of anything like a majority of rank and file Republican voters. The Bush administration was the high water for the neoconservative ascendancy. Many understandably mistook mainstream Republican support for President Bush and the Iraq War as assent to the neoconservative philosophy and agenda. It wasn't.

By 2016 a majority of Americans realized it was time to turn the page. Witness the rise of Bernie Sanders. Sanders' unlikely success in the Democrat primaries speaks to the moral bankruptcy of the Clintons and the impotence of their message. At the same time the cranky Vermont socialist was peddling the warmed-over collectivism of yesteryear to cheering crowds of twentysomethings and aging hippies, Donald Trump was in the process of winning the Republican primary with more votes than any other Republican nominee ever.

Against this backdrop, *National Review* trotted out Glenn Beck as their pointman. But who is more consistent and credible: Donald Trump or Glenn Beck? If they wanted to be taken seriously, why would *National Review* lead off with a piece by the mercurial Beck, who would later be seen rubbing his face on a plate of Cheeto dust?[17]

In his kick-off to *National Review*'s "Against Trump" symposium Beck said this:

> Sure, Trump's potential primary victory would provide Hillary Clinton with the easiest imaginable path to the White House. But it's far worse than that. If Donald Trump wins the Republican nomination, there will once again be no opposition to an ever-expanding government. This is a crisis for conservatism. And, once again, this crisis will not go to waste.[18]

While conservative writers and intellectuals wanted to talk about what was good for conservatism, Donald Trump was talking about what is good for America. And for voters, what's good for America will always trump what's good for conservatism. It was a defining stand for the self-proclaimed leaders of conservatism. These would-be solons turned out to be shortsighted, self-interested, and out of touch, pied pipers leading the country into a future of endless, winless wars, cultural destruction, and crony capitalist plantation economics.

Donald Trump responded to *National Review* on Twitter by saying, "Very few people read the National Review because it only knows how to criticize, but not how to lead."[19]

Jonah Goldberg wanted none of it. He wrote for *National Review*, "Well, if this is the conservative movement now, I guess you're going to have to count me out."[20]

In another of his more or less weekly anti-Trump pieces he continued in the same vein: "And that's probably the main reason I'm so opposed to him: A Trump presidency would destroy conservatism in this country."[21]

National Review contributor and bow-tie OG, George Will, left the Republican Party over Donald Trump. He wrote, "If Trump wins, the GOP ends as a vehicle for conservatism."[22]

NR colleague David French wrote an essay titled, "As Nominee, Donald Trump Would Do Incalculable Damage to the Pro-Life Cause."[23] This is particularly ironic in retrospect as one of President Trump's first actions was to reinstate the Mexico City Policy, which bans the use of federal funding for advocacy of abortion abroad. He also sent Vice President Pence to the annual March for Life with a message of solidarity and support. So much for the incalculable damage to the pro-life cause.

We could list many more examples, but you get the idea. Over at rival conservative magazine the *Weekly Standard*, the criticism was just as vicious. Then-editor Bill Kristol wrote, "If you're for Trump you functionally are for a man unfit to be president, & for the degradation of Am. conservatism."[24]

Russell Moore, president of the Ethics and Public Policy counsel, ratcheted up the rhetoric about as far as it could go by calling into question the state of Trump supporters' eternal souls. Moore wrote in the *New York Times* (where else?) in September 2015, "To back Mr. Trump, these voters (evangelicals) must repudiate everything they believe."[25]

Erick Erickson, former editor of *RedState,* wrote, "Do these people not care about leading others to Christ? Are they so wrapped up in the day to day partisanship of Republican vs. Democrat *that they have abandoned Christ vs. the World. Shame on them.*"[26]

For the writers at *National Review* and the *Weekly Standard,* Donald Trump was and is a repudiation of their secular faith. But their faith was just rehashed gnosticism—a belief in a secret knowledge administered by an elite few to the unknowing many. And Donald Trump crashed their party, heralding a long overdue reformation.

When they were talking about the peril to "conservatism," voters were more interested in the perils to America. And the only one talking honestly and credibly about them was Donald Trump. He didn't emblazon a campaign bus with a focus group–tested slogan about Straight Talk, he just did it. What's more, Donald Trump spoke the language of an elemental American conservatism with a longer and better pedigree than what has been peddled by Conservatism Inc. in recent years.

Ultimately, the media-political-academic insiders who vehemently opposed Donald Trump had become nothing more than a faction of the kind warned about by James Madison in "Federalist No. 10"—just a garden variety, parochial interest group narrowly focused on their own agenda, which they conflated with the national interest. That would be fine but for the fact that their own legitimacy relies upon their speaking for the legitimate interests of the nation. Instead, it led them into inflexible positions from which their pride would not let them retreat.

Many of the very people who accused Donald Trump of intemperance would be known by nothing so much as their own radical rhetoric, and those who accused Donald Trump of lying would themselves play fast and loose with the truth. In their hubris and rage they visited destruction upon themselves.

After the election these same people all wrote articles with the same theme: We never saw it coming. But how could they not? Some of us saw it. Talk radio hosts in particular saw the Trump wave building earlier than most, perhaps because of their close connection to the audience. But they saw only what they wanted to see and what the ecosystem in which they live their professional lives incentivized them to see.

None of Donald Trump's most virulent critics have yet made peace with the president. They continue to take potshots at him from their perches at magazines and on television. They still cling to an air of respectability, but as more people see Donald Trump govern—he's not perfect, but so far he's governed based on the promises he made on the campaign trail—they resemble nothing so much as members of a fading aristocracy. They have lost the estate and the wealth that goes with it, but they cling to the title as the last vestige of a bygone era.

In the 1970s and 1980s all of the intellectual vigor in American politics was on the Right. The broad coalition of generally right-of-center political philosophies that made up the so-called conservative movement was alive with ideas and vigorous debates. It gave the Reagan administration its best and brightest. But the fire slowly dwindled after the Contract with America.

The American Right became monolithic. Dissenters were banished from the pages of the respectable journals and didn't get invited on the cable news shows. It was good for the victors—for a while. But it led to a moribund, inward looking intellectual movement that slowly grew apart from the country it proposed to lead.

How did we get here? How did the system fail? That's a big question, but the short answer is that it went wrong at the beginning.

2

WHAT WENT WRONG

HOW DID THE PUNDITS END UP SO INCORRECT?

IT ALL LOOKS SO OBVIOUS IN RETROSPECT. Things usually do. Eight years of the George W. Bush administration and an unpopular war in Iraq—and a less popular peace, with its concomitant entanglements and gray areas and lack of clear resolution or even clearly identifiable goals—left Americans looking for answers. In response, Barack Obama was elected and re-elected primarily on the basis of his biogrpahy and personal charisma rather than a broad-based adoption of the radical leftist agenda he promised to pursue: Witness the wholesale destruction of the Democrat Party in state legislatures, governor's mansions, and Congress. After nearly three decades of alternating rule by the Clintons and the Obamas, the Democrats are at a low ebb not seen in a century. Yet, for all their electoral success, the national Republican Party is in an equally precarious position.

A few weeks before the election Bush strategist Chris Wallace asked Bush strategist and one-time left-wing bogeyman Karl Rove if Trump would win. Rove replied, "I don't see it happening."[1] He went on to liken Trump's chances to pulling an inside straight. This is the same Karl Rove who confidently predicted just a week before the 2012 election that Mitt Romney would win with at least 279 electoral votes[2] and then went on to have an infamous on-air meltdown on election night arguing that Romney would win the crucial state of Ohio after the Fox News decision desk correctly predicted that Obama would win the state and effectively dash Romney's hopes of winning.[3]

He wasn't alone. Michael Tanner, a senior fellow of the libertarian Cato Institute, wrote in *National Review* in October 2016: "But with each passing hour, it becomes more obvious that he is going to lose this election, and most likely take a Republican Senate down with him. Even Republican control of the House is now in jeopardy."[4]

Kevin Williamson, an unreconstructed Never Trumper, wrote an essay for *National Review* titled "So much (for) Winning" in which he opined:

> It is a curious claim now in that Trump, barring some black-swan-level event, is not going to win. If the election were held today, the most likely outcome would be that Hillary Rodham Clinton would finish with well over three hundred electoral votes, easily besting Trump. Trump has even managed to put Texas and its thirty-eight electoral votes into play. That's a bit short of the "so much winning, you'll get tired of it" that he boasted of; it isn't even a little bit of winning, or even a decent showing.[5]

Do you ever get the feeling they really don't like Donald Trump at *National Review*? The problem is that their visceral dislike of Trump the man irrevocably poisoned their analysis of Trump the candidate. So it is no surprise that they, like Captain Renault in *Casablanca,* were shocked (Shocked!) when Donald Trump won the election by battering down the Democrats' fabled blue wall in the upper Midwest by winning not only Ohio, but Pennsylvania, Michigan, and Wisconsin.

At the *Weekly Standard*, Bill Kristol made his prediction on October 31, 2016, "Now the campaign draws to a close. And one outcome seems increasingly likely: Donald J. Trump will lose."[6]

In the *New York Times*, David Brooks penned a piece whose title made reading it superfluous: "No, Donald Trump Won't Win."[7]

The *Nation* published a feel-good piece for Democrats and leftists titled, "Relax, Donald Trump Can't Win." In it they comforted Clinton supporters and Never Trumpers everywhere (we know they were peeking at the *Nation* before the election, looking for some soothing confirmation bias) with a quasi-scientific sounding conclusion tacked onto a single factoid and an accusation: "Even before you get to his campaign's incompetence and lackluster fundraising, the numbers just aren't on his side."[8]

Not to be outdone, the *Washington Post* published a prediction piece by star politics reporters Chris Cilliza and Aaron Blake titled, "Donald Trump's Chances of Winning Are Approaching Zero."[9] Math nerds everywhere were crushed that the *Post* missed one of the rare chances to use the word *asymptotically* in a headline, inside-the-Beltway people of all political stripes nodded their heads sagely, and Trump supporters everywhere—if they read the *Post*—went back to work knowing better.

Of course, all of these predictions—and there are many, many more—proved not just false but disastrously, monumentally, epically wrong. Donald Trump's victory accompanied victories in the House of Representatives and the U.S. Senate where Republicans retained control of both against what were supposed to be overwhelming odds and a treacherous environment. Republicans had to defend twenty-four of the thirty-four Senate seats on the ballot in 2016 and, as we saw above, the conservative intellectual elite had written them off. Likewise, Republicans expanded their control at the state level, picking up five state House chambers, two state Senates, and adding two more Republican governors for a total of thirty-three. After the 2016 election, which nearly all of the experts relied upon by the national media predicted a defeat for Republicans so total that it could only end with visions of burning buildings, salted earth, and weeping widows, we find ourselves in a country with a degree of Republican electoral dominance not seen since the 1920s. Meanwhile, the Democrat Party is in disarray. A generation of rising Democrat politicians was sacrificed to advance and enrich the Clintons and their cronies and to gratify Barack Obama's ego.

And the smart guys didn't see it coming. It remains a mystery as to why the networks employ people to make political predictions when they are consistently wrong. There is an old saying that success has many fathers while failure is an orphan. In political media the opposite may be true. Would any other profession tolerate consistently bad results? Would anyone hire a doctor with the track record most of the experts on cable news have?

Yet, before Hillary Clinton could compose herself to address the nation with some semblance of dignity in defeat—you will recall that she refused to do so on election night, preferring to send John Podesta out to buy some time—the new narrative was already circulating: The pundits and analysts were all "shocked at Donald Trump's surprise victory."

CBS News called it a "stunner" and a "major upset."[10] The *Washington Post* called it a "stunning upset."[11] The *New York Times* called it a "surprise outcome" that "threatened convulsions around the country."[12]

Even *Recode*, a popular daily news source for the technology business, weighed in with this headline: "With Donald Trump's Surprising Victory, Silicon Valley Is Having a Meltdown." But their subhead might be far more telling: "Back into the Comfy Silicon Bubble, *Stat*!"[13]

The legacy conservative media was no better. They had all made their predictions and had those predictions confidently reinforced by friends, colleagues, and people who matter. Everyone agreed that Donald Trump had to be stopped. He was no good! And besides that *he couldn't win*. Not possible. Not against the Clinton Machine.

It turns out that the Clinton Machine was a paper tiger—a Beltway fable they tell naughty consultants and campaign managers to keep them in line. "Toe the party line or we'll feed you to the Clinton Machine:

They invented the politics of personal destruction. Do you want that to be your fate? Good. Now, do as you're told."

Except Donald Trump didn't do as he was told. He didn't come from the political world. He came from the business world—a particularly tough corner of the business world at that. High profile New York real estate development has its closest analog in Israel's diplomatic relations with her neighbors, most of whom are dedicated to her permanent destruction.

Donald Trump wasn't any more impressed by the Clinton Machine than he was by Jeb Bush's "shock and awe" fundraising strategy that yielded him exactly three delegates to the Republican Convention at a cost of about $50 million each. Trump's detractors underestimated him throughout the primaries and, having learned nothing, did the same thing during the run-up to the general election. Despite running a primary campaign against sixteen opponents, he still ended with more votes than any other Republican nominee ever. And despite running a general election campaign against Hillary Clinton, the Clinton Machine, the media, and legacy conservative media and the Republican establishment, Donald Trump won 62.8 million votes—more than any Republican candidate in history.

But the experts couldn't or wouldn't see it. What is interesting is that the mainstream media, and in particular the explicitly leftist media, were more circumspect than the legacy conservative media. They had at least the recognition that Donald Trump had a chance to win, even if those comments always sounded a bit like their version of touching wood so as to not inadvertently tempt fate with fatal hubris.

The Left was predisposed to miss the Trump wave. They were partisans supporting Hillary, not impartial observers. It was no secret the mainstream were actively working on behalf of Clinton's campaign. Let's not forget that the DNC emails released by Wikileaks disclosed that *Politico* reporter Kenneth Vogel sent his story on Hillary Clinton's fundraising to the DNC's press secretary for markup before publishing it. And Mark Leibovich, a reporter for the *New York Times,* gave Clinton veto power over the quotes used in his story about her.[14]

In case anyone wasn't getting the message, Jim Rutledge, *The New York Times'* media reporter—supposedly an in-house conscience of sorts—mused aloud in the pages of the *Times* about whether or not journalists should abandon long-held standards of objectivity in light of Donald Trump's candidacy. He wrote:

> If you're a working journalist and you believe that Donald J. Trump is a demagogue playing to the nation's worst racist and nationalistic tendencies, that he cozies up to anti-American dictators and that he would be dangerous with control of the United States nuclear codes, how the heck are you supposed to cover him?
>
> Because if you believe all of those things, you have to throw out the textbook American journalism has been using for the better part of the past half-century, if not longer, and approach it in a way you've never approached anything in your career. If you view a Trump presidency as something that's potentially dangerous, then your reporting is going to reflect that. You would move closer than you've ever been to being oppositional. That's uncomfortable and uncharted territory for every mainstream, non-opinion journalist I've ever known, and by normal standards, untenable.
>
> But the question that everyone is grappling with is: Do normal standards apply? And if they don't, what should take their place?[15]

Hint for journalist reading the Rutledge piece on journalistic ethics: Yes, journalists should abandon traditional standards of objectivity and oppose Donald Trump. Many have taken him up on his modest proposal. No wonder the media is trusted less than Congress.

Again, none of this is a surprise. Conservatives have known about the left-wing bias of the mainstream media for decades. That they were shocked by Donald Trump's victory should shock no one. One of the most interesting things about the 2016 election was watching the conservative media imitate their counterparts on the Left.

They had been virtually unanimous in their opposition to Trump during the election. Their predictions were based on their prejudices and desires and produced predictably bad results. As a result they were flat-footed on election night. And just to show that they like hyperbole as much as the next guy, *National Review* opined on election night that Donald Trump had won "the most shocking upset American politics has ever seen." If that wasn't enough, it was also, "the biggest upset in American political history."[16] Wow!

Except that it wasn't. To many Trump supporters—and there were almost 63 million of them—he was the business end of a wave that would submerge Hillary Clinton with as much ease as it had rolled over Jeb Bush and Marco Rubio and Ted Cruz and all the rest. What kind of credible political analyst watches Donald Trump rack up more primary votes than any Republican ever in the most crowded field ever and doesn't sense that something is happening in the country? The kind that, if they were generals, would believe the Maginot Line would defend France from the Blitzkrieg. In other words, someone who doesn't get out much and is still fighting the last war.

The indomitability of the Clinton Machine is a piece of political folklore that passed its expiration date in January 1999 when Bill Clinton—the electable one—left office. But it's been passed down and was accepted as a truth on par with the first law of thermodynamics until the votes were counted on election night. In the aftermath of Donald Trump's decisive victory the media and the public intellectuals closed ranks: It wasn't them. Their predictions were good, but the Trump victory was unforeseeable. After all, if they hadn't foreseen it, and they're the experts (just ask them), then it was by definition unknowable, a freak event like snow in July or Chuck Schumer keeping his word.

The problem is that Donald Trump and the agenda he outlined for America on the campaign trail did not fit the prevailing paradigm. And so the pundits, observers, and commentators on culture and politics lacked the intellectual infrastructure and the vocabulary to understand and describe it accurately. Wine critics are notorious for the idiosyncratic terminology they use to describe the tastes and smells of wines they write about. They have been known to describe fine wines as having hints of bramble, saddle leather, and beef blood. And those are all meant to commend the wine to prospective buyers. The critics and connoisseurs have had to create a language because they are trying to convey a nuanced sensual experience with words. Trump's politics required no ex nihilo creation of a new language, just the reclamation of an old one that American elites have studiously unlearned over the last generation or two. But it was commonly spoken at least among Republicans as recently as Reagan and by Democrats in the time of Kennedy, even if it had a slight German accent. What Donald Trump knew that almost no one inside the Beltway, in elite media, the academy, or the think tank world knew is that for most Americans it's their native tongue. It's the language of America the nation, the people, the Declaration, and the Constitution. Americans love the Declaration and the Constitution not just because they are ours, though that is part of it, but because they are good. For elites they are never good enough. Nor are the American people, for whom they have a not so subtle disdain.

Barack Obama infamously described the residents of middle America as the bitter clingers. The sentiment is shared in some quarters of Conservatism Inc. too. *National Review*'s Kevin Williamson echoed Obama's sentiments when he said that Trumpism is "bound up in a nasty species of white identity politics that crowds out other issues."[17] And writing about "poor white America," he said, "The truth about these dysfunctional, downscale communities is that they deserve to die. Economically, they are negative assets. Morally, they are indefensible."[18] Donald Trump proposed something different, not the radical individualism and profits above all else of the libertarians but an older, better, and more American idea: As Americans we're in this together and government exists for the "benefit of ourselves and our posterity." He wasn't suggesting the dole or wealth redistribution like Bernie Sanders but, echoing Reagan, that the best social program is a job and that government policy has a role to play in building a more prosperous and more productive society.

Supremely lacking in self-knowledge, the elites failed to recognize that they lived their lives in a monochromatic subculture with a scrupulously enforced orthodoxy. Donald Trump doesn't. Most Americans don't. And so we have come to a point where the media and intellectual elite have become largely alienated from the rest of the country.

Victor Davis Hanson, a senior fellow of the Hoover Institution at Stanford University, explains it this way:

> What the media and Democrats see as Trump's outrageous extremism now looks, to more than half the country, like a tardy return to normalcy: employing the words "radical Islamic terror," or asking cities to follow federal law rather than go full Confederate, or deporting illegal aliens who have committed crimes, or building a wall to stop easy illegal entry across the U.S. border, or putting a temporary hold on unvetted refugees from war-torn states in the Middle East. In the eyes of many Middle Americans, all these measures, even if sometimes hastily and sloppily embraced, are not acts of revolution; they are common-sense corrections of what were themselves extremist acts, or they are simply continuances of presidential executive-order power as enshrined by Obama and sanctified by the media.[19]

Without the right hermeneutics elites defaulted back to the strategies and language of the last war. They relied upon the established Right-Left political settlement that has prevailed for the past fifty years or more. But the world had moved on. Trump knew it. Voters knew it. But elites who had learned the lessons of recent political history by rote couldn't see the changed world because of their own blinders.

The conventional view reflected the reality of the 1960s and 1970s. Democrats were the party of unions, of women, and of minorities while Republicans were the party of the wealthy and the white. That describes a world that no longer exists yet still dominates the thinking of political professionals. What's worse, it's a Marxist view of the electorate that sees voters primarily in terms of race, sex, and class. The reality is that Democrats have become the party of the coasts, of university towns, and of those too young to know better. Republicans have become the party of the middle class.

The dirty little secret of American politics is that the rich and super-rich—the much derided 1 percent—has been a segment of the population that has been firmly under control of the Progressive Left for years. In fact, one might reasonably conclude that it's the other way around—that the rich and super-rich are running the American Left as a quasi-feudal enterprise with the very richest and best connected calling the shots and using cynical, lowest-common-denominator identity politics for votes to prop up their rule. Unfortunately, conservative elites bought into the premises of the Left and thereby sowed the seeds of their own destruction.

Republican consultants gazed enviously at the way Democrats moved the pieces of their electoral coalition around the board like chess grandmasters and determined to learn the dark arts of politics and do the same thing for their candidates. The openings were plotted long before, but that was the point of the fatally flawed but much caressed autopsy performed by Republican grandees after the 2012 election. For all of the ink spilled praising its diligence, professionalism, and impeccably scientific underpinnings, the conclusions can be summed as, "We can do identity politics too." But that gives away the game. If you accept identity politics you have already conceded the central point of the American project. The Declaration of Independence explains that we can and should appeal to the "laws of nature and nature's God" and that there are truths that we hold "to be self-evident, that all men are created equal, that they are endowed by their Creator with certain unalienable Rights." And more to the point, that "governments are instituted among men, deriving their just powers from the consent of the governed." The Declaration was a statement by the American nation that led to the Constitution, which created the state that would protect those rights.

It is because of those natural, inalienable rights that just government requires the consent of the governed. Government is instituted to protect and defend—not bestow—those rights for its citizens. This necessarily leads to a high view of American citizenship and belief that that there is a symbiotic relationship between government and its citizens. Each owes the other certain responsibilities and relies upon the other for the protection of its rights. A just government relies on its citizens' consent for its right to exist. And government owes all of its citizens an equal defense of their equal rights. Any political movement that relies upon dividing citizens against each other on the basis of claims to the superior rights of one over the other is fundamentally illegitimate.

More than a century ago Democrats fell victim to the Progressive dream of a post-Constitutional order in which self-anointed "experts" ruled without or over the will of the governed. That's when such pernicious notions as a "living Constitution," which put the wishes of unelected judges above the expressed will of the sovereign people, came to the fore in American politics. More recently many conservatives succumbed to the intellectual fundamentals of Progressivism. They came to it not through the original sources—Kant, Hegel, and Marx—as did the Left, but through secondary and tertiary conduits and a too-close contact with the critical theory that permeates all of modern education and culture.

Conservatives were susceptible to this at least in part because of a failure to appreciate the natural-rights basis of the American founding. It made them unable to comprehend the appeal of the greatness agenda described by Donald Trump, despite the fact that it has a long pedigree in American politics. Many of the themes would have been familiar to presidents of both parties in the first half of the twentieth century, including both Roosevelts and even the oft-overlooked but exemplary president Calvin Coolidge, but certainly not Woodrow Wilson, the godfather of so much of what has gone awry in American politics for the last century.

But if you didn't understand America you couldn't understand the Trump candidacy and can't understand his presidency. Democrats long ago gave up on the promise of America. Politics isn't based on self-evident truths or natural rights but upon the will to power. The Cultural Marxism that drives the modern Left has conflict—what Marx and Hegel called the dialectic—at its core. All relationships are thought of as power relationships—who has it, who doesn't, and how to get it. This is a crude, reductionist view of man and of politics. It deprives man of his humanity and dignity and denies the commonsense understanding of human nature. But it does explain the vicious reaction of Trump's opponents and his detractors in the media-academic-political complex.

At a more basic level, when Donald Trump not only won the election but made it look easy smashing through the Democrats' vaunted blue wall, it made a lot of otherwise smart people look foolish. A lot of ego was tied up in the election results. Because elite opinion was and is so monolithic, the only competition was for who could stake out the most extreme claims about Trump and his impending destruction at the hands of the pants-suited messiah. When it all blew up normal people might have been chastened or regained a sense of humility and fallibility. But the bubble protects its own.

Tears were shed, participation trophies were distributed, and everyone who had just been colossally wrong doubled down. No one rethought their positions. No one reconsidered their over-the-top rhetoric or demonstrably false accusations, no one wrote a retraction. And absolutely no one was fired. There were no firings because the media doesn't understand its job as being correct in its projections or accurate in its reporting. The modern media understands its job as political advocacy. Media personnel are no longer reporters, they are participants and change agents. So instead of looking at the folks who had been wrong during the election as being derelict in their duties, they were viewed as soldiers who fought the good fight and lost—but who lived to fight again.

On this basis they have redoubled their efforts to discredit and delegitimize Donald Trump. It didn't work during the election, but now that he in the White House they can devote even more resources to the project. The *New York Times*, for example, announced that it was doubling the number of reporters it has at the White House.[20] The left-wing *Talking Points Memo* published an essay after the election titled, "Trump, Free Speech, and Why Journalists Must Be Activists,"[21] while the Center for Journalism Ethics at the University of Wisconsin, Madison, advised journalists to practice "pragmatic objectivism,"[22] which can be likened to situation ethics. In other words, what it means to be objective isn't itself objective. Just try to figure that one out. But before you waste too much time let me cut to the chase: It means journalists are justified in doing whatever they feel like.

So just after having been routed on the field of battle, the media elite regrouped, reformed, and took up their positions to rejoin the fight. However, in surrendering their commitment to objectivity they have undermined their own credibility with the public and have retreated further into a false narrative of their creation, nourished and encouraged by peers and colleagues.

Scott Adams explained shortly after President Trump took office:

> The setup is that during the presidential campaign Trump's critics accused him of being Hitler(ish) and they were sure other citizens would see it too, thus preventing this alleged monster from taking office.
>
> They were wrong. The alleged monster took office.
>
> Now you have literally millions of citizens in the United States who were either right about Trump being the next Hitler, and we will see that behavior emerge from him soon, or they are complete morons. That's a trigger for cognitive dissonance. The science says these frightened folks will start interpreting all they see as Hitler behavior no matter how ridiculous it might seem to the objective observer. And sure enough, we are seeing that. . . .
>
> But lately I get the feeling that Trump's critics have evolved from expecting Trump to be Hitler to *preferring* it. Obviously they don't prefer it in a conscious way. But the alternative to Trump becoming Hitler is that they have to live out the rest of their lives as confirmed morons. No one wants to be a confirmed moron. And certainly not after announcing their Trump opinions in public and demonstrating in the streets. It would be a total embarrassment for the anti-Trumpers to learn that Trump is just trying to do a good job for America. It's a threat to their egos. A big one.[23]

Conformity to a minority orthodoxy that is at odds with the facts on the ground and the lived experience of most Americans combined with unhealthy amounts of ego and public embarrassment results in a potent brew that has led media elites to consistently wrong conclusions and repeated public humiliations at the hands of Donald Trump, who pursues his goals with honey badger tenacity.

They claim that no one saw it coming, but what they mean is that no one they know or respect saw it coming or wanted to see it coming. And that willing suspension of disbelief has led to a national media that now takes itself, if anything, more seriously than ever even as it is viewed by normal Americans as a self-important but ineffectual laughingstock.

An energetic and objective press is a necessity for free government. The public does have a right and a need to know "all the news that's fit to print." But the present state of American journalism is such that it must first take the log out of its own eye before presuming to pluck the splinter from anyone else's.

3

DON'T SHOOT FIRST

BURYING THE CANDIDATE WHO SUPPORTS YOUR CAUSES

DID CONSERVATIVES ANALYZING THE 2016 ELECTION actually read their own books?

"Culture wars." It's a phrase noxious and toxic to most Republican political analysts. Abortion. Marriage. Family. Race. Crime. Drugs. Illegal immigration. "Stay away," they say. "Too divisive," they warn. "Those issues caricature the party and movement." "We want 60 to 80 percent issues." "We can't lose the women's vote." "We have to do better with the Hispanic population." The party, after all, aren't we told is economically conservative and socially moderate? That's the comfortable thing for the donor class to say at their donor-class events. "Well yes, I'm a Republican but *not that kind* of Republican. I'm socially moderate but economically conservative." If there is one speech Republican consultants know not to mimic or come close to, it is the speech Patrick J.

Buchanan gave at the 1992 Republican Convention in Houston. The speech where he spoke of a "culture war."

The Buchanan speech in 1992, coming in the wake of the Los Angeles/Rodney King riots, was, indeed, a stem-winder. Its most memorable lines, however, were descriptive not prescriptive—Pat Buchanan was not *calling* for a culture war, he was *describing* one:

> There is a religious war going on in this country. It is a cultural war, as critical to the kind of nation we shall be as the Cold War itself. For this war is for the soul of America. And in that struggle for the soul of America, Clinton & Clinton are on the other side, and George Bush is on our side. And so to the Buchanan Brigades out there, we have to come home and stand beside George Bush.[1]

From there, Buchanan spoke of jobs and the economy—teems of supporters who had told him their stories about lost jobs in shuttered factories. Environmental regulations that cared more about owls than people. Then he spoke of, and concluded his speech with, a story of two policemen he met who helped push back and dissuade rioters in Los Angeles from further mayhem:

> They had come into Los Angeles late in the evening of the second day, and the rioting was still going on. And two of them walked up a dark street, where the mob had burned and looted every single building on the block but one, a convalescent home for the aged. And the mob was headed in, to ransack and loot the apartments of the terrified old men and women inside. The troopers came up the street, M-16s at the ready. And the mob threatened and cursed, but the mob retreated because it had met the one thing that could stop it: force, rooted in justice, and backed by moral courage. . . .
>
> "Greater love than this hath no man than that he lay down his life for his friend." Here were 19-year-old boys ready to lay down their lives to stop a mob from molesting old people they did not even know. And as those boys took back the streets of Los Angeles, block by block, my friends, we must take back our cities, and take back our culture, and take back our country.[2]

That was the gravamen and peroration of Buchanan's "culture war" speech. It wasn't heavy on abortion (it mentioned the issue only twice, and briefly). The words *race* and *affirmative action* appear nowhere in the speech. Its only mention of prayer in school was that George H. W. Bush supported voluntary prayer in school. Opposition to gay marriage received one sentence. Reading or listening to the Buchanan speech that consultants today warn of because it is too incendiary and divisive, one can only conclude candidates are instructed to stay away from the issues of law and order, the defense of police, the celebration of justice, and harmony kept by the moral force of the laws backed by the sacrifice and presence of police.

Re-reading that speech, one might say it was more Richard Nixon 1968 speaking of "the forgotten Americans—the non-shouters; the non-demonstrators," than the Christian Coalition or Moral Majority of, say a Pat Robertson, a Jerry Falwell, or a James Dobson.[3] Or a Franklin Graham. It was about safe streets and putting down or stopping riots. That was the essence of the culture war that we were all instructed was too divisive and turned off the majority of Americans.

To be sure, politicians running for national office stayed away from that kind of talk or phraseology. Try to recall John McCain in 2008 or Mitt Romney in 2012, or, for that matter Bob Dole in 1996 (all candidates who lost) ever talking about those things. But the conservative movement did not stay away from those issues. Nor did the conservative think tanks. And, looking at the losses of Republican presidential campaigns from moderates and traditional Republicans like Bob Dole, John McCain, and Mitt Romney who truly did stay away from anything like "culture-speak," one wonders if *that* may not have been part of their strategic mistake. Of course, yes, George W. Bush did talk about the culture, but when he did it was mostly about welfare reform and integrating it with religious organizations—a mixed blend of culture-speak if you will—speaking of the poor, but speaking to the religious, a Bobby Kennedy meets Mother Teresa effect. But George Bush did not embrace this, he was sure to point out, to sound like a traditional conservative or "culture warrior."*

Indeed, one of George Bush's most famous speeches in the 2000 campaign (delivered in the primaries of 1999) was broadcast from the Manhattan Institute, where he criticized the more well-known cultural conservatives: "Too often, on social issues, my party has painted an image of America slouching toward Gomorrah."[4]

That line was an attack on a legal and cultural hero of the movement, Robert Bork—the legal scholar, author, and former federal judge and solicitor general who had written a best seller by the title, *Slouching Towards Gomorrah*, just a few years earlier. That book, that best seller, did take on domestic cultural issues such as affirmative action, abortion, pornography, feminism, the First Amendment, and religion. And when he heard that speech, Judge Bork struck back, with a strong op-ed in the *Wall Street Journal*, the mainstream editorial page home of the conservative intellectual movement in America. Shortly after Bush's speech, Bork wrote:

> It is a considerable compliment to have one's book, "Slouching Towards Gomorrah," cited, even disparagingly, by a presidential contender whose proud boast it is that he does not read books. (He may not even have realized that he was referring to a book.) . . . A rolodex is a wonderful substitute for actual knowledge.[5]

It would be of some irony, and a point we shall return to later, that George W. Bush's election to the presidency in 2000 became a reality due to a Supreme Court decision from a court Robert Bork should have been sitting on but that was denied him in large part because Democrats and the Left had no problem engaging in political wars-cum-culture wars. Think of the worst (and most traveled) thing said about Robert Bork during his confirmation hearings in 1987. It came from the liberal lion of the Senate, Ted Kennedy:

---

* The Bush family's stock and trade was pointing out their distinctions from traditional conservatism. One recalls George H. W. Bush speaking of a "kinder, gentler" conservatism, prompting Nancy Reagan to ask "Kinder and gentler than what?"

Robert Bork's America is a land in which women would be forced into back-alley abortions, blacks would sit at segregated lunch counters, rogue police could break down citizens' doors in midnight raids, schoolchildren could not be taught about evolution, writers and artists could be censored at the whim of the Government, and the doors of the Federal courts would be shut on the fingers of millions of citizens for whom the judiciary is—and is often the only—protector of the individual rights that are the heart of our democracy.[6]

This was a wholly unfair and untrue attack on the judicial philosophy of Robert Bork, but it had purchase and traveled. The point? The Left, the liberal movement in America, and Democrats had no problem engaging in culture wars—subtly and not-so-subtly. Meanwhile, for decades, Republicans were urged not to so engage; indeed, they were urged (as George W. Bush did) to triangulate those issues, water them down, criticize them, or ignore them. For these kinds of reasons, one of the heroines of the intellectual conservative movement, author and editor Midge Decter, would often say, as one author here heard her say at several meetings and conferences: "The Republican Party is the cross the conservative movement has to bear."

But while the Republican political apparatus thought it knew how to win elections by staying away from what had become known as the cultural issues, what was happening and taking place at the wholesale and intellectual level? What were the think tanks and journals and publishing houses doing and saying? And who was supporting them financially, attending their conferences, and buying their books? They were two very, very different groups.

From the American Enterprise Institute (where Robert Bork worked) to the Heritage Foundation to the Manhattan Institute and beyond: authors and scholars were churning out article after article, essay after essay, conference after conference, book after book, on all of the supposedly untouchable or third-rail cultural issues.

One of the first such books taking on liberal shibboleths, academic political correctness, and multiculturalism was Dinesh D'Souza's *Illiberal Education: The Politics of Race and Sex on Campus*, published in 1991. That was a retail follow-on, shall we say, to the more wholesale indictment of higher education published by Allan Bloom in *The Closing of the American Mind* about four years prior. The same year as *Illiberal Education* came out, Professor Shelby Steele penned *The Content of Our Character: A New Vision of Race in America* about race relations and race preferences. By no means were the early 1990s the beginning of these books. William J. Bennett's *Book of Virtues* was not his first foray into the culture. He had already made a name for himself as an author with his 1979 co-authored book criticizing race preferences and affirmative action, *Counting by Race: Equality from the Founding Fathers to Bakke* (edited by Midge Decter). Of course, Charles Murray's *Losing Ground*, on the failure of the welfare state and system, came just a few years later.

But the 1990s and 2000s saw a tremendous rise in the columnist, publishing, and think-tank communities' taking on all these hot button or cultural issues. Vice President Dan Quayle may have been scorned by the elites for his "Murphy Brown" speech in 1992 warning about the problems of out-of-wedlock births, but conservative icon, columnist, and *National Review* founder, William F. Buckley, would write—before Quayle's speech of the same month—"There is only one question to ask a presidential candidate that makes any sense. It is: What do you propose to do about the rate of illegitimate births?"[7]

Soon followed more conservative intellectual attention to this issue. The famous 1994 Irving Kristol essay in the *Wall Street Journal*, "Life without Father," and a whole series of books and conferences, and non-profits all were dedicated to thinking through and solving the issues of fatherlessness and out-of-wedlock births. A think tank, the National Fatherhood Initiative, dedicated to just this issue, was even created around the same time.

When it came to the issue of race preferences and affirmative action, no conservative in Washington, D.C., could avoid talks, conferences, and books on the issue. Legal scholar (and later Arizona Supreme

Court justice) Clint Bolick, of the Institute for Justice, was writing and debating against race preferences. Linda Chavez had created a think tank called the Center for Equal Opportunity to take on the issue. The Heritage Foundation became a home for panel after panel and conference after conference on the issue. Dinesh D'Souza would write another best seller on the issue, *The End of Racism,* as would the scholars Stephen and Abigail Thernstrom with their book, *America in Black and White.*

Out in California, liberal California, Larry Arnn (then of the Claremont Institute), along with two other California scholars and activist Ward Connerly, established the Civil Rights Initiative in California to overturn race-based preferences in public accommodations and in 1996 actually won that state-wide initiative (Proposition 209) at the ballot by a whopping nine points.[8] Again, this in the West Coast land of liberalism—California. Two years prior, an anti–illegal immigration proposition in California was run (Proposition 187) and prevailed by even larger margins.[9] This is what the conservative movement was up to in California. And it was winning.

Back in Washington, D.C., think tanks were pushing education reform through vouchers and school choice. Again, the Heritage Foundation, along with a host of other think tanks and the litigation prowess of Clint Bolick and his Institute for Justice, were in the lead.

Talk of "virtues" rather than "values" was becoming more and more dominant with run-away best sellers like William J. Bennett's *Book of Virtues* and its sequels for adults and children. Gertrude Himmelfarb, wife of Irving Kristol and mother of Bill Kristol, would add to this by writing *The De-Moralization of Society: From Victorian Virtues to Modern Values.*

And of course there was the issue of crime, associated with welfare and fatherlessness and drugs. Scholars like Heather Mac Donald and John C. Lott were making their names and establishing the locus of conversation from a conservative perspective on crime, guns, and policing while one of the neoconservative heroes of a slightly older generation, James Q. Wilson, was in high demand for speaking and writing on policing and crime. Indeed, Wilson's theory (shared with George Kelling) on "broken windows" would serve as the template for Rudy Giuliani's crime-fighting tenure as mayor of New York City. And, of course, in the East Coast land of liberalism, Rudy Giuliani was elected mayor of New York City in 1993, in large part on the issue of crime.

Illegal immigration would, by and large, become an issue and debate for the conservative think-tank community a little later, with the exception of Proposition 187 in California. But throughout the 1990s and reaching into the early 2000s, issues revolving around English-first, English-only, and English for the children certainly also dominated the think-tank and magazine circuit. Again, liberal California would pass the "Unz Initiative," named after a wealthy businessman who bankrolled the proposition, requiring all public school classes to be taught in English. That proposition passed by even greater margins than Proposition 187 or the Civil Rights Initiative.[10]

Of course, the terrorist attacks of September 11, 2001, refocused a great deal of attention away from these social or cultural issues, but they never fully went away. Indeed, issues like multiculturalism and political correctness—the subjects of Dinesh D'Souza's first and landmark book—were getting worse, becoming more encrusted throughout the academy as well as throughout the cultures and policies of corporate America. And, sure enough, in short order after September 11, those cultural and social issues came roaring back in the language, discussion, and policies surrounding not only immigration but the language and description of the enemy.

By and large, conservatives wanted to name and identify the enemy in descriptive terms such as "Radical Islam" or "Islamo-fascism," but liberals did not, with some exceptions on the Left by the likes of Christopher Hitchens and, later, the comedian and television host Bill Maher. And conservatives embraced them, at least on these issues. The Left, liberals, and the Democratic party would claim such terms were examples of the neologism they created: "Islamophobia." The war became, on the cultural front, a battlefield of language. After the election of Barack Obama, one author here would comment again and again, "the only time you hear the word 'Islam' from the President is when he speaks of the capital of Pakistan."

But even here, the stage was set for conservative pushback against certain politically trendy moderation and linguistic capitulation from elected officials, including, if not especially, from President George W. Bush and his administration. Indeed, just after the attacks of 9/11, it would be fair to say there were two George Bushes. President Bush made headlines, and took a lot of heat, for his early comments on the war that was declared on us. One of his first comments that he would backtrack on was "This crusade, this war on terrorism is going to take a while."[11] "Crusade!?" the Left roared. President Bush would never utter the word again; this, despite a history of the Crusades that most scholars understood were a reaction to the Islamic wars of their initiation. This, despite that Osama bin Laden had no problem talking about the Crusades. This, despite that wartime and liberal hero President Franklin D. Roosevelt, in what was the largest broadcast public prayer up to that point in history,could say: "And, O, Lord, give us Faith. Give us Faith in Thee; Faith in our sons; Faith in each other; Faith in our united crusade,"[12] as he urged Americans to stand and hold fast on the eve of D-Day.

Then, of course, there was President Bush's early statement that he wanted to get Osama bin Laden "dead or alive,"[13] and his equally quick backing off of that statement as it came across too tough for the liberal mindset and domineering politically correct. Indeed, President Bush would later say one of his chief regrets was the use of that phrase.[14] But most Americans loved that kind of talk and wanted their wartime president to speak in the language of the cowboy, of right and wrong, of good and evil, of Marshal Matt Dillon. And the conservative writers from *National Review* to the *Weekly Standard* to *Fox News* and throughout talk radio did, too. But, as mentioned above, political correctness and multi-culturalism had so settled in that even an evangelical, West Texas George Bush had to capitulate on certain of that language—ever reminding Muslims at home and abroad "Ours is a war not against a religion, not against the Muslim faith."[15]

Indeed, President George W. Bush and his administration went out of their way to ensure that Muslims here and abroad knew this was not a war against all Islam—as if that really needed to be said. Did anybody *really* think America was going to war with nearly two billion people? Did anybody *really* think that the wars in Afghanistan and Iraq were wars against Muslims, especially as the United States and her military did everything they could to protect the populations of those countries and even consented in the writing of their new constitutions, dedicated to Sharia (Muslim law) as they were? But President Bush and his administration were relentless in disabusing any notion of such, going so far as to dedicate a page on its White House website to assuring Muslims at home and abroad that there would be no Islamophobia here.[16]

One may be forgiven for thinking some of the following was said by President Barack Obama:

> Here in the United States our Muslim citizens are making many contributions in business, science and law, medicine and education, and in other fields. Muslim members of our Armed Forces and of my administration are serving their fellow Americans with distinction, upholding our nation's ideals of liberty and justice in a world at peace.
>
> America treasures the relationship we have with our many Muslim friends, and we respect the vibrant faith of Islam which inspires countless individuals to lead lives of honesty, integrity, and morality. This year, may Eid also be a time in which we recognize the values of progress, pluralism, and acceptance that bind us together as a Nation and a global community. By working together to advance mutual understanding, we point the way to a brighter future for all.
>
> Islam brings hope and comfort to millions of people in my country, and to more than a billion people worldwide.
>
> According to Muslim teachings, God first revealed His word in the Holy Qur'an to the prophet, Muhammad, during the month of Ramadan. That word has guided billions of believers across the centuries, and those believers built a culture of learning and literature

and science. All the world continues to benefit from this faith and its achievements.

The face of terror is not the true faith of Islam. That's not what Islam is all about. Islam is peace. These terrorists don't represent peace. They represent evil and war.

I've made it clear, Madam President, that the war against terrorism is not a war against Muslims, nor is it a war against Arabs. It's a war against evil people who conduct crimes against innocent people.[17]

Those words were all President George W. Bush's. To his credit, President Bush was not uncomfortable speaking of "Radical Islam." But that phrase, perfectly descriptive and, indeed, quite a good distinction in and of itself between all of Islam and Islamic terrorists, was too much for the Left, liberals, and the Democratic party. And, as mentioned above, President Obama would have none of it. Gallons of ink and millions of words from conservatives were spilt and spent criticizing President Obama for not using this, or like, phrases.

Before we get too far ahead of ourselves, let's get back to illegal immigration. The issue finally boiled upward and outward in the mid-2000s. And it divided the conservative community of intellectuals, journals, and think tanks. It did not unify it in one direction. On one side of the border enforcement argument were such magazines as *National Review*, which favored enforcement first; on the other, the editorial page of the *Wall Street Journal,* which did not. Think tanks such as the Heritage Foundation and the Claremont Institute sided with the *National Review* perspective, and think tanks such as the Hudson Institute and the Cato Institute and, to a degree, the American Enterprise Institute, with the *Wall Street Journal.*

There was no shortage of conservative scholars taking a strong position against amnesty and illegal immigration—indeed that position seemed the dominant one. They would include the likes of almost every talk-radio host and such luminaries as William Buckley and Robert Bork, David Frum and Newt Gingrich, Jonah Goldberg and Rich Lowry,

Heather Mac Donald and Thomas Sowell—to name just a selection.[18] Just a couple of years before this debate took off and dominated what seemed like a year of conservative and internecine conservative think-tank debate, Michelle Malkin, the popular blogger, had penned her first book and best seller on the problems with illegal immigration and lax border enforcement: *Invasion: How America Still Welcomes Terrorists, Criminals, and Other Foreign Menaces to Our Shores.*[19] And all of this was before Ann Coulter's 2015 huge best-seller: *Adios, America: The Left's Plan to Turn Our Country into a Third World Hellhole.*

This, all this and just this, the foregoing, is where the conservative public intellectuals were. The debates and seminars and conferences and essays and speeches and books in the intellectual conservative movement, this is what the think tanks were writing on.* But few of these issues or these matters were ever embraced, or even mentioned, by Republican presidential candidates. After all, Dan Quayle and Pat Buchanan had "proven" the reason why. Consultants hated them, and a lot of candidates (McCain, Romney, Dole, the Bushes) were uncomfortable with them. But not the think tanks and their donors, not the rank and file. And all of these issues, including large parts of the War on Terror and illegal immigration debates, could be folded up into one big, uber-category of what was *never* discussed or taught about from the conservatives' perspective at the elementary, secondary, or post-secondary level, in our schools or universities.

But it wasn't just our schools, it was nearly the entire culture and elite culture itself that was either ignoring these issues or writing about the conservative take on them with scorn and contempt. If they weren't just embracing the liberal line as settled. Entertainment, from music to

---

* To be sure, yes: the think tanks were also publishing on and discussing economic policies and, after the election of Barack Obama in 2008, health care. But for decades, the famous ones, the popular names, were focused more on the culture . . . and illegal immigration. In fact, aside from Stephen Moore, who would also embrace the immigration debate—and become perhaps more famous for it for a spell—one strains to think of a popular name writing from the conservative perspective on the non-cultural issues.

Hollywood, was either anti-cop or entirely left-wing on all of the above issues—from family to race to Islamism. And so too the media and corporate America. Race preferences, affirmative action, and the like—there is no debate about any of that in the corporate board rooms. The U.S. Chambers of Commerce and its state satellites are anti-anti-illegal immigration (or pro-amnesty). When you're up against Hollywood, the music industry,* education, the media, and corporate America, it's one helluva conservative lift to be taken seriously or think you can win elections. And it is, indeed, intimidating to take on.

All of these issues dominated by the elite culture can be rolled into one big category, whether it's about race or family or illegal immigration or Radical Islam or crime: political correctness. That issue, political correctness (along with its attendant intellectual cousin, multiculturalism) has been at the center, at the heart, of almost every conservative discussion of the past two decades, if not beyond. Whether it is a morning coffee discussion among conservative friends before work, a Bible study, a dinner table, or a think-tank seminar, the phrase "political correctness" or "politically correct" is on the lips and very much on the minds. It is the catchphrase or shibboleth conservatives use to signal their understanding of their minority status in the culture, the view that they—we—have held that to the Left, to the liberals, to the Democrats, we simply do not have a right to govern and that our perspective is not only not wanted but plainly wrong. Piercing the veils and policies of political correctness has and had been the stock and trade of Conservatism Inc.—the conservative think tanks and magazines.

But no candidate would try to pierce those veils—at least no winning Republican candidate for president. Sure, the Gary Bauers and Mike Huckabees and Ted Cruzes and Rick Santorums would "go there," as it were. But they'd never get the nominations, and they'd be told that was why. This was the language and talk the base loved, the think tanks efforted, and the meat and potatoes of the conservative blogosphere, book publishing, and talk radio. But George W. Bush, Bob Dole, John

---

* A small exception might be country music.

McCain, and Mitt Romney would not touch it.

Who did? Who, at long last, spoke the words: "The big problem this country has is being politically correct. I've been challenged by so many people and I don't frankly have time for total political correctness. And to be honest with you, this country doesn't have time either. This country is in big trouble. We don't win anymore."[20] That would be Donald Trump in an August debate in 2015. That would be the same Donald Trump who embraced Ann Coulter's book, *Adios America* (a book praised by *National Review* editor and prominent Never Trumper Jay Nordlinger). That would be the same Donald Trump who said, "When Mexico sends its people, they're not sending their best. They're not sending you. They're sending people that have lots of problems, and they're bringing those problems with us. They're bringing drugs. They're bringing crime. They're rapists. And some, I assume, are good people."[21] That would be the same Donald Trump who used the phrase "Radical Islam" in almost every speech or debate or interview where he appeared.

It would seem more than odd, then, that so many establishment conservatives, from *National Review* to the think tanks, would campaign as hard against Donald Trump, if not harder, as against the Democrats or Hillary Clinton. Much of this came to a head when William J. Bennett addressed the Never Trumpers on Fox News in August of 2016—even *after* the Republican convention. Not doing well in the polls at that point, and taking as much heat from the Never Trump conservatives as ever, Bennett was asked what Donald Trump needed to do. His response:

> He does not need to speak to the Never Trumpers, some of my friends or maybe former friends who suffer from a terrible case of moral superiority and put their own vanity and taste above the interests of the country. But he can speak to the middle and he can speak to the problems, as he spoke in Milwaukee, and he can speak, as he does, to some audiences, particularly, Martha, a lot of that Milwaukee address was to black America and I think that's something he should do again. I think he can get 15, 20 percent of that vote.[22]

The Never Trump movement went ballistic. Charles Murray criticized William Bennett; so, too, Jonah Goldberg and Bill Kristol. And not a little. Charles Murray went so far as to tweet: "Because we are morally superior, perhaps."[23] Bennett, they said, had forgotten his writing of the past, his grounding. But was it him or they with short-term amnesia? What one could say in defense of Bennett's position is the same thing that could be said of pretty much the entirety of the conservative think-tank and journalism world up until about 2015, *mutatis mutandis*.

If Bennett's detractors and the Never Trumpers put all of conservatism's work over the years together, they could have seen what they had missed about their own works: a determination to reverse a culture of political correctness aimed at diminishing American and Western intellectual traditions and sovereignty. A determination to win the war against Radical Islam. A determination to fight back against multiculturalism and political correctness. What was it, after all, Donald Trump spoke mostly about and campaigned on—even if indecorously? And what was it that had fed and animated Conservatism Inc. for so many years? The same issues.

Try it this way: Throughout much of the 1990s, Bill Bennett and others were campaigning against rap lyrics and entertainment that applauded and encouraged rape and cop killing. Now there is a grassroots movement invigorated by too many of those encouragements to violence, and Hillary Clinton gave it her support. Meanwhile, Donald Trump stood strongly against it and with the cops. Drug legalization? The Democratic party made plain its ambition to fight for legalization by putting it in the party platform in 2016. Meanwhile, Donald Trump's convention and platform did not. War against terrorism and Radical Islam? The Democratic party wanted none of that language. Clinton scandals of the 1990s and the *Death of Outrage*? Hillary Clinton was part and parcel of the whole problem and would bring her husband (the lead character of those scandals) back into the White House. Donald Trump was trying to, and did, send those protagonists into permanent political retirement.

For more than a decade, the conservative movement has been asking for more talk of American exceptionalism. One candidate centered his whole campaign around it, and the other surrounded herself with the likes of Huma Abedin and a coterie of transnational progressives. Now think about personnel as policy. Better education outcomes? Who was in the pocket of the unions and who knew all too well how much the unions stand in the way of excellence? A quick look at what the union bosses have had to say about Donald Trump should easily have dispatched those questions.

Yes, it *was* actually pretty easy to see the interests of this country were ill-served by not only Hillary Clinton and her record, but by the kinds of people she would have brought with her.

It *was* actually pretty easy to see that "indecorous and infelicitous" language should be just about the last concerns on our minds when it came to saving our country. Every current or former member of any military branch, or reader of military history, learned that lesson long ago, after all.

Too many conservatives were vested in proving they were right in saying Donald Trump could not win. One could never read a word from any of them about the things Trump had done or said right, not even his ongoing outreach to the minority community—something else movement conservatives and party regulars had begged their candidates to do for at least a generation but had proven incapable of doing effectively themselves.

Thus, the oddity of Donald Trump and the conservative movement, or Conservatism Inc. that wanted to bury him and his candidacy. To many Americans, nearly 63 million of them, he spoke their language and thought the way they did. It was also the way the conservative movement, from the intellectual tops to the grassroots bottoms, had spoken and thought for a very long time, as well. For those without blinders, the Trump victory was no mystery—it was founded, in large part, on the very work conservative think tanks and journals had been doing for decades. One might even say, as the old Moliere line has it: Donald Trump was speaking their prose but they didn't know it.

4

CONSERVATIVE STOCKHOLM SYNDROME

WHEN CONSERVATIVES ADAPT TO THE CRITIQUES OF THE LEFT

"STOCKHOLM SYNDROME" IS A TERM used to describe the rare situation when, as the *Encyclopaedia Britannica* puts it, "a captive begins to identify closely with his or her captors, as well as with their agenda and demands."[1] Although the term has not been recognized as an official condition to be diagnosed by professional psychologists or psychiatrists, it has been a part of cultural parlance since the 1970s, based on a Swedish bank robbery and hostage incident and, more familiarly in the United States, in the kidnapping of Patty Hearst in 1974.

The condition, however, is much more prominent when translated into political psychology. Or, at least, that is what we have found in our attempt to explain five different phenomena that otherwise have no reason for the behaviors of many of our fellow or self-described conservatives. It can be seen when Republican candidates or office holders try to soften their positions to come off more appealing or less Republican or conservative in liberal settings. It can be seen when Republican candidates or office holders or conservative scholars or journalists seek recognition from liberal institutions or from mainstream media hosts. It can be seen when Republican candidates or office holders or conservative scholars or journalists choose to appear on mainstream or liberal media outlets instead of conservative outlets. It can be seen when Republican candidates or office holders or conservative scholars or journalists deliberately and actively try to appease or win over liberal audiences on deliberately liberal or left-wing television shows, primarily hosted by comedians. Finally, it can be seen when conservative scholars or journalists condemn fellow conservative scholars or journalists or Republican candidates or officeholders in front of or to the Left.

The etiology, cause, or sometimes active motives for these behaviors tend to be driven by two or three standard interests: often it is ego, often it is for popularity, often (especially when witnessed by candidates and office holders) it is based on the advice of consultants.

Perhaps proving that this is not a true psychiatric disorder but is based on deliberate decision making, there is no counterpart on the Left or in the liberal community, no "liberal Stockholm syndrome." It has long been said by Republicans and conservatives that we tend to "eat our own" while Democrats never criticize one another or apologize. How else to explain, for instance, the long-term success and approval, if not defense, of former United States Senator Ted Kennedy, given not only his actions at Chappaquiddick but his well-documented and legendary escapades with other women? How else to explain not just the toleration of but defense and lauding of Bill Clinton, given his legendary infelicities and worse?

How else to explain the ongoing toleration and ignoring of the absurdly stupid and hyper-politicized comments of certain Democratic law-makers, primarily in Congress? A few conservative columnists and websites list the collected idiocy and race-baiting comments of liberal heroes from Nancy Pelosi to Maxine Waters. Have Democrats ever distanced themselves from them or condemned them? Have any Democrats ever criticized former Democratic Senate leader Robert Byrd's past with the Ku Klux Klan or his use of the "N-word"? No, it is very difficult, indeed, to find Democrats critical of other Democrats.

Almost everyone is prone to saying stupid or outrageous things now and again. Behaviorally, the poor treatment of other people, while more volitional and irrespective of IQ, is also bi-partisan or non-partisan. But Democrats and liberals, convinced of the righteousness of their cause, convinced of the need to uniformly defend their cause, almost never beat up on or criticize one another. Conservatives and Republicans, however, are the first to jump ship on their own. Actually, that is probably not fair but worth leaving on the page—we are often the *second* to jump ship and criticize our own once a liberal or mainstream outlet reports on a member of our party or movement saying something indefensible, stupid, or even just arguably indefensible.

Some of this is a badge of honor. That we police ourselves or hold our movement and party to a higher standard is a good thing—and we should never be in the position of the Democrats or liberals who see politics as more important than *almost anything* else. But, for illustrative purposes and as a way of beginning to understand the conservative desire to be loved versus the liberal desire to just win at all costs, the Republican Party's eternal insecurity versus the Democratic party's eternal convictions about itself, it is worth pointing out who eats their own from time to time and who never does and never will.

It needs to be said here, too, that when the affliction strikes Republicans and conservatives, it is not presented or evidenced uniformly or consistently—but it all came to a head with the candidacy of Donald J. Trump. Moving on to the elements or conditions of the conservative Stockholm syndrome, think of it simply this way. Too many conservatives and Republicans want to be loved or respected by their opponents or enemies, whereas for the liberal or Democratic mindset the point is to defeat their opponents or enemies. Too many conservatives and Republicans appear to believe they aren't quite right, whereas for the liberal or Democratic mindset there is never any such self-doubt.

There are only a handful of conservative or conservative-leaning media outlets—Fox News is one. Talk radio is another. As pointed out in the previous chapter, the entertainment and media culture is, otherwise, primarily dominated by the Left. This is true of almost every other cable television show, as it is true of the late-night talk shows and networks from HBO to Comedy Central. But if Bill Maher reaches out to a conservative or Republican, conservatives and Republicans rush to go on his show. When Stephen Colbert and John Stewart had their shows on Comedy Central, they often tried to book conservative authors and Republican politicians—and the authors and politicians would run to them. And, in almost every case, with very few and rare exceptions, the conservatives and Republicans on those shows looked like the fools the hosts wanted them to look like. It never made any sense.

Stop and think for a sane moment: Knowing the audiences of the likes of a John Stewart or Stephen Colbert or Bill Maher, why would Republican candidates even think there were votes to mine there? And why would conservative intellectuals or office seekers think they— without the teams of joke-writers employed by the comedians—could be funny and hip and witty with those audiences or match wits with the comedians? Comedians, after all, have one goal: to entertain. To make people laugh. To poke fun. Conservative intellectuals and authors have serious points to make about the state of our polity or an issue of public policy. Office seekers have one point, to win elections. The gap between the two could not be further—and, as we say, trying to bridge it almost never worked.

Add to this the problem of self-doubt so many conservatives and Republicans have about their cause, and it becomes all the worse. There were and are, of course, a handful of exceptions of thinkers and authors who could stand up to and do well in these settings. Ann Coulter and Kellyanne Conway come to mind. Christopher Hitchens, when he was alive, was no conservative but was a truly independent thinker and writer who would occasionally embrace conservative positions and even endorsed the re-election of George W. Bush in 2004—and he could spar and parry with the best of them in any environment. After that, the list gets pretty short. In fact, to many of us, it was simply debasing to watch some of our heroes on these shows. Credit goes to a handful of people who understand this game, Laura Ingraham for example, who have made a point of never doing those shows.

But why go to those precincts in the first place? Some, but few, Republicans and conservatives are, in the parlance of our age, "hip." Our group tends to take serious issues very seriously, issues that run the gamut from constitutionalism to the protection of innocent life. And to the credit of most of our scholars and candidates, they have been lifelong passions, studies, and interests. What business, what commonalities, what "win" is there for a Rick Santorum or Ted Cruz to submit to an interview or audience with a Bill Maher? Again, we have causes, but comedians and their audiences seek cynicism and laughter.

Another angle here is worth pointing out: the prejudice and temptation of television. Again, with the exception of several shows on the Fox News Channel, almost all of television—from cable to the networks—is liberal or left wing. Talk radio hosts and their producers know well the challenge about to be described. Many national talk radio hosts have millions of listeners, and several local radio hosts have hundreds of thousands. In a good many cases, a talk radio host will have a much bigger audience than a television (cable or network) host. But talk radio hosts and their producers, with just two or three exceptions, know that in a campaign or with a popular conservative author, the candidate or author will almost always first choose to appear on a lesser-watched television show rather than the more-listened-to talk radio show. Mike Gallagher, as but one example, has millions of weekly listeners—and he will tell you, for as often as Mitt Romney appeared on television networks in the 2012 presidential campaign, he simply did not and would not appear on Gallagher's show. We can tell you, as well, from personal experience, that any number of candidates and conservative personalities would run to CNN's morning television show over and instead of a radio show that had a much larger audience—and that was more favorable to the candidate or personality.

Some of this is a prejudice toward television. Most of it is an ingrained and wholly wrong belief that simply because it is television, or the name CNN or MSNBC is slapped onto something, it is more credible. But the search for that kind of credibility is a fool's errand, a will-o'-the-wisp. It never comes but is continually sought. There is, in other words, this thought inherent in too many Republicans and conservatives that they aren't quite right and they need the approval, imprimatur, kosher stamp of the mainstream media or the more hip entertainment community. Part of this is a desire to be liked, but part of it is an inherent self-doubt that fuels and animates the desire to be liked by a certain network, host, or crowd.

And all of this helps to explain Conservatism Inc.'s miscalling of the election and criticism of Donald Trump during the campaign.

As for miscalling the election: of course when you listen to MSNBC or CNN or read the editorial pages and news coverage from the *New York Times* or *Washington Post,* you will get a distorted view of not only truth, but of what tens of millions of people who don't watch those networks or read those newspapers think or believe. Most of us know these outlets are biased. When it comes to print journalism, the bias is usually in what they do not report. When it comes to broadcast journalism, the bias is usually in what they do report (or emphasize) and the questions they ask their guests. We, as a party and movement, know this and have known it a long time.

This is exactly why we have created alternatives: like Fox News, like talk radio, like the Conservative Book Club (to rival the *New York Times* best-seller list) or the *Claremont Review of Books* (to rival the *New York Review of Books*). But, still, given the choice between putting an op-ed in the *Washington Post* or in *National Review*, the former will usually win out. Given the choice between appearing on Laura Ingraham's or Mike Gallagher's show or a CNN morning show, CNN will usually win out. Somehow, we have not fully embraced our own cause and our own base and outlets as equally credible as the left-wing bases and outlets. Somehow, we still think they matter more—or that they are the only ones that matter at all.

And as for criticism of Donald Trump—yes, that liberal near-monopoly of media got its way and persuaded many of us, too many, to bow to it rather than defend him or go on offense against whatever it was he was being attacked for that day, given that in almost every case Hillary Clinton was a worse violator. Not only was Hillary Clinton a worse violator of almost everything Donald Trump was accused of, there was something else too many in Conservatism Inc. forgot as well: we had a country to save!

Think of it this way: Early on in 2016, Donald Trump and his candidacy were known for two primary things: opposition to illegal immigration and wanting to "make America great again." The first was something conservatives have been begging for going on ten years, the second was a slogan from the Ronald Reagan-George H. W. Bush ticket of 1980. Donald Trump also had a robust tax reform plan that had been praised by the likes of Steve Forbes and Steve Moore, who were the holders of the Ronald Reagan-Jack Kemp tax-cutting tablets, and he spoke a great deal about the problems of Radical Islam. Just so, it turned out he was also winning the GOP nomination—taking upwards of 45 percent of Hispanics in Nevada and proving the ability to win not only Deep South states like Mississippi (as a Manhattanite, no less) but also in purple Michigan and deep blue Massachusetts.[2] Yet many—a great many—conservative think tankers and journalists were, at the same time, excoriating him as well as those who supported him, and those who would not join their Never Trump bandwagon.

Everything above is history and fact, though distantly remembered if at all. So, too, was it a fact that Donald Trump was not a typical Republican candidate. On the positive side of his difference from our standard candidates, he was a businessman who has employed tens of thousands of people. On the negative, he could be crude in his language, even vulgar. And some of his policy prescriptions and positions lacked unifying coherence. His position on Israel early in the campaign was but one exhibit: he condemned Radical Islam but at one point claimed he wanted to be neutral in the Israel/Palestinian conflict. Those problems, inconsistencies, and negatives were not a little concerning. But they were ironed out over the time of the campaign and almost all but the most pure of conservative candidates (who almost never end up winning) have had inconsistencies. (One small example: George W. Bush, we recall, could not answer Gary Bauer in 2000 when Bauer asked Bush why he supported trade with China but not Cuba. And nobody seemed to care much.)

But while Donald Trump's inconsistencies were not a little concerning, they are also not a little overemphasized. The candidate who wanted to be neutral with Israel was not saying anything beyond President Bill Clinton, who was the most beloved of presidents by the Jewish community though he brought Yasser Arafat into the White House. But, as for Donald Trump, it was also true he helped campaign for the most hawkish prime minister Israel has had since Menachem Begin: Bibi Netanyahu. And in time Donald Trump would speak of moving the U.S. Embassy from Tel Aviv to Jerusalem. This was 180 degrees different from Barack Obama, who had done all he could to marginalize Israel and oust Netanyahu.

Yes, Donald Trump flubbed—or worse—a question about David Duke endorsing him. But he also had previously denounced David Duke. And the reason his flub simply had no legs and should have had no meaning was that nobody could seriously believe Donald Trump had any truck or tolerance for David Duke. Sometimes a flub is just a flub and every candidate makes mistakes here and there. Every candidate. As for Trump, a man who has an Orthodox Jewish daughter and grandchildren he is very close to, and who adore him in return, was simply not a David Duke supporter or anything like one. Still, many in Conservatism, Inc., along with the mainstream media piled on rather than defended him.

On the judiciary, early on, Donald Trump had stated his model for a Supreme Court justice would be his sister, a liberal, but a judge who, nonetheless, was first nominated to the federal bench by Ronald Reagan. But Trump had also said his model was Antonin Scalia and in short order would release a list of potential Supreme Court nominees and federal judges crafted with the help of the Heritage Foundation and the Federalist Society. Yet Conservatism, Inc., simply said they did not believe or trust him. Supreme Court Justice Neil Gorsuch proved which way Trump would settle—just as conservatives had hoped.

Oddly enough, the blinders on Conservatism Inc. were thick. Donald Trump spoke of Scalia and his list of strict constructionists while Hillary Clinton gave no doubt as to her potential nominees or policies. Hers would be a presidency of higher taxes and, at best, no action on illegal immigration. On foreign and defense policy she was known for few major accomplishments but among them: ruining Libya just as it was trying to align with the United States and participating in both the ruining of Egypt and antipathy toward Israel.

As for her judicial appointments: think Sonia Sotomayor and Elena Kagan as far as the eye can see. But somehow the mantra "Trump is not a conservative" was heard more from Conservatism Inc. than were the problems of Hillary Clinton's policies and personnel.

Donald Trump had some explaining to do in his candidacy. As did so many other Republican candidates and nominees over the years. But Donald Trump's Democratic party opponent did not. She was clear and consistent—as clear and consistent a liberal as could be. But if Trump had explaining to do, did not his conservative critics also have some explaining to do?

Again, yes, Trump could be vulgar, but is it not of some irony that those who pointed this out the most had worked for, written for, and held up a man—William F. Buckley Jr.—whose most famous line on television may very well have been, "Now listen, you queer, stop calling me a crypto-Nazi or I'll sock you in the goddam face and you'll stay plastered."[3] And that was a line in a day of much more public decorum. Imagine, if you can, the hue and cry from the "respectable right" had

Donald Trump uttered the same words. In a party of family values, it very much appears Donald Trump's relationship with his children and grandchildren stands much better than Mr. Buckley's as well.[4] Too many were blind to their own double standards. Double standards used to be something conservatives abjured as well.

But double standards require the ability to distinguish. Early on, some were scratching their heads and criticizing the likes of William J. Bennett for condemning violent rap lyrics in the past but not being similarly exercised by Donald Trump's vulgarities. Thus, the language of Donald Trump was put on par with commercial industries and musicians who sing about the virtues of rape and cutting off heads. We're sorry, but there is a difference between the sailor's mouth of a political candidate and the commercialization of rape and cop killing. People who could not see that distinction could see nothing. And it was the Clinton candidacy and Democratic convention, not the Trump candidacy or Republican convention, that highlighted the Black Lives Matter movement, complete with the mother of Michael Brown (the BLM hero of Ferguson, MO who arguably catalyzed the anti-cop movement and attitude of the BLM and the Left—the man whose shooting was cleared by every investigation, state and federal, that looked into it).[5]

Before we leave the issue of double standards and Conservatism Inc. there was and is the question of proportion and consistency. This problem comes to us in comparison to campaigns past. Was Rudy Giuliani—a pro-choice, pro–gay rights mayor who endorsed Mario Cuomo for governor—the recipient of anything close to the scorn of Conservatism Inc. when he ran for president in 2007/2008? Or take Mitt Romney—a pro-choice, pro–gay rights one-term governor of Massachusetts who did not even seek a second term, knowing he could not win it. He twice ran for president and was the hero and choice of many on the conservative side of the spectrum in his first run, and the consensus candidate the second time. He was never put through the grinder of the conservative punditocracy the way Donald Trump was for his dramatic changes of position. Indeed, Giuliani had worse and more public marital issues than Donald Trump as well. And Mitt Romney's conversions of convenience or sincerity (whomever you believe) were much closer in time to his presidential campaign than Donald Trump's changes of position were to his. And, yet, both Giuliani and Romney were at once supported by many in the conservative movement and, to this day, remain heroes of it.

The anti-Trump conservative punditocracy, the Never Trumpers, were completely over-wrought in their critiques of and captiousness about Donald Trump. And beyond inconsistent and incoherent when he was compared to candidates past. To be sure, Donald Trump was far from perfect. He was seemingly far from an ideal conservative or Republican candidate for president on paper, looked at in isolation. (Though writing those words today seems a tough sell itself, given he has been the only Republican to beat the Clinton Machine or win the presidency in three presidential election cycles.) But the critique from his conservative critics did morph into some kind of Stockholm syndrome, where every label conservatives had abjured by the Left in the past was now being thrown at Donald Trump by his own party's self-appointed gatekeepers. Including the charges of racism and bigotry. The problem beyond the irony is this: the punditocracy had either not convinced, or forgot to tell, those who actually vote—not thousands of voters, millions of them.

In the end, we conservatives had longed for a president who could talk of American exceptionalism, do something about illegal immigration, and full-throatedly condemn Radical Islam. He was here, in front of our eyes and ears and ballots, and the New York–D.C. Republican and conservative effort was to slay him with all the arrows in their quivers. To those not blinded by their own self-interest, rather than the country's interest they had been talking and writing about for decades, it simply made and makes no sense. After all, when you ask for governance by the first two thousand names of a phone book, appealing to base common sense rather than Ivory Tower intellectualism, as William F. Buckley Jr. famously remarked, this kind of candidate and candidacy may very well be what turns up.

The problem, in large part, may have been this and exactly this: Conservatism Inc. forgot its base and why it existed. Sure, the conferences and papers and books and op-eds on immigration and Radical Islam and American exceptionalism and constitutionalism and tax cuts were one thing, but in the mouth and candidacy of the plain-spoken, that would have to wait. Why? The same reason, in large part, that pollsters could not figure out why people did not want to say they were supporting Donald Trump. Nobody put it better than Peggy Noonan in September of 2016:

> Every four years I ask people if they'll vote, and if they have a sense of how. Every four years they tell me—assertively or shyly, confidently or tentatively. This year is different. I've never seen people so nervous to answer. It's so unlike America, this reticence, even defensiveness. It's as if there's a feeling that to declare who you're for is to invite others to inspect your soul.
>
> "I feel like this is the most controversial election ever," said a food-court worker at La Guardia Airport. She works a full shift, 4 a.m. to noon, five days a week, then goes full-time to a nearby college. We'd been chatting a while, and when I asked the question she told me, carefully, that she hasn't decided how she'll vote, and neither have her family members. I said a lot of people seem nervous to say. She said: "Especially Trump people. They're afraid you'll think they're stupid."
>
> Which is how I knew she was going to vote for Donald Trump.
>
> It's true: Trump voters especially don't want to be categorized, judged, thought stupid—racist, sexist, Islamophobic, you name it. When most of them know, actually, that they're not.[6]

That, after all, had been part of the problem of Conservatism Inc. Our scholars and best thinkers are scholars and thinkers nonpareil. Think of Hadley Arkes or Allan Bloom or David Gelernter or Robert P. George or Harry Jaffa or Harvey Mansfield or Charles Kesler, who had university appointments. Or think of those who left academic postings for the think tanks—the likes of Walter Berns or George Will or Irving Kristol or any number of younger scholars. But to the high or elite culture, and increasingly the college and university class, we conservatives were always the unwashed, the unenlightened, the ones who needed their consciousness and consciences raised. We never really had a right to govern because we were the troglodytes and dumb ones. Sometimes we were the fascists and the bigots, other times we were science-deniers and racists. Although we actually knew we were not, we always knew we operated in an environment that thought we were. Too often too many of us caved to and bent to it, conceding just a bit that we had to denounce messengers whose language may not have been ours even when their popularity and ideology was. We liked our conferences in Washington and Manhattan, and we liked our subscribers. Of those who showed up at our candidates' rallies and what moved them, not so much.

But what was the point of all those papers and conferences and debates and op-eds and magazines if not to, well, actually implement them? And how in a republic or democracy do you implement? Elections and mass appeal. Selling your points. So what of Trump's language? What of his occasional vulgarity? Sure, it wouldn't work at the faculty club, but what about, as we used to ask, Kansas? Or Topeka?

The media had an awfully easy job of making caricatures of the Trump voter—and the rally attendee. Example after example could illustrate how network and cable and print journalists would seek out the most easy-to-caricature conservatives. We give you but a small example from our own witness, but this was repeated thousands of times in 2015 and 2016, as it was with the Tea Party rallies, as it was with almost every grass-roots conservative movement. We hosted a debate-watching party mid-2015 in a rented movie theater. The crowd was lively and all age groups. But here was the description from the reporter in attendance: "Despite sitting in a dark theater that smelled of chicken fingers, nachos, and beer for more than three hours, the crowd's energy never diminished."[7] We will be as honest as we can here: We smelled none of that and didn't really see any beer, not that we noticed anyway.

But that is always the caricature and what the media looks for or smells.

Perhaps all of this is why Donald Trump has been known as the "Blue Collar Billionaire." He spoke to an audience that think tanks and foundations and magazines had long ago stopped speaking to—but needed; an audience the mainstream media long ago began to mock and scorn. But at the end of the day, and end of the campaign, it was clear: a lot more people were taking the conservative message from Conservatism Inc. over the decades more seriously than Conservatism Inc. was taking the people and the voters. Or its listeners and readers.

As for those of us who were not surprised by Trump's victory, we were listening to, as Donald Trump was speaking to, an America with far different concerns from Hollywood's and the mainstays of the elite culture: those who liked nachos and chicken fingers and beer, perhaps, even if their theaters didn't smell of it. We think of it in the context of the central truths that explain the popularity of country music. Without the glitz and style of the postmodern era, country still sings about the bedrock values and verities and hardships of life: patriotism, faith, family, poverty, love, break-ups, divorce, addiction. And in comprehensible lyrics. Country music also gets to a part of America wholly uninterested in what the musicians and coasts find important in clothing or travel or bling. An oldie but goodie that helps explain this divergence, this differential, this disconnect from, say, *The View* and MSNBC and CNN is Loretta Lynn's song (written by Shel Silverstein of all people), "One's on the Way." In it the lives of the elites is quite descriptively contrasted with the lives of everyday people. Hollywood and Washington are all about glitter and glam but back in Topeka 'the rain is a fallin' / the faucet is a drippin' and the kids are a bawlin'.'"

It may seem peculiar that a billionaire understood and spoke to all this, all the while denouncing such things as political correctness. But as his son said of him:

> He didn't hide out behind some desk in an executive suite; he spent
> his career with regular Americans. He hung out with the guys on con-
> struction sites pouring concrete and hanging sheetrock. He listened

to them and he valued their opinions as much and often more than the guys from Harvard and Wharton locked away in offices away from the real work.

He's recognized the talent and the drive that all Americans have. He's promoted people based on their character, their street smarts and their work ethic, not simply paper or credentials. To this day, many of the top executives in our company are individuals that started out in positions that were blue collar, but he saw something in them and he pushed them to succeed.[9]

Other wealthy people have understood "here in Topeka" and could talk to them because they knew them, too. It has been said of Ronald Reagan that he learned as much from his travels for General Electric, meeting with the factory and line employees across the country, as he did anywhere or from anything else.[9] It is also important to remember that, at first, many of the conservative intellectuals disdained Reagan, as well—even supporting his primary opponents in 1979 and 1980 before supporting him. Reagan was not known for harsh language as Trump is or was, but he was seen as an anti-intellectual and someone whose positions had also changed. But, like Trump, his work with actual hourly employees gave him a different view of America and Americans than the Doles or Bushes or Romneys or McCains had. It also gave Reagan and Trump the ability to go over the media and directly to the people in their simple language.

The elites missed it at almost every turn with Ronald Reagan, until he proved victorious in 1980. And they missed it, too, with Donald Trump. But who got these candidates and who these candidates got is what mattered in the end, the American people. It is for shame that so many in the conservative think tanks and journalist community forgot just who it was that mattered most, whose values and country they were there to uphold and defend. It is for shame not because they were proven wrong, but because for many of them, they still cannot see it.

5

THE RISE AND FALL OF
THE SUBTEXT

WHAT THE PUNDITS AND JOURNALISTS MISSED
ABOUT TRUMP

BEYOND THE CONSERVATIVE STOCKHOLM SYNDROME, characterized by the ease in which conservatives became comfortable with using the epithets against Donald Trump and his supporters that they once abjured when the Left used those epithets against them, another indicator was their falling into the "trap of the subtext."

In the 1994 Whit Stillman cult-movie classic *Barcelona*, a short dialogue takes place that explains a volume of both history and logic, and offers a critique of the postmodern pseudo-sophisticated and over-intellectualized world we now live in. Walking down the street, the two main characters are talking:

FRED: Maybe you can clarify something for me. Since I've been, you know, waiting for the fleet to show up, I've read a lot, and . . .

And one of the things that keeps popping up is this thing about "subtext." Plays, novels, songs—they all have a "subtext," which I take to mean a hidden message or import of some kind. So subtext we know. But what do you call the message or meaning that's right there on the surface, completely open and obvious? They never talk about that. What do you call what's above the subtext?

TED: The text.

FRED: OK, that's right, but they never talk about that.[1]

In this short dialogue is found the entire conservative critique of postmodernism, along with its related academic fields such as critical legal studies, the heart of which is not to take central writings of original authors' works at face value but, rather, to take their critics at face value. The critique is more important than the original text or art. Or, alternatively, they try to show inherent biases that animated those original authors' works—showing, or claiming to show, that what they wrote was not so much a product of original thinking and deliberate meaning but, rather, the effect of their race, class, or skin color.

Almost all conservative thinkers and academics in political studies are familiar with this problem in the academy. It is not a small reason many of them left it—or were barred from it. And the same is true of religious practitioners, adherents, or "believers." The orthodox just want to study the Bible or Torah and those who believe in it—and not reformists who try to define (or, really, redefine) what those texts actually said in black and white.

As for conservative thinkers and academics in the political fields—be they the few remnants at the universities or the scholars at our think tanks or journalists and pundits—they all know this trend. Many were schooled on it from that handful of professorial remnants they studied under, for example the likes of Harry Jaffa and Charles Kesler at Claremont McKenna, Robert P. George at Princeton, Hadley Arkes at Amherst, Harvey Mansfield at Harvard, Walter Berns (when he was at Cornell or the University of Toronto or Georgetown), or Allan Bloom at the University of Chicago.

Many journalists and pundits who were too young or not fortunate enough to study with these giants of thought might have picked this learning up along the way at the seminars offered at the Claremont Institute or the Hudson Institute. And when it comes to understanding politics and political thinking, almost all of it starts with a once-obscure political philosopher who taught the likes of Jaffa, Arkes, Mansfield, Bloom, and Berns.

That once-obscure professor was Leo Strauss. It is far beyond the scope of this book to try to explain Leo Strauss and his legacy (a great and handy book that came out this year does it better than anyone before: Steven F. Hayward's *Patriotism Is Not Enough*). A refugee from Germany who would go on to teach at the New School, the University of Chicago, Claremont, and St. John's, suffice to say, Leo Strauss has long been misunderstood by many on the Left, that is, when he was not being maligned. Indeed, a phenomenon of a great deal of that misunderstanding and maligning was to confuse "Straussianism" with "neoconservatism," a confusion or blending no student of Leo Strauss's would ever imagine.

To further compound the errors of this confusion in the commentariat by the likes of Chris Matthews and others obsessed with finding the intellectual roots of President George W. Bush's foreign policy, the "neoconservatism" the Left kept talking about in the 2000s was almost always in the context of foreign policy, something Leo Strauss spoke and wrote little on. In other words, for much of the Left, "Straussianism" became a handy (and sloppy) label for some imagined version of "conservatism" or a synonym with "right-wing."

The irony is that Leo Strauss himself was not very political and certainly not a Republican—nor were many of his prominent students like Allan Bloom. Harry Jaffa, our teacher, started out as a Democrat and remained so during his years studying under Strauss, voting for Roosevelt, Truman, Stevenson, and Kennedy, and did not vote for a Republican until 1964 when he went to work for the Goldwater campaign. But Strauss did stand for something that would become known, at least academically, as "conservative." Or at least not post-modern and intellectually cutting edge.

Almost every introduction to the work of Leo Strauss begins with his students (or students' students nowadays) pointing out that Strauss thought the importance of teaching philosophy, the way to study it, was to understand writers (be they philosophers of old or the founders of this country) as they understood themselves. In other words: study the text. This is the opposite of the postmodern or pre-postmodernist progressive academic trend and ethic of studying the criticism or the ascribed inherent biases of the writers based on their ethnicity or color or economic circumstance.

As Strauss would put it:

According to a saying of Kant, it is possible to understand a philoso-pher better than he understood himself. Now, such understanding may have the greatest merits; but it is clearly not historical under-standing. If it goes so far as to claim to be the *true* understanding, it is positively unhistorical. . . . Historical understanding means to understand an earlier philosopher exactly as he understood himself.[2]

Or, again:

The task of the historian of thought is to understand the thinkers of the past exactly as they understood themselves, or to revitalize their thought according to their own interpretation of it. To sum up this point: the belief in the superiority of one's own approach, or of the approach of one's time, to the approach of the past is fatal to historical understanding. . . . The task of the historian of thought is to understand the past exactly as it understood itself; for to abandon that task is tantamount to abandoning the only practicable criterion of objectivity in the history of thought.[3]

This brings us to what so many missed about Donald Trump. And understanding this point helps understand how so many voters could look at Trump and see and hear one thing while so many critics saw and heard something else. It also helps explain what a contingent of Strauss students and students' students (at least from what is known as the West Coast School of Straussianism) supported Trump.[4]

The same failure to understand Trump and his supporters as he understood himself and they understood him plagued pundits and critics alike. One of the 2016 campaign's popular explanations of the disconnect between the commentariat and polls on the one hand, and Trump's continuing popularity at his rallies and his continued victories in the primaries on the other, was the line from Brad Todd and Salena Zito: "voters take Donald Trump seriously but not literally, while journalists take him literally, but not seriously."[5]

This does not quite get to it. Donald Trump's voters understood and took Donald Trump both seriously and literally when it came to policy, but the journalist community would not take him seriously when it came to policy. That community did not think he meant what he said when it came to making America great again or the policies he would proscribe to do so—they actually took him as unserious, a snake-oil salesman, someone people should not trust. But when it came to his personal life or his strong language, yes, that they would take literally, too seriously. In other words: voters heard Donald Trump *as voters* and heard him *as a candidate*. Journalists heard Donald Trump as a pitch-man. Donald Trump's voters understood him as he understood himself.

Nowhere was this more evident than in a postelection CNN interview between Van Jones and a family in Trumbull County, Ohio. Jones, a left-wing CNN contributor and Trump detractor throughout the campaign season, went to Trumbull County to try to understand, to study, how a middle-America family could actually vote for Donald Trump—a political psychology, sociology, anthropology study of sorts. The father was Scott Seitz, who headed a family of lifelong Democrats. The whole family except Mrs. Seitz, who abstained from voting, voted for Donald Trump in 2016.[6] Why? Mrs. Seitz said she could not vote for Hillary Clinton because "of her morals."[7] Van Jones, taken aback, said:

"So let me give you guys a chance to respond to some of the stereotypes about all the Trump voters. All the Trump voters hate the Mexicans, they hate Muslims, they don't like black people, they're just—it was all this explosive kind of racial talk was what really got everybody going." The son replied:

> One of my jobs is helping counseling individuals recovering from drug and alcohol addictions. And I'm just going by the statistics. At my location, most of them are minorities. I would probably go as far as to say 80 to 85 percent.
>
> So, you know, if that were the case and if I was racist, then I just don't believe that I'd be very good at my job.
>
> But I'm not the stereotype that individuals think we are.[8]

Van Jones seemed to be taken a little aback again—this was a family one might say looked like it came out of central Hollywood casting for the white working class, something, perhaps out of a show like *Roseanne*, complete with flannel shirts and work boots. But the son works in addiction treatment and recovery, and with a mostly racial minority population?!? This is not the Trump voter or rally attendee we got to know when CNN or other networks tried to caricature those supporters. The subtext of Donald Trump's racism was *the text* for the media, not those who actually "lived in Topeka" as the song goes, not those taking the presidential race and candidates, well, seriously. No understanding or thinking about Donald Trump through the lens of race, class, and gender here. They were listening to the text.

The interview went further and was more revealing yet. Van Jones was beginning to "get it." He asked, "But when you hear something about guns and the Second Amendment, you think about meat in your freezer. Tell us about that."

Mr. Seitz replied:

> Absolutely. When we get a downturn in the economy, we need to still feed our families. And when they talk about the Second Amendment or taking our guns away, that's exactly what we think of, all the time

that we have hunting together and, as a family, and we got out and we harvest and we put food in the—in the freezer.

And when we get slow at work, we still have food to feed our families. And that's most important to us. We need to put food on the table.[9]

Earlier, Mr. Seitz would say of the promises of hope and change that Barack Obama brought, and that they all voted for, that they just didn't happen for them—and that Hillary Clinton never spoke to them. Her mission was different, about "special interests." Trump's mission?

We truly want to make America better. . . . We hope that the bleeding can actually stop in our area. The Rust Belt area is filled with United Autoworkers, United Steelworkers and everything trickles down from that. And when they seem to suffer, the rest of us suffer. And we need to stop the bleeding.[10]

For the Seitz family, as for so many others—the vulgarities or offenses of Donald Trump in his speech or in his past were all subtext, irrelevant, commentary. The focus on them was not going to affect jobs or help put food on the table one way or the other. And so far as personal morality went, so far as character: to Mrs. Seitz it was a wash, a pox on both candidates.

For all the critique of Donald Trump's character, his marriages, his language, his 2005 Billy Bush tape, did not Hillary Clinton have, if not salty language, an equal or greater number of scandals attached to her and her family? Or, as we would often put it on our radio show: character, in this election, just was not on the table. What was? Well, for the Trump voters and an awful lot of erstwhile Democratic party or Obama voters: the economy and saving the country. Besides, for all of Donald Trump's censorious and rough language, what family in this day and age did not have that among their own?

As Barton Swaim put it:

Whatever else may be said about the man, his campaign was essentially human in ways ordinary campaigns haven't been for a long time. His "speeches" were unscripted and sometimes aimless, and voters flocked to nearly every one. He spoke the way family members speak to one another in the privacy of their homes: the stupid gibes, the bluster, the candor verging on cruelty. It all sounded too familiar to be fake. Voters judged him based on what they heard from the man himself—not what they saw in ads or heard from surrogates.[11]

But what of the culture? What of the conservative critique of lower standards in our speech and entertainment? What of the ongoing coarsening of our culture that the likes of so many from William J. Bennett to those in the so-called "religious right" or the social conservatives spoke of for so many years?

Well, would any of it have been better under a Hillary Clinton administration? If politics was downstream from culture, what kind of culture would be created from an even more leftward Supreme Court? What kind of culture would come from fewer restrictions on abortions, especially late-term abortions? What kind of culture would come from less religion in the public square, given left-wing interpretations of the First Amendment? What kind of culture would come from less religious liberty? What kind of culture would come from further appeasement of the anti-cop or Black Lives Matter attitude? What kind of culture would come from higher taxes that take away entrepreneurial investment and jobs? Couldn't it have been possible, just possible, that Trump supporters thought of all that, the durables and the enduring, rather than his marriages and statements in the past about women? After all, his marriages and statements had no public policy prescriptions to them—they were personal. And hadn't we all been taught to live with the notion, taught by the Clintons no less, that personal behavior is irrelevant to good or important public policy?

And what, just what, of the social and religious conservative critique of the moral decay or *acedia* of society? Well, were not crime and drugs so much the center of that critique, the tangible or visible representation of the problem? And who spoke to that? Who spoke on behalf of the police—and who spoke on behalf of the "victims" of police? What party's candidate had downgraded the prosecution of illegal drug use and set about commuting drug offenders' sentences, and who spoke of the problem of drug use rather than the problem of drug law enforcement?

J. D. Vance, the author of the bestselling *Hillbilly Elegy*, put it well in an interview in the middle of the 2016 campaign season. Asked about the poverty and hopelessness in places like West Virginia, Vance said:

> The simple answer is that these people—my people—are really struggling, and there hasn't been a single political candidate who speaks to those struggles in a long time. Donald Trump at least tries.
>
> What many don't understand is how truly desperate these places are, and we're not talking about small enclaves or a few towns–we're talking about multiple states where a significant chunk of the white working class struggles to get by. Heroin addiction is rampant. . . . The average kid will live in multiple homes over the course of her life, experience a constant cycle of growing close to a "stepdad" only to see him walk out on the family, know multiple drug users personally, maybe live in a foster home for a bit (or at least in the home of an unofficial foster like an aunt or grandparent), watch friends and family get arrested, and on and on. And on top of that is the economic struggle, from the factories shuttering their doors to the Main Streets with nothing but cash-for-gold stores and pawn shops. . . . From the Left, they get some smug condescension, an exasperation that the white working class votes against their economic interests because of social issues. . . . From the Right, they've gotten the basic Republican policy platform of tax cuts, free trade, deregulation, and paeans to the noble businessman and economic growth. . . .
>
> Trump's candidacy is music to their ears. He criticizes the factories shipping jobs overseas. His apocalyptic tone matches their lived experiences on the ground. He seems to love to annoy the elites, which is something a lot of people wish they could do but can't because they lack a platform.[12]

Indeed, music to the ears of those attending concerts played by the tone-deaf. And that salty or harsh language? It "matches their lived experiences on the ground." Mitt Romney may have had perfectly intact language and character—it meant nothing to these hard-times communities, and he could not relate to them or them to him. Finally:

No one seems to understand why conventional blunders do nothing to Trump. But in a lot of ways, what elites see as blunders people back home see as someone who—finally—conducts themselves in a relatable way. He shoots from the hip; he's not constantly afraid of offending someone; he'll get angry about politics; he'll call someone a liar or a fraud. This is how a lot of people in the white working class actually talk about politics, and even many elites recognize how refreshing and entertaining it can be! So it's not really a blunder as much as it is a rich, privileged Wharton grad connecting to people back home through style and tone. Viewed like this, all the talk about "political correctness" isn't about any specific substantive point, as much as it is a way of expanding the scope of acceptable behavior. People don't want to believe they have to speak like Obama or Clinton to participate meaningfully in politics, because most of us don't speak like Obama or Clinton.[13]

And, as Peggy Noonan put it, while they do not speak like Obama or Clinton (or Romney) and they know that, they also know they are not stupid either—though those who were inclined to back Trump kept being told they were. Barack Obama may have spoken about his presidency meaning "the rise of the oceans began to slow and our planet began to heal"; as "the moment when we ended a war and secured our nation and restored our image as the last, best hope on earth."[14] But (a) that is not how Donald Trump spoke and (b) for too many like Vance's friends and the Seitz family, nothing like that ever even came close to being true.

What did Trump promise? Building a wall (something every blue-collar worker and working-class citizen can relate to and knows how to do); killing off Radical Islam (something every American would like to see done, but was never even spoken of by name for eight years); bringing back jobs and manufacturing (something a little more important to the working class and poor than slowing the rise of oceans, which only exist on the coasts anyway); and making America great again (something any patriot or self-described patriot would want).

And that was the text. That was it. Phoenix, Arizona journalist Kari Lake summed up this notion after the election, after the Screen Actor Guild awards, a week into the Donald Trump presidency: "Darn! I missed the SAG awards. Did any of the speeches mention America's working poor or unemployed?"[15] The elites and Hillary Clinton and her party were talking about everything *but* what Donald Trump was talking about and Donald Trump was talking—simply—about what almost every family in the lower and middle classes talks about.

To Hollywood and the Left, and not a few Never-Trump conservatives, Donald Trump was a sexist or bigot or racist. But weren't all Republican candidates? Always? Trump voters, in Ohio, Michigan, West Virginia, beyond knowing they were not dumb, also knew they were not racists. But Hillary Clinton thought otherwise—and said so, repeatedly claiming all Americans have "implicit biases," sometimes it's even "in our DNA going back probably millennia." Ah, the subtext about conservative or Trump policies again: not law and order, not racially neutral, but biased. America has come a very long way on race policies, but the Left has used that cudgel, as academia has, for a very long time—and a lot of non-racists, the vast majority of America, is and was sick and tired of it. Does a racist work in a rehab facility dominated by a minority population, after all?

The Never-Trump conservatives who denounced Trump for the color of his skin as "the orange guy"[16] or the "orange haired authoritarian hoodlum,"[17] or as someone who did not mean what he said may have felt good and clever about themselves for that kind of talk, but it was not how Trump saw or understood himself any more than it was how his supporters saw or understood him. In fact, nearly everything said about Trump by his detractors was ignored as irrelevant by his supporters. It was all subtext. They wanted America—and their communities and households—to be great again. And they understood one thing about Donald Trump: he did, too. That's what he said after all—and again and again and again and again. That's not what his critics said about him—that was so much modern and postmodern academic analysis—but it is what he said, what he understood about himself, and what nearly 63 million Americans understood about him, too.

6

IDENTITY GROUP POLITICS

THE FOOLISHNESS OF DIVIDING TO CONQUER

THE GREEK POET ARCHILOCUS is remembered for saying that a fox knows many things while a hedgehog knows one important thing. That observation became the subject of Isaiah Berlin's most famous essay, "The Hedgehog and the Fox," in which he classified some of history's great philosophers and writers as either foxes or hedgehogs. It is a useful framework for understanding the divide between what Professor Angelo Codevilla called the country class and the ruling class.[1] It also sheds some light on President Trump.

We don't want to stretch this metaphor too thin, but it remains a useful entry point for understanding the 2016 election and the broader movement that supported Donald Trump and continues to advocate for the Greatness Agenda. What Codevilla calls the ruling class—those in and around government and the Davoisie oligarchy of globalists and their fellow travelers—was nearly unanimous in its visceral reaction to Donald Trump and implacable in its opposition to his candidacy. The Queens born real estate magnate was not their cup of tea. He had the wrong accent, came from the wrong borough, and his red power ties were too brash. But they could have swallowed that had he toed the line. But he didn't. In fact his platform stood as rebuke to the central tenets of the faith. In his seminal "Flight 93 Election" essay, Decius (Anton) describes these as "open borders, lower wages, outsourcing, de-industrialization, trade giveaways, and endless, pointless, winless war."[2] Donald Trump opposed them all and the ruling class hate him for it.

In a famous phrase, Julius Krein, the editor of *American Affairs*, called Trump a traitor to his class. Krein meant it as a compliment, but while the ruling class no doubt agree with the substance they feel betrayed. And it clouds their judgment, allowing them only to see the strawman they created. It leads them not only to misunderstand Donald Trump and the Greatness Agenda, but to underestimate him. During the election it surely hastened the spread of Trump Derangement Syndrome.

In fact, political and intellectual elites wield great power, controlling as they do the commanding heights of the culture. Their institutions are fully staffed and well financed. Everything was going along just fine, thank you very much, until Donald Trump gave voice to the legitimate issues of middle America. Everyone knew their place. The Progressive Left would set the agenda and D.C. Republicans would grouse and complain about the pace of the country's leftward motion, not the movement itself. The Left's project of growing the government and empowering the administrative state at the expense of the people's elected representatives in Congress, and then rubber stamping it through a judiciary that no longer believes it is bound by the actual text of the Constitution, proceeded year after year.

Republican elites did not show much interest in taking serious action to change the direction of the car; they just wanted it to go a little slower and to get a chance to drive every now and then. Washington was of, by, and for the ruling class. And that works for a while, when things are good. But when wages stagnate for years, when people are told they possess an unforgivable original sin based upon the color of their skin, and when young people believe their prospects are worse than their parents', then a free people will wake up and ask what their leaders have been doing. They will demand an accounting.

In response, all the Left can offer is the politics of race, sex, class, and any number of other demographic identifiers. Republicans, for their part, rely on checklist conservatism, mostly a set of talking points and pet policy changes of late '80s and early '90s vintage that amount to little more than a cosmetic reordering of the existing political furniture. It turns out the term *conservative* described the temperament of many of its ruling class adherents rather than a principled political philosophy grounded in the natural rights upon which the country was founded. Donald Trump intuitively recognized this, perhaps because he came of age in an era of American confidence and because he spent his career away from Washington in a world that demands results. Thus he is an existential shock to the system of a town that runs on words not deeds.

Politicians, writers, and intellectuals who broke the social compact that held within the ruling class were shown the door. In some cases the money dried up—no more fellowships, writing gigs, or cruise invitations. Political candidates saw bundlers stop bundling and super pacs stop supporting their campaigns. Upstart candidates who challenged the prevailing bipartisan orthodoxy were ignored until they went away. Occasionally one would break out, sometimes dramatically, as when an unknown economics professor named Dave Brat unseated Eric Cantor in the Republican primary in 2014. Cantor was the sitting House Majority Leader at the time. The Tea Party election of 2010 was the most notable of these moments. Taken individually these were isolated tremors set off by surly voters who, Republican leaders hoped, could be lulled back to sleep with some tough-sounding rhetoric. In retrospect they were fore-shocks of the earthquake that was to come. All of this led to a stifling and self-reinforcing homogeneity of acceptable political opinion, which was out of step with the needs and beliefs of a large part of the country.

Congressional Republicans failed to deliver on their promises to voters. What's more, voters came to understand that the leadership had no intention of delivering on the issues important to their base. In some sense this was because they really didn't know what motivated the core conservative base of the Republican Party. But mostly it's because the leadership and the base disagree on the most important issues. And so the party leadership and much of Conservatism Inc. hoped the base would go away. They could afford to give the natives a few wins every so often, even a House Majority Leader. Don't shed too many tears for Eric Cantor; he was able to land a lucrative job as vice chairman of an investment banking firm immediately after leaving Congress. Now, that's failing up! But it wasn't enough. Voters—citizens!—expected the people they sent to Washington to represent their interests. When they didn't, they got Donald Trump. It all looks clear in retrospect. But during the campaign, ruling class elites were blinded. They thought they could shut down Trump using the tried and true tactics that had worked for so long: isolation and social shaming.

It came from all quarters. The conservative writers and intellectuals shrieked that Trump was not a "true conservative." Bill Kristol, then the editor of the *Weekly Standard*, told CNN that Donald Trump "is discrediting conservatism. He needs to be separated and severed from conservatism," Kristol said. "And every Republican and conservative who cares about the future of the Republican Party and conservatism needs to say now, I really do believe this, needs to say now, 'I'm not with Trump.'" This was nearly a month after Donald Trump had officially received his party's nomination.

When pushed on the issue and asked if Hillary Clinton's appointments to the Supreme Court would not do more damage to the country, Kristol replied, "I'm happy to take that responsibility compared to your taking the responsibility of supporting a man who is utterly unfit to be president of the United States."[3] When faced with the practical reality of who would name Supreme Court justices, Kristol made clear that he would prefer Clinton's picks to Trump's. Normal people saw this as foolishness born of petulance. They would have to live the consequences of a Clinton Court. This is particularly poignant in light of Trump's nomination of Neil Gorsuch, a scholar and originalist on every conservative's Supreme Court dream team. That Kristol would have preferred a Clinton nominee in the mold of Kagan or Sotomayor is itself an indictment of the corruption of the conservative ruling class.

On the Left, the *Huffington Post* made the decision in July 2015 to cover Donald Trump in its entertainment section. It was a not so subtle display of disrespect meant to diminish Trump in the eyes of voters and deflate his campaign. When that didn't work they announced in January 2016 that they would add the following warning to every story they ran about Trump: "Note to our readers: Donald Trump is a serial liar, rampant xenophobe, racist, misogynist, birther and bully who has repeatedly pledged to ban all Muslims—1.6 billion members of an entire religion—from entering the U.S."[4]

That was typical across virtually the entire space occupied by the media bubble. In the early stages of the campaign they tried mockery. When Donald Trump just kept winning they switched to vitriol. And when even that didn't work they began vilifying not just the candidate but his supporters.

It wasn't just Hillary Clinton who thought that approximately half of America was nothing more than a "basket of deplorables." Bret Stephens wrote in the *Wall Street Journal*, "If by now you don't find Donald Trump appalling, you're appalling."[5] Note that Stephens has since left the *Journal* for the vehemently anti-Trump *New York Times*. And the *Christian Post* opined that "Trump is a scam" that Christians should "back away."[6]

Talk show host Michael Medved wrote in *National Review*,

If Trump becomes the nominee, the GOP is sure to lose the 2016 election. But the problem is much larger: Will the Republican Party and the conservative movement survive? If Asians and Latinos come to reject Republican candidates as automatically and overwhelmingly as African Americans do, the party will lose all chance of capturing the presidency, and, inevitably, it will face the disappearance of its congressional and gubernatorial majorities as well.

This quickly became the accepted wisdom on the respectable Right. It was a way to shame Trump supporters—a tactic learned from the radical Left. When the Left hears something they don't like from a conservative they yell "Racist!" or "Hitler!" Conservatism Inc. learned that lesson well, but the first and only time they decided to use their new weapon was on the man who was elected to become their party's nominee. Somehow Donald Trump was a "threat to conservatism" while Mitt Romney, the father of Obamacare, was not.

This is not new. Alexis de Tocqueville wrote in *Democracy in America*:

> Tyranny in democratic republics does not proceed in the same way, however. It ignores the body and goes straight for the soul. The master no longer says: You will think as I do or die. He says: You are free not to think as I do. You may keep your life, your property, and everything else. But from this day forth you shall be as a stranger among us. You will retain your civic privileges, but they will be of no use to you. For if you seek the votes of your fellow citizens, they will withhold them, and if you seek only their esteem, they will feign to refuse even that. You will remain among men, but you will forfeit your rights to humanity. When you approach your fellow creatures, they will shun you as one who is impure. And even those who believe in your innocence will abandon you, lest they, too, be shunned in turn. Go in peace, I will not take your life, but the life I leave you with is worse than death.[7]

Bear in mind that this is from the same author credited with first identifying the soft despotism of what would come to be known as the administrative state, and so he was well aware of the real threat to liberty posed by unaccountable and unelected bureaucrats ruling by fiat. He was a product of post-revolutionary France after all. But you can clearly see what the ruling class is trying to do to Donald Trump and his supporters. They wanted to make it so that, in Tocqueville's words, "When you approach your fellow creatures, they will shun you as one who is impure." When Amanda Carpenter published a list of Trump supporters it was so they could be shunned by polite society—the winners. Except "the winners" didn't win this time. So long had they marinated in the globalist cocoon that they couldn't tell the difference between their own talking points and objective reality.

Like the fox in the metaphor, the media and intellectual elite that arrayed against Donald Trump know many things—many of them wrong and most of them useless. But Donald Trump knows one big thing: America. And that's all it takes, because that's what matters to voters. While elites imagine their cities in speeches, everyone else is living in the real world with families and jobs, school, church, sports, and all the other things that make up a normal life. People whose jobs are in and around politics don't appreciate how far removed they are from the life of the average American.

In *Democracy in America*, Tocqueville also noted the unique advantages bequeathed to the nation by America's Puritan founding. It is virtual heresy today to speak of the Puritans as anything other than evil white oppressors, but because of their religious convictions they established a society in which all men were understood to be equal before God and as such equal in social and political status. This principle led the Puritans to establish the first system of public education. They were largely products of the English middle class and established America as a middle-class country, which stood in distinction to the class-based world they had left behind in England with its landed gentry and hereditary monarchy. Today's globalists, whether they lean Left or Right, are the intellectual heirs of the Old World aristocracy who saw in themselves a self-perpetuating class of natural rulers. Those on the Left believe they are in the vanguard of an historical revolution that leads inexorably onward, while the Buckleyite Right have Tory inclinations and as such are highly protective of what they view as their rightful political perquisites. This represents a detour from the historic American politics, especially those of Lincoln, that clearly identified government's just basis and primary responsibilities to its citizens as the natural right of the Declaration. Tocqueville argues persuasively that a similar basis for government was made as early as the Mayflower Compact in 1620.

Though a Roman Catholic, William F. Buckley had high church, throne and altar, social and political sensibilities that his preternatural charisma made infectious. They were endearing, even admirable, because they reflected his lived experience—he was the product of prep schools in France, England, and the United States before he matriculated to Yale—and were thus thoroughly authentic. Too many Buckley admirers conflated his distinctive style with American conservative politics. The American founding was revolutionary in its principles, but high church conservatism became an entropic defender of the status quo increasingly defined as whatever the Left forced on the country a generation earlier.

What ruling class elites don't understand is that for most Americans, politics is the plumbing of the country. You use it every day and it makes life better, but you don't want to think about it too often. You just expect it to work. Americans are fortunate in that way and most of them know it. They respect politics, but more the system than its practitioners. That is usually appropriate. Rare is the statesman who can uplift and ennoble his fellow citizens. That's why Washington, Lincoln, and Reagan enjoy so much esteem. What's more the average American citizen loves this country and, despite what the armchair Machiavellis believe, they love their fellow citizens as well.

The media and intellectual elite failed to see what was happening in the country because they were trained to abhor much of what middle America loves about the country. On the Left, the Constitution and the Declaration are just the tools that white male slave owners used to keep power and subjugate a nation. As such, ignoring or replacing them is a moral imperative. And on the Right, they just want to make sure no one calls them a racist or fascist. This is not to say that they don't love America—it's to say that they don't understand it and that much of what they think they know is wrong. And this is just as true, though more subtle, on the Right as it is on the Left.

For many voters much of politics is non-ideological. They may broadly identify with the Right or the Progressive Left, but what they really want is government that works and broadly comports with a commonsense notion of fairness. There is a sense in which this is the basis for the political philosophy grounded in natural right that was behind the American founding. Today that would be identified with conservatism, but it is nonetheless a minority view within intellectual conservatism. Rightly understood such a political philosophy is just an expression of what is: The common nature shared by all mankind is a reality that all people implicitly recognize. The Founders simply sought to describe it accurately and to assert it as the only just basis for legitimate government. Having done that with the Declaration of Independence, they took the further step of adopting a Constitution, the principle aim of which was to create a government that would protect the natural rights asserted in the Declaration for its citizens. That is it. It's straightforward and easy to understand. And perhaps for that reason many intellectuals distrust it.

On the Left, however, everything is ideology and struggle. The political systems built on the philosophy of Kant, Hegel, Marx, and others rely upon the dialectic—the struggle to push forward to a future beyond good and evil. But this view must be taught because it is antithetical to the self-evident truths identified as fundamental at the American founding. At root it is a rebellion against human nature that is dehumanizing because it has as its ultimate goal to break the bonds of humanity itself. That's not freedom, it's chaos, confusion, and destruction.

This highbrow philosophy becomes real when elites try to force their vision of social progress—open borders, trade giveaways, and nation building abroad—on a public that would prefer their government tend to its core responsibilities: protecting the natural rights of its citizens to be secure in their persons and property. When people finally understand that is the choice, they overwhelmingly prefer the latter.

Victor Davis Hanson is not only a renowned classicist and senior fellow of the Hoover Institution at Stanford University, he is also a fifth-generation farmer who still lives on the family farm in rural California. One does not need to subscribe to agrarian social philosophy to notice the positive correlation between the distance one keeps from centers of elite influence and one's practical and political wisdom.

Hanson doesn't seem to have much patience for the know-it-alls and busybodies who presume to lecture their fellow citizens on virtue without much evidence that they can offer a coherent definition of it, let alone demonstrate any in their own lives.

> In sum, the architects of Democratic-party reform are themselves the problem, not the solution. On key issues, they represent a minority opinion, one confined to the entertainment industry, academia, race/class/gender elite activists, and the wealthy scions of Silicon Valley, Hollywood, and Wall Street. In addition, minority activists themselves do not get out in the heartland and mistakenly believe that the demeanor, mindset, and, yes, guilt of white urban liberal elites in their midst characterize the white working and middle classes in general. And they mistakenly assume they themselves cannot be out-of-touch elites, given their ethnic and racial heritage, when in fact many most certainly are. Do Eric Holder and Colin Kaepernick know more about poverty and hardship than a West Virginian miner or an out-of-work fabricator in southern Ohio? Does an affluent Van Jones visit depressed rural Michigan to lecture out-of-work plant workers and welders about their endemic white privilege?[8]

Contrast this with Craig Mills, a writer for the left-of-center *The Daily Beast*, who views the election this way:

> Further, "white working class" seems to be *the* identity that matters when considering how Trump won. I hear continually this is the group we should concern ourselves with understanding to the exclusion of others. How absurd. I cannot recall any of those who exhort us to empathize with the white working class asking us to question their racist

or sexist motives, as if this group's decision-making occurs in economic isolation. . . .Millennial, boomer, veteran, senior, female, black, Latino, gay, Muslim, white. These are but a few groups both parties court for a reason: Identity personalizes politics. Addressing income alone will not address badly needed police reform, education disparities, or a woman's access to reproductive services. Neither will it address religious freedoms or climate change. Nor will it address the institutional structures that make dismantling barriers to fairness difficult. National parties and politics are messy because of the multiple interests—identities—they encompass. Until and unless we move to a multiparty political system, we must focus on speaking to those identities.[9]

Mills is representative of the modern Progressive Left. Identity politics is fundamental to their political philosophy. The multicultural world boils down to a binary choice between Marx and Marcuse, who was himself a Marxist and the father of what we now know as cultural Marxism. Marcuse accepted Karl Marx's core argument, but where Marx saw a class-based struggle, he substituted race, class, gender, and other demographic classifications as the combatants in what is always and everywhere nothing more than a struggle for power fought with force and fraud. Reason, which they reject as a means to knowing truth, becomes the handmaiden of passion, and human beings become dogs fighting over meat.

This worldview was projected onto Donald Trump. When he said he wanted to Make America Great Again, all leftists heard is the representative of one demographic group—white, male, of a certain age—challenging the other groups for power. In their worldview it is a zero-sum game and to the victor goes the spoils. It does not occur to them that Donald Trump has a commonsense view of the world and that there is no subtext to what he says. He means what he says. Conservatives and non-political people are often frustrated by the stridency of the Left but their understanding of the world demands it. If one group wins the others lose.

Meanwhile conservative intellectuals became lost in the details. Most never knew or understood the basis of the American founding. They believed conservatism was bow ties, seersucker suits, and a list of slogans from the 1980s. Checklist conservatism failed because it became irrelevant.[10] But before it became irrelevant it became complacent, in many ways a victim of its own success. For all the talk, there was never really a single conservative movement. There was an electoral coalition of broadly right-of-center political philosophies that came together to oppose communist imperialism abroad and collectivism at home. The debates between these groups were vibrant and gave rise to wise consensus positions that were able to win substantial electoral majorities in the 1980s and early 1990s. But the underlying divisions remained.

Taken for granted was an understanding of and appreciation for the principles of the American founding. For most of our history those things were proudly taught and broadly understood. As the Left exerted more influence on the education system, curriculums changed, especially after the 1960s but accelerating in the 1990s and 2000s. Yet conservative institutions like talk radio and Hillsdale College have done an excellent job educating that part of the public that wants to know America better. If only the intellectuals had been listening.

In the wake of their public rebuke on Election Day, the Left and the legacy conservative institutions that comprise the Never-Trump archipelago imagine that they are brave warriors defending the republic against imminent destruction. That storyline is entirely a creation of their own overactive imaginations reinforced by an aggressively orthodox peer group and strong psychological need to avoid embarrassment in front of the American public. In reality, they are Don Quixotes jousting with windmills while the Trump administration does the people's business and the rest of America goes back to work.

In the end the political pros and intellectual elites whose job it is to educate and enlighten missed what was readily apparent to many Americans because their educations trained them to see the world through an artificial construct while the people who live in the real world, results-oriented Americans, can afford no such high-brow illusions. Their criticisms of Donald Trump grew more shrill and hyperbolic the more successful he became. And they still cannot give him credit for his successes as president, which strips them of all claims to have their criticisms taken seriously when he, like all presidents, suffers failure. It also renders them incapable of offering counsel. But this may be for the best, as it is these same people who have overseen decades of policy blunders that have cost the nation dearly in blood and treasure. Bad political philosophy inevitably leads to bad outcomes in the real world—it's like trying to steer a ship through stormy seas with the wrong map.

Those wrong maps have led President Trump's critics to distort what he has said or done to fit the narrative that complements their worldview.

Dr. Larry Arnn, president of Hillsdale College, offered a useful corrective. When asked what the election of Donald Trump would mean for the country, he said:

> Some say it will mean the denigration of immigrants based on race or religion. Trump has not said that: he has said that our country belongs to its citizens. Think of consent of the governed, the principle of the relationship between the people and the government in America. That cannot mean just the will of the people, that they can do whatever they want. Otherwise they would be giving consent to governments that would immediately take away their right to consent. It must mean, if it means anything, that consent is rightly given only to governments that protect their right to consent.
>
> Moreover, it cannot mean that anyone has a right to be a citizen of the United States, even if it is truly said that the principles of the nation are universal. It means rather that the United States, alone among the nations of the earth, is a set of practices and beliefs, available in principle to every people to believe those beliefs and adopt those practices. It means also that citizens have the right to determine who becomes a citizen. In the Declaration of Independence, one of the complaints against the King is that he expanded the borders of

Quebec down into the American colonies, having given that province a government by his fiat alone. The King was attempting to choose the people, whereas the people have the right to choose the government. Trump and the American people seem to favor the latter, and in that vital respect they are on the side of the Founders.[11]

Most Americans are on the side of the Founders too. Donald Trump has expressed a high view of citizenship—the idea that being an American citizen is both unique and valuable. Citizenship and civic virtue have not been popular with the smart set in recent years, but many Americans continue to place a high value on both.

It is no surprise that Democrats could not understand Donald Trump, though if for no other reason than self-preservation they should at least try to understand Trump as he understands himself. It is the only basis for reasoned discourse. But you can almost hear them scoff, "Reasoned discourse and Trump do not belong in the same sentence." And therein lies the problem—the Left believes it has transcended reason, so there is no reason to engage their opponents, just force them to bend the knee.

Conservatives weren't much better. Those who have been trained to believe that the purpose of politics is to stand athwart history yelling, "Stop!" would do well to learn the difference between prudence and principle and to reengage with the American people. Unfortunately, like the Progressive Left too many conservatives have come to believe they can achieve near eschatological satisfaction through politics. They can't. When they try, they necessarily begin to resemble the Left and alienate their own base.

7

UTOPIANISM

HOW THE AMERICAN REVOLUTION WAS
SUPERIOR TO THE FRENCH REVOLUTION

THE UTOPIAN SCHEMES OF THE PROGRESSIVE LEFT have been the bane of modern politics and a danger to both humanity and civilization. They have racked up a staggering death toll, to say nothing of the cost in human suffering and moral degradation. In the twentieth century alone Communism killed 100 million. The Nazis—national *socialists*—killed as many as 20 million more. And this does not even touch the other tragedies motivated and justified by left-wing utopianism, from the French Revolution to the evil that is on-demand abortion, which has killed nearly 60 million in the United States alone since its legalization in 1973.[1]

Unfortunately, the Progressive Left has been so successful in influencing the culture that even American conservatives have picked up a hint of their utopianism over the past few generations. This is a departure not just from historic American conservatism, but from the principles of the American founding. Though close together in time and, on the surface, related in spirit, the American and French Revolutions represent political opposites. The American Revolution and founding were based upon the natural right ideas common to both classical political philosophers like Aristotle and to the Bible. These ideas are behind the most memorable and important phrases in the Declaration: "We hold these truths to be self-evident, that all men are created equal, that they are endowed by their Creator with certain unalienable Rights, that among these are Life, Liberty and the pursuit of Happiness." The Declaration also appeals to "the laws of Nature and Nature's God." The signers of the Declaration argued that their natural rights were knowable, self-evident, and common to all mankind. They also argued that they had been repeatedly violated by the government of King George III, that it had failed to redress their grievances, and that as a result they had a right to revolt. Their public appeal to natural right as a basis for the right to establish a new country is unique in human history. It also obligated them to establish a government that was consistent with those principles.

The French Revolution was almost the exact opposite. Rather than drawing its legitimacy from the natural rights of man—from the classics—its instigators drew their inspiration from the modern political philosophers of the Renaissance and the Enlightenment, who explicitly (and sometimes esoterically) rejected the natural right of both Athens and Jerusalem. In its place—I'll save you a lot of reading—they relied upon the will to power. Philosophers like Marx and Hegel spilled a lot of ink dressing it up, but when it's all said and done it's a politics of force or fraud. Robespierre himself linked republican virtue of the French variety with terror: "If the mainspring of popular government in peace time is virtue, its resource during a revolution is at one and the same time virtue and terror; virtue, without which terror is merely terrible; terror, without which virtue is simply powerless."[2]

The Left believes that all human relations can be understood in terms of oppression and conflict. For philosophers in this modern school, there is no search for truth, virtue, or the good. There is only the struggle—what Marxists call the dialectic—of one group (class, gender, race, etc.) against the other. In their understanding it is an explicitly evolutionary struggle with a sure outcome—thus the term "progressive." Central to the project is belief that human history moves inevitably toward a better, more evolved, enlightened future. This is why we hear progressives say things like "you're on the wrong side of history." They fetishize the new, different, or alien over the known or traditional, because their ideology demands it. After all, if the train of history leads to an earthly promised land, wouldn't you want to hurry it along?

Whereas the American Revolution was unique because it relied for its legitimacy upon a recognition and respect for the rights arising out of human nature, the French Revolution was radical because it rejected human nature. That same tension exists between Left and Right today.

Jean-Jacques Rousseau, the philosopher of the French Revolution, is known today as a precursor to Marx. He wrote the following, which sounds like nothing so much as a first draft of Communism:

> The first man who, having fenced in a piece of land, said "This is mine", and found people naïve enough to believe him, that man was the true founder of civil society. From how many crimes, wars, and murders, from how many horrors and misfortunes might not any one have saved mankind, by pulling up the stakes, or filling up the ditch, and crying to his fellows: Beware of listening to this impostor; you are undone if you once forget that the fruits of the earth belong to us all, and the earth itself to nobody.[3]

In other words, if only man weren't so self-interested we would live in a state of peace and plenty. Rousseau was a native of Geneva, the former home of theologian John Calvin (whose academy would eventually become the University of Geneva), and though professing the Reformed faith of Calvin he rejected the doctrine of original sin, writing in *Emile,* "There is no original perversity in the human heart." This is consistent with his other writing on what he called primitive man or man in the state of nature, which he argued was a superior state to that of political man. He said, for example, "Nothing is so gentle as man in his primitive state, when placed by nature at an equal distance from the stupidity of brutes and the fatal enlightenment of civil man."[4]

This is the basis for modern leftism. But it stands in stark contrast to the political wisdom of Athens and Jerusalem upon which the American founding was based. And it stands in contrast to the commonsense understanding of the world that most people have from their lived experience. It reminds one of George Orwell's famous aphorism that there are some ideas so stupid that only an intellectual could believe them.

In contrast, Aristotle taught us that man is by nature political. That is to say that humans are naturally social, reasonable, and morally aware. The Bible teaches much the same thing as the progressive revelation of God's redemptive work for His people is primarily an eschatological and not a political document. That is to say that it is primarily concerned with the ultimate issues that are beyond even politics and philosophy: eternal salvation. That said, biblical revelation and classical political philosophy are consistent in some of the fundamentals required for a just political system:

A recognition of the equal humanity of all mankind. For Aristotle—as for Jefferson—this was a self-evident truth. Our reason allows us to distinguish between a man and a dog. No human is any more or less human than any other regardless of what other distinguishing features he may have. Those features—height, intelligence, etc.—are lower order variations. This is consistent with the biblical teaching that all of mankind is created in the image of God.

The necessity of politics. Aristotle taught the necessity of politics as beginning with man's sociability and his reason. The Bible teaches that the civil government is ordained by God to establish temporal (not eternal) justice. This is seen throughout the Old Testament[5] and is confirmed in the New Testament, most notably in Romans 13:1–7.

The centrality of the family. Aristotle argued in his *Politics* that the family is the model for and building block of the state. Likewise the

Bible teaches that the family is fundamental to human society. It exists from creation and is ratified in the fifth commandment and again in Ephesians 6:2, among other places.

Man's human nature is prone to vice rather than virtue. The Bible proclaims a doctrine of original sin that has corrupted human nature. Aristotle views the questions differently. Men can cultivate either virtue or vice. This sets the stage for Aristotle's *Politics,* because politics ought to promote justice and seek the good. Yet Aristotle is keenly aware of mankind's vicious proclivities and thus finds common ground with the Bible in terms of practical ethical and political questions. There can be cooperation if not complete agreement.

With these principles for a foundation, the American project set itself on an entirely different trajectory than the one begun in the French Revolution. The French promised eternal peace, an end of poverty, and the brotherhood of man based upon a fanciful rejection of the reality of human nature. They got Robespierre, the Reign of Terror, and the guillotine. In contrast, the American regime embraced human nature—the good and the bad—and produced Washington, Jefferson, and a Constitution that has produced more good for more people than any political document in the history of the world.

We see these contrasts and conflicts continue to play out in modern American politics. The Left is in the tradition of modern political philosophy and the French Revolution, while American conservatism historically is in the tradition of the classical political philosophy and the American Revolution. Yet in recent decades too many conservative intellectuals have tacitly accepted some of the key philosophical under-pinnings of the Left, which has weakened the conservative, republican, and Republican cause.

William F. Buckley Jr. played a key role in creating the post–World War II conservative political movement. He was instrumental in many things for which Americans can be thankful, not least of which is helping to galvanize the resistance to Communist imperialism, advocating the nomination of Barry Goldwater, and supporting the election of Ronald

Reagan. One of Buckley's triumphs that is too little remembered is that he popularized the phrase, "Don't let them immanentize the eschaton" and made it a conservative rallying cry. It means don't fall for utopian political schemes, because they can't work.

The idea if not the exact phrase comes from Eric Voegelin's 1952 classic, *The New Science of Politics*. He put it thus: "The problem of an eidos in history, hence, arises only when a Christian transcendental fulfillment becomes immanentized. Such an immanentist hypostasis of the eschaton, however, is a theoretical fallacy." By comparison, Buckley's version sounds almost pithy. Perhaps because of its unapologetic awkwardness, the phrase had more staying power than most focus-group-tested marketing slogans born on Madison Avenue. That it was a short way to express a central component of American conservatism and of the Founders' understanding of human nature gave it additional resonance. Under Buckley's influence it became a conservative rallying cry in the 1950s and 1960s and became a shorthand expression for the conservative understanding of the world. It was popular enough that in the 1950s and 1960s that twentysomething conservatives printed it on T-shirts and buttons. More remarkable was that people actually wore them. To paraphrase General Jack D. Ripper in *Dr. Strangelove,* "How does that coincide with your postwar right-wing conspiracy?"

Yet Buckley—and Voeglin—were right. There can be no heaven on earth. Biblical Christianity recognizes this. It's why Peter calls Christians "strangers and exiles" and why Jesus' prayer to the Father on the eve of his crucifixion is often cited by Christians as a call to be "in the world but not of it." It is also consistent with the prophet Jeremiah who wrote that God's people must seek "the welfare of the city where I have sent you into exile." In other words, work for the good of your city but recognize that man's sinful nature represents a permanent constraint that precludes the possibility of anything like a perfect society. Certainly there can be good societies—thus the admonishment to seek the welfare of the city—and there are surely societies that, despite what modern multicultural orthodoxy says, are better (freer and more just) than others. But that's it. What Augustine called the city of God is separate and distinct from even the best city of man.

That's the view of orthodox Christianity and it's a view shared in the essentials by classical political philosophy and by the Founders. But it is at odds with modern philosophy and thus with its political expression, Progressive Leftism.

The Left promises too much and has left death and destruction in its wake. That's not hyperbole. The body count attributable to leftist utopianism is staggering, to say nothing of the destruction and dehumanizing tyranny, whose costs cannot be counted. Whether it be the viciousness of the French Revolution, the uprisings of 1848, the Russian Revolution in 1917, Mao, Central America, etc., the revolutionary political impulses throughout the world have been largely motivated by leftist utopian ideologies like communism and fascism. Even the political street violence of the 1960s and 1970s that has seen a resurgence since early in the 2016 election cycle and has continued since the election is motivated by left-wing politics.

At the heart of the modern project is the radical liberation of the self. The freedom the Left seeks is the impossible freedom from human nature which is dehumanizing and destructive. Thus the degeneracy and the focus first on hedonism and then on death. What can you expect from a philosophy that rejects man's self-evident nature and thus that any objective notion of "the good" is knowable or even exists. This has been at the heart of the conflict between conservatives and liberals for a century.

After the Cold War the messianic tendencies of the neoconservatives took on an outsized role in American policy. They are tendencies that frankly were not evident in the first generation of neoconservatives, who were serious scholars and intellectuals. Many, though not all, of that first generation supported Donald Trump. These are people like Dr. William J. Bennett, Norman Podhoretz,[6] and Michael Ledeen. Those claiming the name "neoconservative" today were almost uniformly Never Trump and were clustered in certain prominent political journals and think tanks.

This highlights the remarkable but little commented upon fact that the second and third generation neoconservatives successfully remade neoconservatism specifically, and intellectual conservatism more generally, into an interventionist, Wilsonian political movement that saw America as being largely beyond politics in the highest sense. They were not explicit, but the rhetoric and the policy agenda made clear that in some important ways they saw (and see) America as the first nation to reach the end of history predicted by the historicist philosophers such as Marx and Hegel. This occurred during the period after the disintegration of the Soviet Union and the ensuing neoconservative ascendancy. It is a fundamental departure from post–World War II American conservatism and from the historic American politics that were tied directly to the founding.

Yet neoconservatism in its current iteration remains a fringe view shared mostly by D.C. intellectuals but never fully embraced by rank and file Republican voters. There are perhaps three to five thousand neoconservatives in the country, but they occupy many of the high places of Conservatism Inc. and have been profoundly wrong about the most important matters of national consequence of the last twenty years. Most significant of course is their determination to engage in what has been called "moral imperialism." Woodrow Wilson committed the country to World War I that we might "make the world safe for democracy." For the current crop of neoconservatives, making the world safe for democracy is not enough: the United States must actively engage in nation building. It is imperialism without the economic benefits to the mother country of mercantilism. In others words, America doesn't get anything for its efforts other than the bill. That the policies have spectacularly failed in Iraq, Afghanistan, and Libya does not seem to have chastened them. Why should it if such endeavors are in fact a moral imperative? Just get back up to the plate and keep your eye on the ball next time. Because there's always a next time.

Neoconservatism was not always this way. The first generation had departed the Left and its Marxist ideologies for a reason. They knew their Hegel and had rejected it. One of the original neoconservative intellectuals of the first generation, Jeane Kirkpatrick, Reagan's Ambassador to the United Nations, put it this way when asked about President George W. Bush in 2006—in the heat of the Iraq War: "George Bush junior was 'a bit too interventionist for my taste.'" As for moral imperialism, "I don't think there is one scintilla of evidence that such an idea is taken seriously anywhere outside a few places in Washington, D.C."[7]

This dramatic expansion of the U.S. foreign policy priorities and more emphasis on intervention abroad was based on what some intellectuals defined as a moral imperative. Only when it comes to immigration do they hit the same fever pitch and for the same reasons. There is a belief that America exists beyond the normal bounds of human nature and politics. It is a misreading of American capabilities and responsibilities. They are based on the mistaken notion that America's core beliefs make her responsible not primarily to her citizens—the view of the Founders and of the classics—but to the world. It is a bastardization of Tocqueville's oft-quoted and little understood claim that America is great because she is good. Yet Beltway conservatives can't understand why actual American citizens (as opposed to the notional citizens that populate their models and the potential citizens who lie just over the border) object when Jeb Bush says that illegal immigrants "do jobs Americans won't do" or when Bret Stephens writes in the *Wall Street Journal*, "Entire U.S. industries, agriculture above all, depend on illegal immigrants, without whom fruits and vegetables would simply rot in the field."[8]

It's not just because such a statement is self-evidently false and plays readers as gullible rubes—produce did not rot in the field when the United States actually controlled its border, and the basic market economics the *Wall Street Journal* advocates from its editorial pages dictates that the market will respond to a need for agricultural labor. What he really means is that agribusiness has become addicted to the low wages it pays illegal immigrants to work in the fields. What voters mean when they reject such pablum is that they expect their own government to fulfill its raison d'etre and advance their interests and not the special needs of domestic lobbying groups or foreigners. To the extent that the U.S. government—or any government—owes other countries and their citizens any obligation it is to be a good neighbor, but not to prioritize our understanding of their interests over those of American citizens.

Refusing to put American interests first was not always the way. In fact, it represents a repudiation of much that was taken for granted by the first generation of neoconservatives. For example, Jeane Kirkpatrick, was a former socialist, remained a Democrat until 1985, and was in the vanguard of the early neoconservative intellectuals. Here's what she said with regard to foreign interventions and nation-building projects (think Iraq and Afghanistan):

> No idea holds greater sway in the mind of educated Americans than the belief that it is possible to democratize governments, anytime and anywhere, under any circumstances. . . . Decades, if not centuries, are normally required for people to acquire the necessary disciplines and habits. In Britain, the road [to democratic government] took seven centuries to traverse. . . . The speed with which armies collapse, bureaucracies abdicate, and social structures dissolve once the autocrat is removed frequently surprises American policymakers.[9]

Were she to say these things today she would be excoriated by the current generation of neoconservatives who became utopian in their politics and thus interventionist and internationalist in their politics. The election of Donald Trump on an explicitly non-interventionist platform of putting tangible American interests first represents a repudiation of the utopian detour in conservative politics. It also represents a return to the commonsense views held by prominent neoconservatives at the highest levels of the foreign policy establishment just a generation ago. For all of the tributes to Reagan and invocations of his name, perhaps some of the D.C. intellectuals could find the time to learn actual history.

Kirkpatrick had more to say that cuts even deeper. She was once socialist, a utopian herself and a student of the modern philosophers who opposed everything behind the American Revolution. But she got over it. She explained it this way:

> As I read the utopian socialists, the scientific socialists, the German Social Democrats and revolutionary socialists—whatever I could in either English or French—I came to the conclusion that almost all of them, including my grandfather, were engaged in an effort to change human nature. The more I thought about it, the more I thought this was not likely to be a successful effort. So I turned my attention more and more to political philosophy and less and less to socialist activism of any kind.[10]

In other words, she was a utopian, but reality intervened. All Jefferson was doing in his appeal to human nature in the Declaration of Independence was appealing to an objective, commonsense reality known or knowable to all people at all times and in all places. And that in itself was a revolutionary political statement. It still is. Mankind wants a promise of something better in the here and now, and so radical utopian politics has a strong allure despite all of the evidence against it.

Margaret Thatcher famously quipped that the problem with socialism is that eventually you run out of other people's money. In other words someone else has to be living and working in the real world to finance utopian fantasies, and eventually they get tired of it. For example, a study published in 2017 found that 92 percent of left-wing activists live at home with their parents, 50 percent have been arrested for a crime, and nearly one-third are unemployed.[11] Leftist ideology is predicated on the promise that there is a free lunch and that it is just out of reach because of an oppressor. It makes politics a means for justifying and even encouraging social and political conflict. For Marx it was the capitalist system, so he insisted on class war. For Marcuse and the rest of the prophets of critical theory, what we now call cultural Marxism, it is some other demographic indicator like race or gender. Machiavelli and Nietzsche at least were honest about it—they recognized that the real conflict was with human nature itself.

Progressive ideology requires an enemy oppressor to function. Identity politics, constant conflict, and even the street violence perpetrated against Trump supporters before and since the election are all perfectly consistent and predictable manifestations of that ideology. The politics of the American founding stand as a beacon of light beating against the false promises of the progressive prophets.

Unfortunately even conservatives have unknowingly swallowed too much Marx, Hegel, and Marcuse. It is perhaps not their fault—the culture is so marinated in the language of historicism and cultural Marxism that it requires an affirmative defense to avoid it. But it's available and it's part of our culture.

Abraham Lincoln captured the essence in a speech in 1858. Speaking of what it means to become an American citizen, he did not make false promises about eternal peace and prosperity. Instead he made the same appeal that Jefferson did:

> If they look back through this history to trace their connection with those days by blood, they find they have none, they cannot carry themselves back into that glorious epoch and make themselves feel that they are part of us, but when they look through that old Declaration of Independence they find that those old men say that "We hold these truths to be self-evident, that all men are created equal," and then they feel that that moral sentiment taught in that day evidences their relation to those men, that it is the father of all moral principle in them, and that they have a right to claim it as though they were blood of the blood, and flesh of the flesh of the men who wrote that Declaration, [this received loud and long continued applause] and so they are. That is the electric cord in that Declaration that links the hearts of patriotic and liberty-loving men together, that will link those patriotic hearts as long as the love of freedom exists in the minds of men throughout the world.

For conservatives it is a time for choosing between the messy but true politics of human nature and the destructive utopian dreams. Will they return to the politics that made this country great because they were based on indelible truth? Will they recognize that man is inherently political, but made as he is in God's image, is also capable of temporal good? Or will they become a pale imitation of the Left—simultaneously nostalgic for the good old days and slowly but inexorably following the path the Left blazes?

Government should be simple, transparent, and responsible to its citizens for a discrete set of needs—not a mechanism for coercion, social experimentation, or temporal salvation. These are not new ideas but they remain radical. When government is most effective, it limits its activities to those spheres that are beyond the capacity of individuals or small groups: national defense, enforcement of borders and citizenship laws, protection of the citizens in their person and property, international diplomacy, and management of the government's own finances. The Constitution had just four Cabinet secretaries when it was ratified: State, War (now Defense), Treasury, and the Attorney General. At the time private currencies issued by banks were common—that's why they're called bank notes—and they may someday be again. This is not to say that there are no other legitimate activities of government, but that they should be left to the level of government closest to the problem while still competent to address the issue. Who is going to pave the roads? The federal government? No, the local or state government has both the competence and the ability to do so, and Washington should stay out of it.

To go beyond these natural limitations is not only to become less effective but to undermine the legitimacy of the regime itself. Too often the American people have witnessed the federal government utterly fail in its core responsibilities—protection of the border and enforcement of immigration laws comes to mind—while zealously pursuing the optional. For good reasons ordinary citizens come to the conclusion that the whole system is in some sense random and not to be taken too seriously. Such behavior has ill effects on the character of citizens, who are encouraged to take less personal responsibility. Alexis de Tocqueville observed it this way:

This disinterest in himself [i.e., the citizen] goes so far that if his own security or that of his children is finally compromised, instead of occupying himself with removing the danger, he crosses his arms to wait for the nation as a whole to come to his aid. . . . He submits, it is true, at the pleasure of a clerk; but it pleases him to defy the law like a defeated enemy, as soon as force is withdrawn. Thus one sees him swinging constantly between servitude and license.[12]

This undermines the responsible exercise of personal agency and thereby undermines the continued efficacy and existence of free government. In this way governmental overreach ultimately undermines the leviathan state, but left untreated it tends toward corruption and chaos, not a return to first principles.

When government functions well and within its appropriate boundaries, its citizens are left free to pursue their own ends: family, church, art, sports, commerce, science, technology. Those are the pursuits Jefferson referred to in the Declaration. Like an elegantly designed computer operating system, it should run quietly in the background. However, because of the near monopoly on legal force and other forms of power held by government, it also becomes the object of intense desire by those who would use that power to enforce their utopian visions on their fellow man. What they miss is that a free government operating within well-defined boundaries and guaranteeing its citizens the ability to pursue their own legitimate ends is as close to utopia as mankind can get this side of glory. That's the framework the Founders gave us, and it remains as revolutionary today as it was when twenty-seven men pledged their lives, their fortunes, and their sacred honors to bringing forth this new nation.

8

AMERICA FIRST?

NATION BUILDING ABROAD OR PROTECTING CITIZENS AT HOME

"FROM THIS MOMENT ON, IT'S GOING TO BE AMERICA FIRST." When Donald Trump made this declaration during his inaugural address, there was an audible gasp from the anchors on every major television network. It was as though the new president had just made a terrible faux pas, and he left them momentarily wondering whether they were supposed to denounce his heresy or just silently avert their eyes in embarrassed silence. Yet, even as the anchors grasped for words, the crowd cheered. They were thrilled to hear the president speak about the country with confidence and authority. More significantly they found his unapologetic preference for America and acknowledgement of his responsibility to seek its interests above all others refreshing.

When did this become controversial? For Republicans the answer is easy: January 20, 1989. That was the dawn of the age of Wilsonian internationalism and moral imperialism within the Republican Party. There were two historic foreign policy factions within the Republican Party—the practitioners of realpolitik in the Kissinger school (think James Baker and Brent Scowcroft) and those skeptical of the foreign entanglements Washington warned against in his farewell address. The second group in particular put much stock in the Monroe Doctrine, which held that the United States should stay out of Europe's internal affairs but also warned foreign powers to stay out of the Western hemisphere. The tension between the factions was largely put on hold during the Cold War against communist imperialism, which both sides agreed was a necessary part of American national security.

The debate began again during the 1990s but was unresolved by the time of 9/11. Yet by 2001 a third group had gained political power. The Kissinger-school realpolitik types were getting older, and the success of the Cold War had not only accustomed Republicans to international commitments and the conflicts that come with them, but also made many dream of new foes they could conquer in the name of democracy. Had not the United States and its allies just defeated communist totalitarianism and democratized eastern Europe? Surely this was the beginning of an evolutionary leap by mankind that just needed a little help from American money and guns. Into this context a new generation of neoconservatives thrust themselves armed with a self-confidence that looks an awful lot like hubris in retrospect and a constellation of books and journals repackaging the Wilsonian progressivism that overturned a century and a half of settled American foreign policy. Natan Sharansky's 2004 book *The Case for Democracy: The Power of Freedom to Overcome Tyranny and Terror* was seen as a justification for the United States to engage in nation building abroad. The central argument was that all of mankind yearns for freedom and therefore, if some outside force can prime the pump, then people of any culture will more or less instantly become liberal democrats.

The argument was simplistic, beguiling, and wrong. It failed to take into account the power of religion, culture, civic education, family ties, unenlightened self-interest also known as greed, the desire for security, and the attachment to the familiar. It failed to take into account the seven hundred years necessary to get from Runnymede and the Magna Carta to Philadelphia and the Constitution. But from the 1990s until today this passed for wisdom in Washington. Less so in the rest of the country.

For Democrats, putting a date on when a preference for America became declasse is a bit harder because they've been at it so much longer. But it happened at least a generation earlier and had its beginnings in the early twentieth century. By the time of World War I Woodrow Wilson had explicitly repudiated historic American foreign policy goals in favor of utopian internationalism. It was Wilson, after all, who asked Congress for a declaration of war on Germany in 1917 so that the world would "be made safe for democracy." One does not have to strain to hear echoes of Wilson's call for war in the words of Bill Clinton and both Bushes' justification of their own wars for democracy.

The post–World War I League of Nations—the precursor to the United Nations—was Wilson's brainchild, but the American people wanted no part of it and the U.S. Senate refused to ratify the Treaty of Versailles, which would have made the United States a member. Wilson had dragged a mostly unenthusiastic country into the war in pursuit of international prestige and the desire to put into practice theories he had taught as a scholar. Unfortunately, this became a model for idealistic academics who came to see the world as their laboratory and the United States as their change agent. But the American people were steeped in an America First foreign policy that provided for a strong defense, hemispheric primacy, and active avoidance of other countries' fights. Despite a century of intellectual gravitas, that hasn't changed much. The American people are generally more disposed to the historic America First foreign policy than are political and intellectual elites.

So why did President Trump's America First pledge sound so strange to modern ears? Or at least to the ears of American elites? It is, after all, a simple statement of priorities and everyone knew this. When asked during the campaign what he meant when he talked about

America First, here's how Trump responded, "Not isolationist. I'm not isolationist, but I am 'America First.' So I like the expression." He soon began using it at almost every rally.

In another interview with the *New York Times,* on the eve of the Republican National Convention, he offered a refinement. He said he did not mean for the slogan to be taken the way Lindbergh meant it. "It was used as a brand-new, very modern term," he said. "Meaning we are going to take care of this country first before we worry about everybody else in the world."[1]

That's really the heart of it—"we are going to take care of this country first before we worry about everybody else in the world." That commonsense perspective on the primary responsibility of government was somehow lost on many conservatives, who have more in common with their leftist counterparts than they'd like to acknowledge. They may have different policy preferences—lower taxes or more money for the military—but too often they share the same philosophical foundation whether they know it or not. And they reject the basic truths that the man in the street takes for granted, for example, that you can't maintain a state without first having a nation, that the government exists because of and for the benefit of its citizens, and that there are just limitations on the legitimate foreign policy goals of the country.

Just because doing something would be good—for example, bringing free government to a foreign country—does not mean that we have the capability or the right to do it. More important is that just government cannot exist separate and apart from its citizens for very long. It cannot have different values and goals. Rather, it must necessarily reflect the interests of the citizens who form the government through their elected representatives. Ruling-class values have long since parted ways with those of the rest of the country. There is a palpable sense that the ruling class sees itself as both different and at least semi-autonomous. And there's more than a whiff of condescension, the sense that the American people should be thankful that the country's elites even put up with them.

Witness Bill Kristol's appalling response to a question from the audience about immigration. It took place at an American Enterprise Institute panel with Charles Murray in February 2017:

> "Look, to be totally honest, if things are so bad as you say with the white working class, don't you want to get new Americans in who aren't going to be—I'm serious, "You can make a case that America has been great because every—I think John Adams said this—basically if you are in free society, a capitalist society, after two or three generations of hard work everyone becomes kind of decadent, lazy, spoiled—whatever," Kristol said.
>
> "Then, luckily, you have these waves of people coming in from Italy, Ireland, Russia, and now Mexico, who really want to work hard and really want to succeed and really want their kids to live better lives than them and aren't sort of clipping coupons or hoping that they can hang on and meanwhile grew up as spoiled kids and so forth. In that respect, I don't know how this moment is that different from the early 20th century," he added.[2]

He offered his interlocutor, Charles Murray, the chance to rebut him, which Murray declined.

Kristol here is an excellent spokesman for the default position held by political and cultural elites but not often uttered with such candor in public: We don't like the Americans we have, so let's get new ones. There are any number of reasons behind this: multicultural ideology, white guilt, a desire for cheap labor, a false morality that places the interests of foreigners over the interests of Americans, and a sense of frustration with the American people for not recognizing and deferring to their betters, e.g., people like Bill Kristol.

Kristol called his fellow countrymen lazy, decadent, and spoiled. He said they should be replaced by "new Americans." But he betrays more than a patently offensive level of elitism. He betrays a profound misunderstanding of what it means to be an American. For Kristol, it clearly means nothing more than residing within the country's borders and being able to work diligently for lower wages than the native population. Being an American is much more than that. Kristol's view—the view shared by all of the Left and much of the Right—misunderstands and cheapens American citizenship. It makes it a disposable, fungible commodity rather than the precious inheritance that it is. We are heirs to the most valuable civic legacy the world has ever known. It is a legacy that took centuries to develop and is being squandered by the political and cultural equivalent of trust-fund babies.

Citizenship requires civic education, an attachment to the nation, its culture, its people, and its founding principles. But this must be taught to every succeeding generation. You cannot love what you do not know, and it has become increasingly clear that a shockingly large segment of the country's elites do not know America. As President Trump would say: Sad!

Alexander Hamilton explained it this way:

> The safety of a republic depends essentially on the energy of a common national sentiment; on a uniformity of principles and habits; on the exemption of the citizens from foreign bias, and prejudice; and on that love of country which will almost invariably be found to be closely connected with birth, education, and family.
>
> The opinion advanced in the Notes on Virginia is undoubtedly correct, that foreigners will generally be apt to bring with them attachments to the persons they have left behind; to the country of their nativity, and to its particular customs and manners. They will also entertain opinions on government congenial with those under which they have lived; or, if they should be led hither from a preference to ours, how extremely unlikely is it that they will bring with them that temperate love of liberty, so essential to real republicanism? There may, as to particular individuals, and at particular times, be occasional exceptions to these remarks, yet such is the general rule. The influx of foreigners must, therefore, tend to produce a heterogeneous compound; to change and corrupt the national spirit; to complicate and confound public opinion; to introduce foreign propensities. In

the composition of society, the harmony of the ingredients is all-important, and whatever tends to a discordant intermixture must have an injurious tendency.[3]

This runs directly counter to the prevailing view of intellectual conservatives. Take, for example, the view of Jonah Goldberg writing in *National Review*. His view is that America is just a set of beliefs. This is false and runs counter to the explicit views of the Founders. It is true that America was founded on the basis of an appeal to universally knowable natural rights, but those rights were asserted on behalf of a specific people living in a specific place. The Constitution established a government to protect those rights for the American people—and only for the American people. To do more would be to attempt too much and to encroach on the rights of other people and nations. What is more, sustaining a just system of self-government in one nation is quite challenging enough without attempting to do the same for foreign nations. Yet Goldberg still claims that "Up until very recently, American exceptionalism—i.e., we are a creedal nation dedicated to certain principles reflected in our founding documents—largely defined the conservative understanding of patriotism."[4] Nowhere does he mention a devotion to one's fellow citizens—to the actual nation as it exists. In Goldberg's telling patriotism is reduced to a mere abstraction and sucked of its vitality.

Immigration absolutists like Kristol and far too many Republican officeholders have explicitly rejected the wisdom of the Founders in favor of saccharine platitudes about the unalloyed value of immigration always and everywhere. Hamilton is, after all, favorably quoting Thomas Jefferson's *Notes on Virginia*. The Founders understood that immigration is a prudential issue: It can be good or bad, beneficial or harmful depending on a number of factors that change over time. Moreover, it is a political decision that the citizens of any country have a right to decide for themselves, and they have a right to be "wrong" in the eyes of "the experts."

More important, the Founders understood citizenship. They

understood what makes a nation and what binds it together. America has done a remarkably good job assimilating immigrants over the years, but it takes time and diligence. It also takes an understanding of and a belief in the country, its culture, and its principles, and that is in remarkably short supply today. Citizenship is learned partially by instruction and partially by example. And in today's climate of multiculturalism and extreme skepticism of all things American, the urgently important job of making patriots of every generation is much more difficult.

Because so much is viewed through a racial lens let me be clear: American citizenship is explicitly not racial in nature despite the brazenly unAmerican identity politics practiced by the Left that serve only to divide, antagonize, and alienate the American people from their government and from each other. Abraham Lincoln expressed it best when he explained that all Americans who hold firm to the principles of the Declaration of Independence "have a right to claim it as though they were blood of the blood, and flesh of the flesh of the men who wrote that Declaration."[5]

A desire for economic opportunity and prosperity do not make an American. Everyone wants more material wealth, but not everyone believes in the principles of the Declaration of Independence—that all men are created equal and that we are endowed by our Creator with certain inalienable rights. That conviction is a necessary but insufficient requirement for citizenship. Kristol and Goldberg represent a very common school of thought that profoundly misunderstands the nature of citizenship and that undermines and leads to foolish statements like Kristol's spoken desire to replace the American people with "New Americans." Politics based on such thinking is destructive of the conditions necessary for self-government.

It is no wonder that people holding such views would find President Trump's pledge to put America First bewildering and even threatening. Right after President Trump spoke the words Kristol tweeted: "I'll be unembarrassedly (sic) old-fashioned here: It is profoundly depressing and vulgar to hear an American president proclaim

'America First.' "[6] What did he want to hear an American president say, that he would put America second?

Michael Anton explains:

> There is now, and has been for some time, a broad consensus from the center-right all the way to the far left that America's only legitimate role is to be a kind of savior of and refuge for the world. It's not a country with citizens and a government that serves those citizens. It belongs to everyone. Everyone has a right to come here, work here, live here, reap America's bounty. We have no legitimate parochial interests. Rather America exists for others. This standard does not seem to be held to any other country, although one sees it increasingly rising in Europe.
>
> So Donald Trump's forthright stance against that, insisting that this country is *ours*, belongs to us, and demands that we prioritize our *own interests*, sounds like the most horrible blasphemy against this universalist consensus.[7]

Two thoughts: (1) More likely lazy, decadent, intellectual, and political elites should be replaced with ones who believe in America and Americans. (2) This betrays a profound misunderstanding what it means to be American. This from the same guy who was "embarrassed" at hearing the president say "America First." For Kristol no doubt that represents advocacy and pride in the decadent, lazy America, i.e., the actual America that exists and that he finds in need of replacement. New Americans first? This is an elite, a thought leader in search of a new people, people who will come and work cheaply and take orders. And most important who, he hopes, will owe some debt of gratitude and fealty to him and his likeminded brethren and thus keep them in a position of comfortable influence.

The commentators who were aghast at hearing President Trump say he would put America first did not seriously think he was thinking of resurrecting the America First Committee of the 1930s that sought to keep America out of World War II, though Kristol did go on to compare Michael Anton, a member of President Trump's National Security Council, to Nazi theorist Carl Schmitt. Anton had published in the *Weekly Standard* and was friendly with Kristol, but he committed the unforgivable sin: Not only did he support Trump and work in his White House, he had insisted that America was not just a state but a nation and that the American government (the state) exists primarily to protect the natural rights of its citizens, chief of which is their continued right to govern themselves.

Everyone talks about America in the reverential tones reserved exclusively for the great and the good. This is appropriate. But one must ask, "What America?" Are they talking about the America that respects the Founders and the founding? The America that believes that the Constitution both expresses the principles of the Declaration of Independence and exists to protect them? Is it the America that believes that just government must by nature be limited? Is it an America that recognizes the proper limits of government power? Is it an America by and for Americans?

9

WISE FOREIGN POLICY

AMERICA FIRST AND THE RECLAIMING OF COMMONSENSE AMERICAN FOREIGN POLICY

WHEN, THROUGHOUT THE PRESIDENTIAL CAMPAIGN and at his inauguration, Donald Trump spoke of United States foreign policy based on the principle of "America First," the foreign policy establishment and journalist community exploded in both shock and anger—on the Left and Right. Many did not hear what Donald Trump was saying the phrase meant but, rather, what the phrase meant more than seventy years ago. In its original incarnation in the 1940s, the "America First Committee," stood for isolationism, especially with regard to intervening in the war in Europe and taking up arms against Adolf Hitler's Germany.

Donald Trump had made himself vulnerable on the charge that he was a foreign policy isolationist as he had been a critic of the Iraq war—and the only Republican candidate in the 2016 Republican primary to continually and vociferously state he opposed the war in Iraq.

His talk against the North American Free Trade Agreement (NAFTA) and stating that the United States needed to "rethink" its relationship with the North Atlantic Treaty Organization (NATO) had created an environment of thought that Donald Trump wanted to upend international alliances, commitments, and long-standing ethics of defending America by defending our allies.

The closer read of what Donald Trump had been saying, though, was not what the most extreme interpretation and criticism of his comments were. He did not say the United States should pull out of NATO, he did not say (or desire) that the United States would not defend our allies, and when he spoke of decimating or "destroying" Radical Islam, one could hardly think that was the talk or policy of someone believing in a Fortress America or Charles Lindbergh-Pat Buchanan ethics of foreign and defense policy.

First things first: It is true the America First Committee, along with the phrase "America First," had and has a negative connotation and dangerous legacy—*if one is speaking of the 1940s America First Committee* and *if one is speaking of what that committee stood for.* In the 1940s, that phrase stood for non-intervention in Europe as Hitler was marching through it. Given some of its leadership and that it was uniquely organized to keep America out of the fight with Hitler, it also had a legacy and reputation for being anti-Semitic and even, in some cases, pro-Hitler.

As the journalist Krishnadev Calamur captured *that* America First's history, its most prominent spokesman was Charles Lindbergh who, to this day, is the name most associated with the America First Committee. But:

> At its peak, it had 800,000 members across the country, included socialists, conservatives, and some of the most prominent Americans from some of the most prominent families. There was future President [Gerald] Ford; Sargent Shriver, who'd go on to lead the Peace Corps; and Potter Stewart, the future U.S. Supreme Court justice. It was funded by the families who owned Sears-Roebuck and the *Chicago Tribune,* but also counted among its ranks prominent anti-Semites of the day.[1]

Such anti-Semites included Henry Ford and Avery Brundage, "the former chairman of the U.S. Olympic Committee who had prevented two Jewish runners from the American track team in Berlin in 1936 from running in the finals of the 4 x 100 relay."[2] As anti-Semitism goes, it is fair to say, the America First Committee was known more for those prominent members and spokesmen than for the others. And Charles Lindbergh, as the leading spokesman for the group, only served to perpetuate the organization's reputation.

In one well-known speech in 1941, Lindbergh—who had received the German Service Cross from Hermann Goering on behalf of Adolf Hitler in 1938[3]—would say, "Instead of agitating for war, the Jewish groups in this country should be opposing it in every possible way for they will be among the first to feel its consequences. . . . Their [the Jews'] greatest danger to this country lies in their large ownership and influence in our motion pictures, our press, our radio and our government."[4] As for anti-Semitic boilerplate, that is about as good or as clear as it gets. Indeed, it is remarkable those are the kinds of charges and sentences classic and standard anti-Semitism still sounds like: the ownership of Hollywood, the media, and the infiltration of government (sometimes known by variants such as the "Zionist occupation of government" or "dual loyalty").

Whatever the legitimate debates about entering war, any war, in the light of history—and in the daylight of what was known even in the late 1930s and early 1940s—clearly, the America First Committee was wrong. Given Hitler's objectives and actions, it was wrong to argue for keeping America out of that war and it was wrong to have perpetrated anti-Semitic spokesmen for its cause, or at all. Again, Donald Trump did leave himself open to criticism for using the phrase "America First." But leaving oneself open to criticism is not the same thing as embracing all of the gravid and worst—or even main—parts of the 1940s America First Committee.

Looming over Donald Trump's use of the phrase "America First," first stated in a *New York Times* interview in March of 2016, was a flub he had made about the neo-Nazi and former Ku Klux Klan leader David

Duke. In a CNN interview the month before, in February, CNN's Jake Tapper asked Donald Trump about David Duke:

TAPPER: I want to ask you about the Anti-Defamation League, which this week called on you to publicly condemn unequivocally the racism of former KKK grand wizard David Duke, who recently said that voting against you at this point would be treason to your heritage.

Will you unequivocally condemn David Duke and say that you don't want his vote or that of other white supremacists in this election?

TRUMP: Well, just so you understand, I don't know anything about David Duke. OK? I don't know anything about what you're even talking about with white supremacy or white supremacists. So, I don't know.

I don't know, did he endorse me or what's going on, because, you know, I know nothing about David Duke. I know nothing about white supremacists. And so you're asking me a question that I'm supposed to be talking about people that I know nothing about.[5]

This was a flub—and it would have repercussions a month later when Donald Trump spoke of "America First." But it was only a flub. Most political consultants would rightly say something like "When you hear the name David Duke, don't think—just denounce." But, again, to be fair, David Duke himself would clarify that he did not endorse Donald Trump.[6] And the notion that Donald Trump is or was anti-Semitic in any way is beyond preposterous. This, after all, is a man whose famous daughter, Ivanka, converted to Orthodox Judaism and is raising her children—Donald Trump's grandchildren—Jewish. This, after all, is a man whose son Eric married a Jewish woman in a Jewish wedding ceremony.[7] This, after all, is a man who cut a campaign video in 2013 for Israeli Prime Minister Benjamin Netanyahu's re-election, saying:

Frankly, a strong prime minister is a strong Israel, and you truly have a great prime minister in Benjamin Netanyahu—there's nobody like him! He's a winner; he's highly respected; he's highly thought of by all.

People really do have great, great respect for what's happened in Israel. So vote for Benjamin. Terrific guy, terrific leader, great for Israel.[8]

To say this was a more pro-Israel statement than Barack Obama ever made would not be controversial. To say this could come from the mouth of an anti-Semite would be absurd and cause for dismissal from any anti-Semitic club or cabal worth its salt.

So the backstory of an anti-Semitic tinge or underpinning to Donald Trump or his lines about "America First" simply hold no water. Were Israel becoming a state when the America First Committee existed in the early 1940s, the committee would have opposed Israel's creation and the United States' support of it. Clearly, that is not and was not Donald Trump. So, what does he mean when he invokes the phrase "America First"? He did not mean and did not say the United States should cut off or end its alliances—not even with NATO. He explained this twice in March of 2016. In an interview with the *Washington Post*:

CHARLES LANE, *WASHINGTON POST*: So, I'd like to hear you say very specifically, you know, with respect to NATO, what is your ask of these other countries? Right, you've painted it in very broad terms, but do you have a percent of GDP that they should be spending on defense? Tell me more, because it sounds like you want to just pull the U.S. out.

TRUMP: No, I don't want to pull it out. NATO was set up at a different time. NATO was set up when we were a richer country. We're not a rich country anymore. We're borrowing, we're borrowing all of this money. We're borrowing money from China, which is sort of an amazing situation. But it was a much different thing. NATO is costing us a fortune and yes, we're protecting Europe with NATO but we're spending a lot of money. Number one, I think the distribution of costs has to be changed. I think NATO as a concept is good, but it is not as good as it was when it first evolved.[9]

Later that day, with Wolf Blitzer of CNN:

BLITZER: Do you think the United States needs to rethink U.S. involvement in NATO?

TRUMP: Yes, because it's costing us too much money. And frankly they have to put up more money. They're going to have to put some up also. We're paying disproportionately. It's too much. And frankly it's a different world than it was when we originally conceived of the idea. And everybody got together.

But we're taking care of, as an example, the Ukraine. I mean, the countries over there don't seem to be so interested. We're the ones taking the brunt of it. So I think we have to reconsider keep NATO, but maybe we have to pay a lot less toward the NATO itself.

BLITZER: When we say keep NATO, NATO has been around since right after World War II in 1949. It's been a cornerstone of U.S. national security around the world. NATO allies hear you say that, they're not going to be happy.

TRUMP: Well, they may not be happy but, you know, they have to help us also. It has to be—we are paying disproportionately. And very importantly if you use Ukraine as an example and that's a great example, the countries surrounding Ukraine, I mean, they don't seem to care as much about it as we do. So there has to be at least a change in philosophy and there are also has to be a change in the cut out, the money, the spread because it's too much.

BLITZER: So you're really suggesting the United States should decrease its role in NATO?

TRUMP: Not decrease its role but certainly decrease the kind of spending. We are spending a tremendous amount in NATO and other people proportionately less. No good.[10]

"Not decrease its role but certainly decrease the kind of spending." Have not similar things been said by a whole host of conservatives from across the spectrum about the United Nations as well? And to no great criticism? And, has not, indeed, NATO seen an increase of its budget share come from European countries since Donald Trump's remarks?[11]

Donald Trump's use of the phrase "America First" has little or nothing to do with pulling out of alliances but, as with his statements about trade deals like NAFTA, reforming them. And organizations like NATO are indeed going through exactly that kind of financial reform. Donald Trump's use of the phrase "America First" also has nothing to do with Charles Lindbergh's organization or the 1940s. As we like to say on radio, "What do you want an American president to say or believe, 'America Second? America Third?'"

What Donald Trump meant and means by a policy guided by America First principles is twofold—and it is not that difficult to understand for those not stuck in the 1940s. First, it is a commitment to American exceptionalism. Second, it is a commitment to common sense and lessons learned from the immediate past when it comes to military deployments.

The issue of American exceptionalism couched in the language of "America First" was music to a lot of ears. True: Never Trumpers went to the 1940s, but they should have known better. Donald Trump was not speaking of the 1940s, and the only threat to the free world that came close to Adolf Hitler's was and is the threat of Radical Islam. That phrase was never far from—indeed, always was on—the lips of Donald Trump. It would be a hard case to make that an isolationist, much less a 1940s isolationist, would speak so strongly and so often about destroying ISIS or Radical Islam. But to the ears of ordinary Americans—"Topeka" or the Seitz families of the Trumbull counties—"America First" meant something. Something important. Something big. Something lost. It meant, precisely, *not America Second* or *Third* or farther down the line.

Barack Obama had cast himself as a transformative world figure, more of the world than of America. Indeed, he commenced his presidency with what would become known as his "apology tour" abroad, in his first year in office.[12] It was Barack Obama and his Secretary of State, Hillary Clinton, who spoke about "resetting" United States foreign policy—particularly with Russia but, truly, with the rest of the world, and it began with Obama's apologies. First he went abroad to explain—and apologize—that America had "shown arrogance and been dismissive, even derisive" of its allies in the past, of course meaning the recent past.[13] As the *London Telegraph* put it about his 2009 speech in Strasbourg, "His speech in Strasbourg went further than any United States president in history in criticizing his own country's action while standing on foreign soil."[14] It was Barack Obama in his first year in office who decided to travel to several Muslim nations, from Egypt to Saudi Arabia to Turkey, all the while bypassing our long-standing ally Israel, a country he did not visit until his second term, in 2013.

When asked about American exceptionalism, given his obvious doubts about the subject that would give rise to such a question, he famously said, "I believe in American exceptionalism, just as I suspect that the Brits believe in British exceptionalism and the Greeks believe in Greek exceptionalism."[15] The notion that all countries are exceptional and that they have equal claims to exceptionalism is a Lake Wobegon theory of achievement and excellence: "where all the women are strong, all the men are good-looking and all the children are above average."[16] But if everyone is above average, or everyone's *belief* that they are exceptional is all that matters, nobody is exceptional. Hell, we know Islamists believe theirs is the one and true way, that everyone else must submit to their version of Islam. Does that make Saudi Arabia or ISIS or Al-Qaeda's caliphate exceptional, too? Does someone's belief they are Napoleon make them Napoleon?

This view that America is exceptional does not take a course in political philosophy to figure out. To blame and apologize for America, especially while abroad, and to claim the same right of uniqueness as, say, modern-day Greece, is to renounce exceptionalism. And American conservatives, along with good, working-class, everyday Americans, hate this kind of relativism. Trump, though, a can-do builder who spoke of "America First" and who would say again and again "America is tired of losing," and "We don't win anymore,"[17] understood the notion of winners and losers. Which is to say he understood and spoke to not only objective absolutes but to the point that *we, as Americans, should be winning*. This was not a far cry from what Jeane Kirkpatrick, Ronald Reagan's ambassador to the United Nations, would be famous for saying: the election of Ronald Reagan was, at least in part, an election to take the "kick-me" sign off our backs. As one of the stories about Kirkpatrick is told:

> Not long after beginning her assignment at the UN in 1981, Kirkpatrick was asked, "How will the Reagan administration change foreign policy?" She said, "Well, we've taken down our 'kick me' sign." And then someone said, "Well, does this mean that if the United States is kicked it will kick back?" "Not necessarily," she said. "But it does mean we won't apologize."[18]

The entire notion of American greatness or American exceptionalism or making America great again is *defined* by the notion that America *deserves* to be thought of (and think of herself) as exceptional and great. Anyone who signs up in our all-volunteer military must think that. Why else fight for—and possibly die for—a country that is just as good as Greece? Most Americans think that, too. Democrats as well as Republicans join the military and stand for and sing the national anthem. Patriotism is not a partisan ethos—but it can be defined downward. And whether Barack Obama was speaking about everybody's claim to exceptionalism or a foreign policy that was best described as "leading from behind,"[19] he defined it downward. Donald Trump, by speaking of American greatness and America First, defined it upward again. Just as Ronald Reagan had and just as almost every American president had, but not Barack Obama.

To Donald Trump, the first meaning of America First was restoring American greatness and exceptionalism and asking if our trade and foreign relations policies benefitted America before they benefited others. This, really, should not have been a complicated notion to understand. One could go to the 1940s to look for a critique of Donald Trump if one wanted. Or, one could ask any farmer or rancher or almost any

American not focused on the history of the 1940s what America First meant. They would know. And Donald Trump knew they would know. It is a good phrase. It may have been hijacked and it may have had (it did have) a lousy meaning decades ago. But to today's ears, it meant winning again, it meant putting America back in its unique and exceptional place. A place it did not feel like it had been in for a very long time.

As to Donald Trump's second meaning of America First, a commitment to common sense and lessons learned from the immediate past, this, too, should not have been a difficult reach to understand or appreciate. America's involvement in Iraq was a cause for much patriotic fervor early on, and it was the cause of great defense and support by most conservatives. But it did not eventuate that way. Interestingly, before the war went south, opposition to that war was Barack Obama's calling card, even as early as 2002 when he was a little-known Illinois State Senator. Domestic terrorism here in America was on the rise during the Obama presidency. Libya was another story altogether. And then, of course, there was Syria and our relationships with the superpowers of Russia and China. And, as we are about to detail: the second notion of America First—for Donald Trump as much as for his supporters—took on, and stood for, all that.

—10

THE END OF HISTORY

HUBRIS AND FOREIGN POLICY

IF THERE WAS TO BE ANY DOUBT that Donald Trump was not a 1940s "American First Committee" isolationist, it should have been easily enough dispelled by his continual call to destroy ISIS and Radical Islam. It was also refreshing, coming off eight years of an administration that actually *defended* the non-use of the phrase. Indeed, while the Obama administration would speak of Radical Islamist terrorism as "violent extremism," conservatives—and not a few Independents and some liberals—longed for the actual use of phraseology such as Donald Trump used, longed for calling our enemy by its proper name.

President Obama, even as late as 2016, was scolding those who kept asking for the use of some phraseology to identify Islamic terrorism by name:

What exactly would using this label accomplish? What exactly would it change? Would it make ISIS less committed to trying to kill Americans? Would it bring in more allies? Is there a military strategy that is served by this? The answer is none of the above. Calling a threat by a different name does not make it go away. This is a political distraction.[1]

Well, it would accomplish a great deal, actually. In other speeches, President Obama had said he abstained from using phrases like Radical Islam because it would sound as if we were "painting all Muslims as a broad brush, and imply that we are at war with the entire religion."[2] But using a modifier in front of the word *Islam* would do the exact opposite of what President Obama worried about, wouldn't it? Placing a limiting modifier in front of the word *Islam* would be showing it was not all "all Muslims." Claiming it was a sect, a part, a sub-set, an extremist distortion even, would more than imply we were not at war with all of Islam. Those of us who wanted to identify the enemy did not say we wanted the word *Islam* used, we wanted modifiers to Islam such as "Radical Islam" or "Political Islam" or "Islamo-fascism" used.

Donald Trump, who had already stated we had no more time for political correctness, understood this—and understood that the vast American population understood this. He opened his 2016 speech in Youngstown, Ohio, by stating:

> In the twentieth century, the United States defeated Fascism, Nazism, and Communism.
>
> Now, a different threat challenges our world: Radical Islamic Terrorism. This summer, there has been an ISIS attack launched outside the war zones of the Middle East every eighty-four hours.
>
> Here, in America, we have seen one brutal attack after another.[3]

He then spoke of several attacks that had taken place inside the United States, from Fort Hood to San Bernardino to Orlando, among others, and then several attacks committed by Islamists in Europe. He used the phrase "Radical Islam" some sixteen times.[4] In his plan to defeat Radical Islam, he not only spoke of working with Russia to do so, he spoke of working with NATO: "We will also work closely with NATO on this new mission. I had previously said that NATO was obsolete because it failed to deal adequately with terrorism; since my comments they have changed their policy and now have a new division focused on terror threats."[5]

Donald Trump continued to campaign on these themes. He did not forget about them and placed them square and up front in his inauguration speech as well, boldly saying: "We will reinforce old alliances and form new ones—and unite the civilized world against radical Islamic terrorism, which we will eradicate completely from the face of the Earth."[6]

Why does all this matter? For those concerned that Donald Trump's use of the phrase "America First" had anything to do with the isolationist movement of the 1940s and the appeasement of Germany's Hitler or a signal toward a new era of isolationism, the concern was anti-historical and anti-intellectual.

In the first order, if there was any modern-day analogue to Nazism, it was Radical Islam—and that, Donald Trump swore to fight root and branch. Second, yes, it was long past time for America to rethink its foreign and defense policies—a rethinking required from the errors of several past administrations, and not just Barack Obama's.

As for the modern-day analogue between Radical Islam and Nazi Germany, few wrote on this better than the liberal scholar Paul Berman[7] or the peripatetic and sometimes liberal, sometimes conservative writer Christopher Hitchens. It was Hitchens who brought back the phrase "Islamo-fascism" after September 11, 2001.[8] He would go on throughout the decade in books, columns, speeches, and debates to defend the connection of the phrase to the ideology of political Islam and to the recrudescent movement embodied by Osama bin Laden, his followers, his associates, and other Muslim terrorist organizations.

Much more could be said here, but as a brief primer here is Hitchens explaining the connections:

The most obvious points of comparison would be these: Both movements [Radical Islam and Nazism] are based on a cult of murderous violence that exalts death and destruction and despises the life of the mind. . . . Both are hostile to modernity (except when it comes to the pursuit of weapons), and both are bitterly nostalgic for past empires and lost glories. Both are obsessed with real and imagined "humiliations" and thirsty for revenge. Both are chronically infected with the toxin of anti-Jewish paranoia (interestingly, also, with its milder cousin, anti-Freemason paranoia). Both are inclined to leader worship and to the exclusive stress on the power of one great book. Both have a strong commitment to sexual repression—especially to the repression of any sexual "deviance"—and to its counterparts the subordination of the female and contempt for the feminine. Both despise art and literature as symptoms of degeneracy and decadence; both burn books and destroy museums and treasures. . . .

Technically, no form of Islam preaches racial superiority or proposes a master race. But in practice, Islamic fanatics operate a fascistic concept of the "pure" and the "exclusive" over the unclean and the kufar or profane. In the propaganda against Hinduism and India, for example, there can be seen something very like bigotry. In the attitude to Jews, it is clear that an inferior or unclean race is being talked about (which is why many Muslim extremists like the grand mufti of Jerusalem gravitated to Hitler's side). In the attempted destruction of the Hazara people of Afghanistan, who are ethnically Persian as well as religiously Shiite, there was also a strong suggestion of "cleansing." And, of course, Bin Laden has threatened force against U.N. peacekeepers who might dare interrupt the race-murder campaign against African Muslims that is being carried out by his pious Sudanese friends in Darfur.[9]

So, again: if the thought was Donald Trump would have been isolationist against Hitler, how? The contemporary enemy or movement most resembling Hitler's was the one Trump would spend nearly his entire campaign declaiming against and promising to destroy. And if any further comparisons between Nazi Germany and Radical Islam were needed, it was the mainstay and thesis of the father of the neoconservative school of foreign policy, Norman Podhoretz, the former editor of *Commentary* magazine and author of the 2007 book *World War IV: The Long Struggle Against Islamofascism.*[10] That book and thesis were endorsed by a wide range of thinkers and commentators from Rush Limbaugh to Fouad Ajami, from Rudy Giuliani to John Bolton and George P. Shultz.[11]

As for the ushering in of a new commonsense foreign policy based on the concept of America First, Trump was actually a progressive in the sense of the word C. S. Lewis once provided: "If you are on the wrong road, progress means doing an about-turn and walking back to the right road; and in that case the man who turns back soonest is the most progressive man."[12]

And had we not been on the wrong road for a very long time? In the 1990s, just after the fall of the Berlin Wall, we—or many—had thought liberal democracy had vanquished all or most of our foreign-policy twilight struggles. It is hard to understate the influence of Francis Fukuyama's neo-Hegelian thesis of "The End of History and the Last Man," first outlined in *National Interest* in 1989 and later fleshed out more fully in his bestselling book three years later. Wittingly or not, most of the foreign policy thinking out of Washington, D.C., had adopted the notion that a new Pax Americana would take place now that communism was essentially vanquished politically and its remaining superpower in Asia, China, was moving ever more forward toward free market reforms.

Something deeply interesting and important, however, was missing— and missed—in Fukuyama's thesis: Radical Islam. In his 1989 essay, the word *Islam* received only two mentions, most importantly (or most wrongly) this one: "In the contemporary world only Islam has offered a theocratic state as a political alternative to both liberalism and communism. But the doctrine has little appeal for non-Muslims, and it is hard to believe that the movement will take on any universal significance."[13]

Dr. Fukuyama wrote that sentence the same year Iran's Ayatollah Khomeini famously put a fatwa (or declaration of war) on the head of the novelist Salman Rushdie; one year before Saddam Hussein invaded Kuwait and set off the first Gulf War; he wrote that sentence one year after the bloody and check-mated outcome of the Iran-Iraq war; he wrote that sentence one year after Pan Am Flight 103 was blown up over Lockerbie, Scotland; and he wrote that sentence four years before the first attack on the World Trade Center.

His book, to appear on the scene in 1992, said more than two things about Islam, but still little, and still this: "Despite the power demonstrated by Islam in its current revival, however, it remains the case that this religion has virtually no appeal outside those areas that were culturally Islamic to begin with. The days of Islam's cultural conquests, it would seem, are over: it can win back lapsed adherents, but has no resonance for young people in Berlin, Tokyo, or Moscow."[14] Well, we give you the world we and Berlin and Paris and Moscow and London and so many others inhabit today. Or, rather, al-Qaeda, Hezbollah, ISIS, Boko Haram, Hamas, gives you that world.

The sad story of how we arrived at September 11 has been told and documented well enough by now. But the sad story of how we dealt with it in our foreign policy was, simply put, on a seeming auto-pilot of cascading errors committed by both political parties, by both the George W. Bush administration and the Barack Obama administration. And while it made no sense to Americans generally, the Washington, D.C. "experts" in both administrations continued the engagement and perpetuation of those errors. Few stood against them, or called them out. Donald Trump was one of them.

Barack Obama came to prominence from Illinois as an early opponent of the Iraq war. In 2002, as a state senator, he would say of the ramp-up to the war in Iraq: "That's what I'm opposed to. A dumb war. A rash war. A war based not on reason but on passion, not on principle but on politics."[15] And that was his foreign policy calling card—both when he ran for the United States Senate in 2004 and when he ran for the presidency of the United States four years later. He was the one who promised to get us out of Iraq; he was the one who saw it for the folly that it was.

Most conservatives and Republicans had supported the Iraq war, and so did a lot of Democrats, at first—including Hillary Clinton who, as a United States Senator, had voted to authorize it in 2002.[16] Obama, who saw it as folly from the beginning, would take the United States out of Iraq. How we went in, though, and what we did in Iraq, as much as how we got out, would all prove a colossal failure. As one of the early intellectual defenders of the liberation of Iraq and a prominent neoconservative, Kenneth Adelman, would later say: "The policy can be absolutely right, and noble, beneficial, but if you can't execute it, it's useless, just useless. I guess that's what I would have said: that Bush's arguments are absolutely right, but you know what, you just have to put them in the drawer marked can't do."[17]

We can relitigate the justifications for going into Iraq, but what was clear to most is that the idea that we could transform a hardened tyranny into a democracy through the use of ebbing and flowing American power must always and forever be put in the drawer marked "can't do." Iraq might have been transformed to a degree, it might have been pacified. But by the time we were actually beginning to see the signs of that pacification after the famous Surge and the expenditure of billions of dollars in treasure and thousands of lives in blood, Barack Obama snatched the ultimate pacification from its possible completion, against the advice of his generals.[18] Billions spent, thousands of lives lost—for what? ISIS? Putting Iraq *back on the plate* of the next president? Now, what of Iran? What of Libya? What of Syria?

Iran had been at war with the United States since 1979. We were never going to invade Iran, and hopefully never will. But when Iran stood on the cusp of a possible organic and internal revolution away from the Mullahcracy, President Obama snuffed it out in 2009 with his now famous words: "It is not productive, given the history of U.S.-Iranian relations to be seen as meddling."[19] The "green revolution" in Iran was nearly immediately snuffed out with those very words. Of course, when it came to the history of U.S.-Egypt relations, Egypt actually being our second strongest ally in the Middle East, Barack Obama had no problem in being seen as meddling. In 2011 he publicly urged our ally, Hosni Mubarak, to step down from office in Egypt.[20] This put Egypt into several years of turmoil it still has not recovered from—first giving power to the Muslim Brotherhood there, then seeing a military takeover back to a Mubarak-style government.

As for Israel, our strongest ally in the Middle East, Barack Obama would pressure it as no U.S. president before, going so far as to publicly lecture Israel on the appropriate size of its country, its borders, and that it should actually cut itself across the middle to unite Hamas and PLO factions of a future Palestinian state: "We believe the borders of Israel and Palestine should be based on the 1967 lines with mutually agreed swaps, so that secure and recognized borders are established for both states. The Palestinian people must have the right to govern themselves, and reach their full potential, in a sovereign and contiguous state."[21]

One can debate, as nearly every Middle East expert has debated, the merits and demerits of Israel ceding portions of land to Palestinians based on 1967 lines. But President Obama's second sentence, above, calling for a "contiguous Palestinian state," was the shocker. Such a state would mean cutting a line through the middle of Israel to connect Gaza and the West Bank; such a state would mean slicing Israel in half. It would mean there would be no-fly zones against Israel, no-go transportation areas for Israel and Israelis, and a free transfer of movement for Palestinians through the center of Israel with no checks and no security.

For allies, Barack Obama was all for meddling. And that would include what he, himself, said was his worst mistake: Libya. The president who won a Nobel Peace Prize in his first year in office, who had campaigned to take the United States out of Iraq (only to start putting troops back in Iraq, about five thousand as of the writing of this book),[22] was now interested in toppling and removing from power Libya's Muammar Gaddafi. Gaddafi was a long-standing tyrant, to be sure, but had he not been aligning more and more with the United

States since 2001? In 2009, two of the United States Senate's most well-known hawks, Joe Lieberman and John McCain, supported the Obama administration's efforts to send arms to Gaddafi in 2009.[23] Senator Lieberman went so far as to call Gaddafi "an important ally in the war on terrorism."[24] Two years later, caught up (or hoodwinked) by the Arab spring, the Obama administration would change course when President Obama "pushed our allies to adopt a broad and risky intervention" in Libya.[25]

The efforts in Libya were, indeed, a grave mistake, but his "worst," as President Obama put it, would have a lot of other competing decisions.[26] Gaddafi was dragged through the streets in Sirte, Libya, and publicly maimed and killed by violent mobs for the world to see on smart phone videos broadcasting the drunken bloodlust of the Arab street. And, since, Libya has been a failed state by any definition: at least two different governments and heads of state claiming legitimate authority there; a United States ambassador and three other Americans killed in Benghazi in a terrorist attack that is still mired in controversy; and President Obama continuously ordering bombings of ISIS terrorist camps in Libya as recently as three days before he left office in 2017.[27] Smart power, indeed.

And while President Obama had also quietly sent United States troops to Yemen,[28] United States policy toward Syria would prove to be, at once, the most confusing and telling of fiascos. In August of 2012, President Obama, in one speech, twice threatened the Assad regime of Syria that it would be crossing a "red line" should it deploy chemical or biological weapons against its people:

> We have been very clear to the Assad regime—but also to other players on the ground—that a red line for us is we start seeing a whole bunch of chemical weapons moving around or being utilized. . . .
> We have communicated in no uncertain terms with every player in the region that that's a red line for us and that there would be enormous consequences if we start seeing movement on the chemical weapons front or the use of chemical weapons.[29]

The Assad regime heard President Obama's threat as loudly and clearly as it was intended—and then proceeded to ignore it and use chemical weapons against its populations from Aleppo to Damascus.[30] The United States? President Obama? The "red line" had been crossed and the United States did nothing. To be sure, Syria was a terrorist-sponsoring state aligned—oddly enough—with both Iran and Saddam Hussein's Iraq, and a failed state long before President Obama was elected and long before the threat against the use of chemical and biological weapons. But after the non-enforced threat, it would go on to become something worse than a human charnel house, unleashing a world-wide refugee crisis and a death toll conservatively estimated at three hundred thousand people.[31]

Many blame the rise of ISIS on President Obama's actions in Iraq and Syria. But the larger, unarticulated geo-political problem put squarely in the face of Americans may very well be antecedent to Syria's use of barrel bombs, prior to the non-enforced "red line." *What made Syria and the Assad regime think it could violate a red line threatened by the United States in the first place? And, then, be proven right?* The French philosopher Montesquieu wrote, "If the chance loss of a battle, that is, a particular cause, ruins a state, there is a general cause that created the situation whereby this state could perish by the loss of a single battle. In a word, the principal trend carries along with it the outcome of all particular accidents."[32]

In other words: What was the *general cause* that allowed Syria and Bashir al-Assad to thumb its nose at America? What was the *principal trend?* In a name: Obama. President Obama had mistreated friends and allies from the Czech Republic to Poland, from Israel to Egypt to Libya; he had appeased Russia and the Iranians again and again; he had precipitously taken the United States out of Iraq and publicly promised to do the same in Afghanistan. All the while, he refused to speak of the cause of terrorism and continued to blame the United States whenever and however he could.

When, throughout the 2016 campaign, Donald Trump said,

"America doesn't win anymore" and "We don't win anymore," Americans knew exactly what he was talking about. We had put the "kick me" sign back up on our own backs. This was not exceptionalism. This was not American greatness. This was not any way for a superpower that had thought of itself as "the last best hope of earth" to behave. And so when Donald Trump spoke of "America First," this is all precisely what he meant—it was a summoning as old as Plato's *Republic*: to do good to the just and harm to the unjust.[33] It was a summoning to an ethic of George Washington's: "we may safely trust to temporary alliances for extraordinary emergencies."[34] It was a frame of mind established by John Quincy Adams: "Wherever the standard of freedom and independence has been or shall be unfurled, there will her [America's] heart, her benedictions and her prayers be. But she goes not abroad, in search of monsters to destroy. She is the well-wisher to the freedom and independence of all. She is the champion and vindicator only of her own."[35] Or, without wending through the subsequent history of America's great wars, entered only at the point of no other choice, but aiding allies where possible, one might simply say a sound foreign and defense policy of America First in the twenty-first century is "don't do stupid [stuff.]"[36]

A foreign policy based on America First principles is, quite simply, a policy that takes the mandate of the United States Constitution to heart: "provide for the common defense." It is a foreign policy based on treating allies well and when having to take up arms for *our* common defense, doing so as Alexander Hamilton once said: "Whenever the Government appears in arms it ought to appear like a Hercules, and inspire respect by the display of strength."[37] This would mean true shock and awe and not bogging down in non-democratic societies as we help them rewrite Sharia-based constitutions. This would mean, quite simply, destroying terrorist networks that reach into America and staying out of conflicts that do not touch America. It means asking not only is any foreign engagement in America's interest but *is it in Americans' interests?*

Subsidiary to asking these questions is, indeed, not doing stupid stuff. That would include the avoidance of all that had been done in and with the countries mentioned above. That would include recognizing a menacing terrorist organization like ISIS as it was growing rather than calling it "jay-vee" (or "junior varsity") as President Obama did in 2014.[38] That would mean not putting a legitimate police shooting as took place in Ferguson, Missouri, in 2014 on par with the vast network of Radical Islamic terrorism.* That would include not using the language of the fatwas from the Middle East and Afghanistan to blame the Crusades and a belief in Jesus Christ for our current wars.**

Or, it might just mean avoiding all subtext and reading what Donald Trump actually said when he spoke of a foreign policy based on the principle of America First on the campaign trail:

> I'm not isolationist, but I am "America First." So I like the expression. I'm "America First." We have been disrespected, mocked, and ripped off for many, many years by people that were smarter, shrewder, tougher. We were the big bully, but we were not smartly led. And we were the big bully who was—the big stupid bully and we were systematically ripped off by everybody.[39]

Or:

> Our goal is peace and prosperity, not war and destruction. The best way to achieve those goals is through a disciplined, deliberate, and consistent foreign policy.

---

* Speaking to the United Nations in 2014, President Obama denounced terrorism around the world but then said: "In a summer marked by instability in the Middle East and Eastern Europe, I know the world also took notice of the small American city of Ferguson, Missouri—where a young man was killed, and a community was divided. So yes, we have our own racial and ethnic tensions." https://www.washingtonpost.com/news/post-politics/wp/2014/09/24/at-the-un-obama-invokes-ferguson-we-welcome-the-scrutiny-of-the-world/?utm_term=.1c7a1abd85aa]

** At the National Prayer Breakfast in 2015, President Obama criticized terrorism, and then said: "And lest we get on our high horse and think this is unique to some other place, remember that during the Crusades and the Inquisition, people committed terrible deeds in the name of Christ. In our home country, slavery and Jim Crow all too often was justified in the name of Christ." That is the language of Osama bin Laden, language only familiar in the Middle East and parts of Asia.

No American citizen will ever feel that their needs come second to a citizen of a foreign country.

We will no longer surrender this country or its people to the false song of globalism. . . . I'm skeptical of international unions that tie us up and bring America down. And under my administration, we will never enter America into any agreement that reduces our ability to control our own affairs.[40]

Or:

Our current strategy of nation-building and regime change is a proven failure. We have created the vacuums that allow terrorists to grow and thrive. . . .

As President, I will call for an international conference focused on this goal. We will work side-by-side with our friends in the Middle East, including our greatest ally, Israel. We will partner with King Abdullah of Jordan, and President Sisi of Egypt, and all others who recognize this ideology of death that must be extinguished.

We will also work closely with NATO on this new mission. I had previously said that NATO was obsolete because it failed to deal adequately with terrorism; since my comments they have changed their policy and now have a new division focused on terror threats.

Just as we won the Cold War, in part, by exposing the evils of communism and the virtues of free markets, so too must we take on the ideology of Radical Islam. . . .

Our administration will be a friend to all moderate Muslim reformers in the Middle East, and will amplify their voices.

This includes speaking out against the horrible practice of honor killings, where women are murdered by their relatives for dressing, marrying or acting in a way that violates fundamentalist teachings. . . .

The common thread linking the major Islamic terrorist attacks that have recently occurred on our soil—9/11, the Ft. Hood shooting, the Boston Bombing, the San Bernardino attack, the Orlando attack— is that they have involved immigrants or the children of immigrants.

Clearly, new screening procedures are needed.[41]

Or, what Donald Trump said in his Inaugural Address:

Every decision on trade, on taxes, on immigration, on foreign affairs will be made to benefit American workers and American families. . . .

We will seek friendship and goodwill with the nations of the world, but we do so with the understanding that it is the right of all nations to put their own interests first. We do not seek to impose our way of life on anyone, but rather to let it shine as an example. We will shine for everyone to follow. We will reinforce old alliances and form new ones, and you unite the civilized world against radical Islamic terrorism, which we will eradicate completely from the face of the Earth.[42]

Throughout the campaign and even after his Inaugural Address, common sense-oriented Americans understood all this. They did not go to the 1940s. They appreciated the recognition of who the enemy actually was and naming it. And they put together the notion of American exceptionalism and greatness with a foreign policy that put America's *and* Americans' interests first. It may have offended the intellectual class that thought Davos was more important than Youngstown, Pennsylvania, or Ohio; the class that had somehow bought into the notion that America was just another place among the nations, that Americans were just another people among the world. This thinking plagued both parties for far too long and seemed to be a settled coin of the realm of political thinking. Not to Donald Trump. His was a breath of fresh air and sanity to an America, and millions of Americans, who were tired and frustrated with exactly that kind of thinking. They saw, and heard, in Donald Trump someone who remembered their—our—interests, someone who said he would always put those interests first.

11

THE PURITY RITES

PURPORTED FLAGSHIP MAGAZINES THAT PURGE AND DESTROY THEIR OWN COALITIONS

THE FOUNDING OF THE INTELLECTUAL CONSERVATIVE MOVEMENT comes with a now familiar history. It centers around several books and a great magazine—to be joined over time by more books and magazines, think tanks, and radio shows.

In chapter 3, we discussed the conservative movement's long-standing concerns with the academy and its entrenched leftism, multi-culturalism, and political correctness—a left-wing intellectual dominance of speech and thought that had seeped upward and outward to other institutions, from the mainstream media to Hollywood to corporate America. Dinesh D'Souza's book *Illiberal Education* became a best seller and landed him on the intellectual conservative map when he took on the issue in the early 1990s. Of course there was also Allan Bloom's *Closing of the American Mind* in the late 1980s. But it is interesting to note that the entire kick-off of the modern American conservative movement began with this issue, with the publication of William F. Buckley's first book, *God and Man at Yale* in 1951.

With that book, William Buckley created not only a stir but a movement that would lead to the founding of *National Review* four years later and establish Buckley as the father of the modern American conservative movement. What Clinton Rossiter wrote of the conservative movement as far back as 1962: "Conservatism, I have learned the hard way, is not a subject on which it is easy to communicate clearly,"[1] is, in many respects, still true today and was eminently true when William Buckley appeared on the scene. It was, after all, his and *National Review*'s effort to harness the movement and communicate its ideas clearly.

The maiden issue of *National Review* contained a now-well-known mission-statement essay by Buckley, both explaining and justifying the magazine's founding. The most famous line: "[*National Review*] stands athwart history, yelling Stop, at a time when no one is inclined to do so, or to have much patience with those who so urge it."[2]

It is here important to note that a Republican administration was in the White House. But the conservative movement as it was building had not, in its own opinion, yet enmeshed itself into the Republican Party. What was it in history Buckley and the *National Review* founders were trying to stop in the 1950s? It was trying to stop the cultural and institutional trends of liberal progressivism. Buckley told us:

> [T]he United Nations and the League of Women Voters and the *New York Times* and Henry Steele Commager are in place. [*National Review*] is out of place because, in its maturity, literate America rejected conservatism in favor of radical social experimentation. Instead of covetously consolidating its premises, the United States seems tormented by its tradition of fixed postulates having to do with the meaning of existence, with the relationship of the state to the individual, of the individual to his neighbor, so clearly enunciated in the enabling documents of our Republic.[3]

Already in the 1950s, never mind polls of the young that worry many conservatives today, "we feel gentlemanly doubts when asserting the superiority of capitalism to socialism, of republicanism to centralism."[4] Buckley and his co-founders then attacked with a founding creed, or *credenda* as they called it. Parts of that credenda included the following:

> The growth of government (the dominant social feature of this century) must be fought relentlessly.
>
> The century's most blatant force of satanic utopianism is communism. We consider "coexistence" with communism neither desirable nor possible, nor honorable; we find ourselves irrevocably at war with communism and shall oppose any substitute for victory.
>
> The largest cultural menace in America is the conformity of the intellectual cliques which, in education as well as the arts, are out to impose upon the nation their modish fads and fallacies, and have nearly succeeded in doing so.
>
> No superstition has more effectively bewitched America's Liberal elite than the fashionable concepts of world government, the United Nations, internationalism, international atomic pools, etc.[5]

In sum and substance, *National Review*, William Buckley, and the conservative intellectual movement commenced their cause on a dedication to smaller government, fighting communism, fighting political correctness, and opposing international organizations and treaties that conformed the United States to their ethics rather than the reverse.

Perhaps two of the foregoing main points of the movement's founding could be, *mutatis mutandis,* heard and seen in most Republican talking points today, or at least in the campaign efforts of the other Republicans who ran against Donald Trump in the 2016 election: reducing the size of government and fighting the "satanic" enemy of the day, Radical Islam. Few, if any, of the other candidates or Republicans generally speak of our "cultural menaces" or international treaties and organizations. Few besides Donald Trump, that is.

Within about a decade of the founding of the modern intellectual conservative movement, the candidate whom Buckley and his movement would support—and who won the Republican nomination—was Barry Goldwater. With the Goldwater nomination of 1964, the Republican Party was changed. At least temporarily. It offered the voters, in Phyllis Schlafly's words, in the book title of the same name, *A Choice, Not an Echo*. This was to say, it offered the American public a true conflict of ideas in the nominee of the Republican Party, not liberalism versus a moderate Republican, not "an identifiable team of Fabian operators . . . bent on controlling both our major political parties" as *National Review*'s creed had criticized as being the case for too long.[6] In Barry Goldwater, the Republican nominee offered Right versus Left, conservatism versus liberalism.

If Barry Goldwater was the apotheosis of what Buckley, *National Review*, and the new conservative movement wanted in a presidential candidate—and he was—it is also fair to say the country was not ready for that kind of unvarnished conservatism. Yet. George Will would remark in various ways over the years: Barry Goldwater won; it just took sixteen years to count the votes.[7] This obviously referenced the 1980 election of Ronald Reagan.

But before we move the clock up to 1980, two things are still worth pointing out from the 1964 Goldwater campaign, the two most important speeches of that campaign: Barry Goldwater's acceptance speech at the Republican convention and Ronald Reagan's televised political advertisement speech on behalf of the Goldwater candidacy.

In his acceptance speech, written by Harry V. Jaffa, the intellectual founder of the Claremont Institute and of the West Coast school of Straussiansim, all that *National Review* and the new intellectual conservative movement Buckley had harnessed was present. It was not a cheerful speech, but a rather strong dose of medicine and complaint about the trajectory of the world, the United States, and our politics. It began with an appeal to "freedom" and then moved on to foreign policy blunders and failures, particularly in Asia and in Cuba. It complained about the lack of "useful jobs" and how they were being replaced by "bureaucratic 'make work'" jobs. It complained of "violence in our streets" and how "[s]ecurity from domestic violence, no less than from foreign aggression," should be government's first concern. It spoke to the concerns of unarrested communism abroad and the need to restore "our constitutional form of government" here at home. And then, Barry Goldwater's most famous words of the speech, the year, and perhaps his life, came: "I would remind you that extremism in the defense of liberty is no vice. And let me remind you also that moderation in the pursuit of justice is no virtue."[8]

To this day, Barry Goldwater is remembered for those words. Indeed, they may be the most famous words of any candidate's nomination speech. While Barry Goldwater was unlikely to win the 1964 election for a host of reasons, they are still cited as words that helped him lose in that they helped reify the notion that he was defending "extremism" or was himself an extremist. Of course, that was *not* Goldwater's (or Jaffa's) point in uttering those words—they were a response to the moderate or eastern wing of the Republican Party and movement that kept claiming Goldwater was an "extremist." That kept claiming the new conservative movement was extremist.

But those, as stated above, were not the only memorable words from the Goldwater campaign. The other important speech—perhaps even more important—was Ronald Reagan's televised address on behalf of the Goldwater campaign. Known as *A Time for Choosing*, this was Ronald Reagan's first major national address proclaiming his Republican and conservative credentials. It would be his political calling card. It would create his political career, first as a candidate for governor of California two years later, and then in every subsequent race he would run in. In a lifetime of delivering well-known and still-cited speeches, this would prove his most important.

If there is a now obvious connection between the *National Review* founding principles and creed, the Goldwater candidacy, and Donald Trump's emphases in 2016, so much the more is this evident with

Reagan's 1964 speech and Donald Trump's campaign.

In *A Time for Choosing*, Reagan outlined the philosophy he would hew to for the rest of his political life, the philosophy that ultimately brought around other conservative thinkers, think tanks, and magazines toward supporting not just Ronald Reagan in 1980 and beyond but conservatism generally. In Ronald Reagan in 1980, one would see the uniting of the various factions within the conservative movement, be they libertarians, traditionalists, neoconservatives, social conservatives, or economic conservatives. What Buckley and *National Review* tried to harness and fuse over the course of the 1950s and 1960s would be joined by others in the 1970s and 1980s. Magazines and editors like *Commentary* and Norman Podhoretz, *The National Interest* and Irving Kristol; think tanks from the American Enterprise Institute to the Heritage Foundation, from the Hudson Institute to the Claremont Institute and the Manhattan Institute and a host of others—they were all now on board, not just for Reagan but for the general consensus of what conservatism had come to stand for and who the Republican Party's standard-bearer should be.

But, again, what was it Reagan actually spoke about in 1964 and what were the themes he would continue to sound throughout his career? In *A Time for Choosing*, Reagan spoke, in a rather strong tone, about getting beyond thinking his positions were necessarily partisan. Rather, he said, "You and I are told increasingly we have to choose between a left or right. Well I'd like to suggest there is no such thing as a left or right. There's only an up or down."[9]

He spoke of reducing the size of government and of the perils of big government:

> [The Founding Fathers] knew that governments don't control things. A government can't control the economy without controlling people. And they know when a government sets out to do that, it must use force and coercion to achieve its purpose. They also knew . . . that outside of its legitimate functions, government does nothing as well or as economically as the private sector of the economy.[10]

He spoke of the elites in Washington and the loss of the notion of self-government: "This is the issue of this election: whether we believe in our capacity for self-government or whether we abandon the American revolution and confess that a little intellectual elite in a far-distant capitol can plan our lives for us better than we can plan them ourselves."[11]

He spoke of American exceptionalism in telling a beautiful story of a Cuban immigrant who reminded his friends how lucky they were to be Americans, concluding with the line, "If we lose freedom here, there's no place to escape to. This is the last stand on earth."[12]

He spoke of lower taxes and he spoke of America not winning its wars. And, of course, he spoke of socialism and communism. "You and I have the courage to say to our enemies, 'There is a price we will not pay.' 'There is a point beyond which they must not advance.' "[13]

Yes, it is true, come 2016 and years prior, Republican candidates would speak to various pieces of these themes of Buckley's and Goldwater's and Reagan's—but only Donald Trump spoke to all of them, especially with his inclusion of elites in Washington, the loss of self-government, and American exceptionalism.

Larry Arnn, a founder of the Claremont Institute and the president of Hillsdale College, explains how his eyes were opened to the Trump candidacy when he read an op-ed of Donald Trump's in a January 2016 issue of the *Reno Gazette-Journal*. It opened, "The United States of America is a land of laws, and Americans value the rule of law above all. Why, then, has our Congress allowed the president and the executive branch to take on near-dictatorial power?"[14]

For years, conservatives had been condemning the administrative state in nearly these exact words, or, certainly, these kinds of familiar words. But few Republican candidates spoke of it. They, after all, were deployers of that "power." Big government, or the growth of government, was, after all, not just a problem inherent to the Democratic party. Heck, government's size had even grown under Ronald Reagan's presidency—and certainly both Bush presidencies.

But Trump's op-ed went further in its appeal to Nevada voters, speaking to the encroaching of rights on Nevadans from the Bureau of Land Management and Department of Energy. It also spoke of the costs to Nevadans from illegal immigration. If Reagan could declaim against such things as the Civilian Conservation Corps in 1964, and Barry Goldwater could speak against the Tennessee Valley Authority, was not Donald Trump following in just those footsteps in speaking of the Department of Energy and the Bureau of Land Management? If Reagan and Goldwater could warn of the loss of self-government due to the aggrandizement of power by "elites" in Washington, was not Donald Trump following in just those footsteps as well?

But that is *not* what the conservative magazines of yore were seeing in or saying about Donald Trump in 2016—not *National Review*, not *Commentary*, and not the erstwhile supporters of Ronald Reagan at the *Weekly Standard*. Not even the conservative D.C. columnists who wrote syndicated columns. No. That group constituted the core of the Never Trump movement.

Indeed, in January of 2016, *National Review* published a special issue condemning the Trump candidacy, titled *Against Trump*.[15] It contained an unsigned editorial of the same name and an attendant series of essays by inside and outside contributors under the heading *Conservatives Against Trump*.[16] The unsigned editorial started by condemning Trump for switching positions over the years: "Trump's political opinions have wobbled all over the lot. The real-estate mogul and reality-TV star has supported abortion, gun control, single-payer health care à la Canada, and punitive taxes on the wealthy."[17] Of course one could have said some of the same things about candidates like Ronald Reagan and Mitt Romney as well—and their changes of mind or position took place over much shorter courses of time than some of Donald Trump's. But those outlets supported Reagan and Romney; they did not condemn them.

The editorial went on to challenge Trump on his positions, taking a hard stance on illegal immigration and ISIS—not that they fully opposed Trump's positions per se, but that they were, according to the editors, impractical as Trump articulated them. It condemned his "brash manner" and said when they heard him speak of making "America great again" it reminded them of Andrew Jackson. Why couldn't it remind them of Ronald Reagan's 1980 campaign slogan of the same name, one might have asked. But for Never Trumpers, the easier way to condemn Trump a priori was to go to the 1830s. Trump supporters heard Reagan, while the *National Review* editors heard Andrew Jackson.

Calling Trump "a menace to conservatism," the editorial said:

> If Trump were to become the president, the Republican nominee, or even a failed candidate with strong conservative support, what would that say about conservatives? The movement that ground down the Soviet Union and took the shine, at least temporarily, off socialism would have fallen in behind a huckster. The movement concerned with such "permanent things" as constitutional government, marriage, and the right to life would have become a claque for a Twitter feed.[18]

In the light of a year after this was written, one could see that the editorial board of *National Review* would not be the place to go to for stock tips. Donald Trump did become the nominee and a successful— not failed—candidate. His first actions were to nominate a Supreme Court justice as highly qualified and admired in conservative legal circles as possible, to impose a temporary refugee ban from terrorist-sponsoring countries, and to restore the Mexico City policy, which takes the United States out of the business of supporting abortions abroad. As for his Cabinet—Jeff Sessions, Tom Price, Ben Carson, James Mattis, Betsy DeVos, and others—it could be argued that his is the most conservative first-term presidential Cabinet in modern history, even more conservative than Ronald Reagan's first Cabinet.

But that was just the *National Review* editors. What of their constellation of contributors, the so-called "Conservatives against Trump"? It may seem odd that *National Review* would include the radio host Glenn Beck in this group. It is true Beck had supported Ted Cruz for the presidency, but he was hardly a conservative intellect, or even, really, a conservative, and he was even more of an entertainer and huckster than Donald Trump. If Donald Trump had switched positions over the years, Beck had done quite a bit of that himself—and as recently as 2010 was bragging about giving money to liberal causes like hemp farms, believing in the dangers of manmade global warming, and saying such things as "I don't think Ronald Reagan was a real Republican."[19] This same Glenn Beck would say "Barack Obama made me a better man" and that he supported the Black Lives Matter movement.[20]

Still, in trying to leave no Never Trumper behind, *National Review* led off with Beck's critique for its symposium. And what did one get from Beck at the *National Review*? A critique of Donald Trump's support for stimulus spending, and then this:

> Sure, Trump's potential primary victory would provide Hillary Clinton with the easiest imaginable path to the White House. But it's far worse than that. If Donald Trump wins the Republican nomination, there will once again be no opposition to an ever-expanding government. This is a crisis for conservatism. And, once again, this crisis will not go to waste.[21]

"Easiest imaginable path to the White House." "No opposition to an ever-expanding government." Why should anyone take Glenn Beck seriously again? Why should he have been taken seriously in the first place? To be fair, there were others in the *National Review* symposium, too, many of them long-standing and actually credible and smart conservatives. But, again, so much of the critique of Donald Trump was personal and speculative. None of it took Donald Trump's positions as Donald Trump took them, or as his supporters did. We were told he was "immature." We were told he "made a career out of egoism." We were told "he advocates" "a rejection of our Madisonian inheritance and an embrace of Barack Obama's authoritarianism." We were told he had "hair like the tinsel on discarded Christmas trees." We were told he was "the very epitome of vulgarity." We were told "Donald Trump is no conservative" and that he flirted with "racism."[22] And on and on and on. When it wasn't personal or ad hominem, it was simply unbelieving in his seriousness.

And it all rang hollow. Meanwhile, John Podhoretz, the editor at *Commentary*, gave us such Buckleyesque language as Donald Trump "is a lunatic" and is "F***ing insane" but without the ellipticals.[23] Not wrong, mind you, a lunatic and f***ing insane. Then there was Bill Kristol and Steve Hayes at the *Weekly Standard*, documented in chapter 6 above.

If it was true that Donald Trump could speak strongly or even be vulgar—what of this kind of language? If it was true Donald Trump could change his positions over the years, what of all of these people supporting a Ronald Reagan or a John McCain or a Mitt Romney? What were these magazines and editors and writers doing? The opposite of working to harness the coalition for which Buckley had worked so hard, that the entire movement of the 1950s, 1960s, 1970s, and 1980s had worked so hard for. They were writing Democratic party talking points and using the same kind of language against Donald Trump they had objected to when liberals and leftists had used it against them—classic conservative Stockholm syndrome.

And they were purging the coalition they claimed to be trying to uphold. We have had any number of callers and listeners tell us they voted Republican in the past, but some of Donald Trump's language bothered them. Okay—what of some of Hillary Clinton's support for her husband's behavior? What of calling us a "right wing conspiracy," "deplorable," and what of her policies? We can all regret the state of our language today—but what of the state of a country that gives support to the peddlers of that language? What of the actual policies that would be instituted by Clinton versus Trump? What of the court nominations? What of the personnel? In short, we Trump supporters had a country to save, and the salty language would have to wait. Especially if it was language most people had become used to. And especially if it came from a candidate—likely the only candidate—who could actually beat the Democratic party nominee.

Of course not all conservative intellectuals were Never Trump—and maybe, though somewhat and in many precincts lesser known—they made a very strong affirmative case.

-12

FOLLOWING, NOT LEADING

HOW CHECKLIST CONSERVATISM
FAILED AMERICA

THE CENTRAL CONCEIT OF CONSERVATISM INC. has been that only it could save America and return her to her former glory. The glory was not primarily martial, economic, or even cultural, but political. The American regime of constitutional self-government predicated upon the acknowledgment and defense of natural human rights represents the pinnacle of human politics. But it turns out that the conservatives charged with acting upon those principles—the intellectuals, government functionaries, and politicians—weren't anywhere near as interested in doing anything as they were in talking about it. And when they came face to face with a candidate who explicitly called for action that would restore power to the sovereign people at the expense of D.C. fiefdoms, and did so in the name of making America great again, not only did they fail to support that candidate—they actively opposed him.

But why?

What became known as the "conservative movement" that traces its post–World War II lineage back through Reagan and Goldwater to William F. Buckley Jr. and the founding of *National Review* in 1955 was in fact a coalition of distinct political philosophies united by their opposition to collectivism at home and communist imperialism abroad. By the 1990s Reagan had won the Cold War, Soviet communism had collapsed and with it the threat of war in Europe and of aggressive communist states destabilizing what used to be called the Third World (countries that were not officially aligned with either the NATO allies or with the Communist bloc). The end of that threat marked a significant victory. It was a great good for the country and for mankind.

At home the story was more mixed. Republicans in Congress even under Ronald Reagan were more eager to cut taxes than to reduce the size and scope of government. Recall that it was recalcitrant Republican senators who blocked Ronald Reagan's plan to shut down the Departments of Education and Energy as he had promised during the campaign. Reagan was never able to shrink government and return power back to the people. During his administration government spending exploded and the federal deficit tripled. In 1980, the last year of Jimmy Carter's presidency, the executive branch had 2.82 million employees. In 1988 that had expanded to 3.05 million.[1] Much of the blame can be laid at the feet of Congress, where the House of Representatives was controlled by Democrats throughout the 1980s. (Thanks, Tip O'Neill!)

During this time Republicans grew accustomed to big government. Roosevelt's New Deal and Johnson's Great Society programs, which had dramatically increased the size and cost of the federal government, were once the bête noire of Republicans, who longed for the day to roll them back. But by the 1980s and 1990s a younger generation of Republicans went to Washington. They had grown up with those programs and were motivated not to eliminate the administrative state but to control it. In practical terms that meant accepting a federal government that had grown well beyond the parameters prescribed by the Constitution and had encroached on the part of life reserved for the citizen.

In 1950 left-wing intellectual Lionel Trilling famously wrote that

in the United States at this time Liberalism is not only the dominant but even the sole intellectual tradition. For it is the plain fact that nowadays there are no conservative or reactionary ideas in general circulation. This does not mean, of course, that there is no impulse to conservatism or to reaction. Such impulses are certainly very strong, perhaps even stronger than most of us know. But the conservative impulse and the reactionary impulse do not, with some isolated and some ecclesiastical exceptions, express themselves in ideas but only in action or in irritable mental gestures which seek to resemble ideas.[2]

The leftist view of American conservatives hasn't changed much, but now rather than dismissing notions of constitutional government based on natural right as an irritable mental gesture, they call people who hold such unenlightened ideas "deplorables" and "bitter clingers." The complacent go-along-to-get-along club of Republican insiders hasn't changed much either. In 1964 George Romney (Mitt's father) called nominating Barry Goldwater "suicidal destruction"[3] and actively worked against him, even leading a walk-out of Goldwater's acceptance speech at the Cow Palace in San Francisco. For his part, Mitt called President Trump "a phony, a fraud"[4] before reversing course and asking him for the job of Secretary of State after the election. Self-knowledge is a wonderful thing—if only more of our pols had it. Keeping with the theme, John McCain mocked Tea Party activists as "hobbits" in 2011 and turned to the *New Yorker* when he wanted to vent his spleen about conservative voters whom he called "the crazies" in 2015.

For these people conservative voters are just ignorant rubes who can be exploited for votes every other November by tickling their ears with key phrases and promises to "do something" about their pet issues—things that sophisticates in Washington know better than to take seriously. These are things like enforcement of immigration laws, pro-worker trade and economic policies, and a national security policy that prioritizes American interests over starry-eyed nation-building schemes. But you have to hand it to them, they know the buttons to push that keeps the cash rolling in and gets conservatives to the polls.

If you want to pass a trade deal that will export jobs abroad, attach the words "free trade act" to the name. Everyone is in favor of freedom and trade, so putting them together must be even better. If you want to import cheap foreign labor, call them "New Americans"[5] and label the policy "compassionate" and "in keeping with our values." If anyone opposes it they can be shamed by saying that is "not who we are as a nation"[6] (Lindsey Graham) or just "that's not who we are"[7] (Paul Ryan). In other words, if you don't agree with us you're hard hearted and you don't belong.

This is the language of smarmy political opportunism. For such people conservative politics is just a set of slogans tied to a meal ticket. It's not principled, it's not prudent, and it's no way to govern. The Left at least believes in governing according to the ideology they profess at election time. Without any attachment to foundational principles, the politics of Conservatism Inc. has been reduced to pithy aphorisms and worn-out policy proposals. They are like the citizens of a post-apocalypse dystopia that finds the old technology and totems of the old civilization but has no idea what they mean or how to use them: they have access to the Declaration and the Constitution but the plain meaning and political implications of the text elude them.

Conservatism has come to describe not the political philosophy embodied in America's founding documents but a psychological attachment to the status quo—any status quo. So where conservatives once objected strenuously to the expansion of government beyond its constitutional bounds and to the plainly absurd distortions of the Constitution by the Supreme Court to justify them, they now just wait a generation to ratify as given and salutary whatever the Left did a few decades ago. Witness Charles Krauthammer's praise in 2013 for the New Deal programs. He called them "the great achievements of liberalism—the achievements of the New Deal, of Social Security, Medicaid, Medicare. The idea that you rescue the elderly and don't allow the elderly to enter into destitution is a consensual idea [accepted by] conservatives, at least the mainstream of conservatives."[8]

Conservatives have reduced their political philosophy to efficient management of the welfare state through reforms they call "market oriented solutions" and acceptance of the permanent cession of power to the administrative state. This took the form of an explosion of Cabinet-level departments and administrative agencies. Seven Cabinet-level departments have been created since 1953. Another thirty-two major federal agencies such as the EPA, Federal Election Commission, the Federal Trade Commission, and the Equal Employment Opportunity Commission wield significant power. Only four of the agencies existed before 1933 and only one, the post office, before 1900.

With the proliferation of these departments and agencies has come a massive expansion of federal powers to regulate American life at all levels, with little or no oversight or accountability. The sprawling complex of federal bureaucracies that we call variously the administrative state or the deep state represent an as yet unconfronted challenge to self-government. These unelected and therefore unaccountable mandarins are lawgivers unto themselves. Worse, they also operate their own administrative law courts to adjudicate violations under and challenges to their rules, and they maintain their own enforcement power.

The *Washington Times* reports that "since FY 2006, 44 traditionally administrative agencies have spent over $71 million on items like body armor, riot helmets and shields, cannon launchers and police firearms and ammunition, according to federal spending data from watchdog group OpenTheBooks.com."[9] Agencies like the Environmental Protection Agency and the Food and Drug Administration maintain their own armed police forces. In 2013 armed EPA officers raided the town of Chicken, Alaska, looking for violations of the Clear Water Act.[10]

In *Federalist 51* James Madison warned against the concentration of all the powers of the state—executive, legislative, and judiciary—in one set of hands. Human history has taught nothing if not that such a concentration of power leads to tyranny. He explained it this way:

> But the great security against a gradual concentration of the several powers in the same department, consists in giving to those who administer each department the necessary constitutional means and personal motives to resist encroachments of the others. The provision for defense must in this, as in all other cases, be made commensurate to the danger of attack. Ambition must be made to counteract ambition. The interest of the man must be connected with the constitutional rights of the place. It may be a reflection on human nature, that such devices should be necessary to control the abuses of government. But what is government itself, but the greatest of all reflections on human nature? If men were angels, no government would be necessary. If angels were to govern men, neither external nor internal controls on government would be necessary. In framing a government which is to be administered by men over men, the great difficulty lies in this: you must first enable the government to control the governed; and in the next place oblige it to control itself. A dependence on the people is, no doubt, the primary control on the government; but experience has taught mankind the necessity of auxiliary precautions.
>
> This policy of supplying, by opposite and rival interests, the defect of better motives, might be traced through the whole system of human affairs, private as well as public. We see it particularly displayed in all the subordinate distributions of power, where the constant aim is to divide and arrange the several offices in such a manner as that each may be a check on the other—that the private interest of every individual may be a sentinel over the public rights. These inventions of prudence cannot be less requisite in the distribution of the supreme powers of the State.

The administrative state represents just such a concentration of power. In the face of not the threat but the reality of the encroachment upon the natural rights of the sovereign people, Conservatism Inc. offers a frustrating mix of platitudes and acquiescence. Marshall Wittman explained the change this way: "Big-government conservatism is the animating principle of the Bush presidency. It is a radical departure from the conservatism of the past 40 years." Yet during his presidency George W. Bush enjoyed broad support from conservatives despite departing from the historic principles of Republican foreign policy and dramatically expanding the size of the federal government with power grabs like No Child Left Behind and the largest entitlement expansion since Lyndon B. Johnson in the Medicare Prescription Drug Benefit. This was marketed with the Orwellian name "compassionate conservatism," which is notable mostly for the ruthless efficiency of the deceit: two words, two lies. Expanding government power at the expense of the people is neither compassionate nor conservative.

When the Constitution was ratified there were just four departments. They represented the four things that only government can do and for which people come together to form governments: the Department of Defense (originally the Department of War) exists to oversee the military and protect the country from foreign enemies, the State Department conducts diplomacy with other nations on behalf of the country, the Treasury Department collects taxes and administers the government's budget, and the Attorney General enforces the nation's laws. The purview of the departments formed after that is an encroachment on the things citizens can do for themselves individually or through private associations. What's more, as government gets bigger it grows more remote from the people it governs. Limited government is also responsive government. The defenders of big government would have us believe these other departments and agencies are necessary. But I ask, before the Department of Labor, did no one work? Was there no commerce before the Department of Commerce? Was no one educated before the Department of Education?

These are hard questions of politics—the questions upon which turns the fate of the regime and the nation. Conservatism Inc. has marketed itself as the sole defender of the American project. But it turns out mainstream American conservatism was built on sand. From the beginning, it rallied the faithful around simple negation: "standing athwart history yelling 'Stop!'" What started as a clever slogan became a guiding principle, but that's weak tea for a country birthed in a revolution based on the natural right of man to govern himself.

Perhaps conservatives took for granted the principles underlying the American founding and the basic decency and morality of the American people. They relied upon a cultural and political inheritance that they believed was a given, never realizing that it needed to be renewed every generation with civic and moral education. Nor did they realize that the inheritance upon which free government relied was (and is) under a purposeful and sustained attack from the Left. Younger conservatives may believe that Barack Obama was the first president to talk about "fundamentally transforming" America, but in fact he follows a path first marked out by Woodrow Wilson a century ago.

The assault began with the Progressives in the early twentieth century. Under Wilson they initially used constitutional means to pursue radical ends. Witness the passage of the Sixteenth and Seventeenth Amendments. By the late 1930s, Franklin D. Roosevelt realized he could get the Supreme Court to rubber-stamp his unconstitutional New Deal power grabs simply by threatening to pack the court with new justices. It is hard to underestimate the consequences of Roosevelt's actions in 1937, but they represented a sea change in American constitutional law that stripped power from the people and their representatives in Congress. The conservatives of the day complained but didn't sense the mortal threat or the ruthlessness of the Left in pursuing its goals.

Conservatives certainly should have gotten the message that the rules had changed and that this was a fight for the soul of the country at least by the time Gore Vidal called Bill Buckley a "crypto-fascist" on television in 1968. By then the "politics of personal destruction" were in full effect and Progressives were leading the way. The Left was and remains engaged in a project to undo the American experiment in constitutional government, and it will use any weapon at hand to do it.

The conservative response to the Left's will-to-power politics was to create a catechism of approved policy positions and talking points, but they forgot—or never knew—the basis of the faith. In this way the modern Right resembles the mainline Protestant churches hollowed out by one hundred years of replacing the Christian Gospel with the social gospel. The forms are still there—the buildings, the Sunday services, the hymnals—but the substance is long gone.

Pledge fealty to the conservative trinity—strong military, free markets, and family values—and you can consider yourself a True Conservative. But these worthy goals evolved into something else altogether, something not recognizable as historic American conservatism, constitutionalism, or, in the ultimate analysis, in the interests of the American people.

The goal of a strong military became instead endless foreign wars "for democracy"[11] rather than for the defense of the American people, though they never seem to end in victory. (Conservatives interested in reclaiming free government in their country would be better off reading *How Democracies Perish* than the neoconservative favorite, *The Case for Democracy*.)

"Free markets" became a slogan to pacify Republican voters at election time, but is really just cover for globalism that benefits the few[12] at the expense of the many and crony capitalism.[13]

Family values became "compassionate conservatism," which in turn is used to justify everything from open borders[14] to Obamacare.[15]

Congressional Republicans became adept at this form of checklist conservatism, using it to gin up support from the base during elections but abandoning even the pretense by the time they get back to Washington. Even the checklist was abandoned. Marco Rubio campaigned for the Senate as an immigration hawk, only to turn his back on his constituents and join the Gang of Eight amnesty project. Had he not, he might have been the Republican nominee squaring off against Hillary.

Checklist conservatism degrades politics and fails the American people by promising salvation from the depredations of the Left—salvation from the steady, incremental undermining of the sovereignty of the people—but it fails again and again because, in a famous phrase, it is not a choice but an echo. The Left offers a dramatic vision of a utopian future complete with a messianic morality, which the Right counters with warmed-over policy ideas from the 1990s complete with pie charts. Progressives describe their mission as a world historical voyage of discovery, and conservatives' only response is to ask how much the ship costs and if they can take a turn at the helm, without ever thinking to ask where the ship is going or why.

So little does the messianic Left value the consent of the governed that when they are unable to persuade the American people of the rightness of their ideas, they bully and berate them. When that doesn't work they force permanent political changes through the unaccountable and unelected branches of the State and impose their will from above. In the biggest and most infamous cases like *Roe v. Wade* and *Chevron, U.S.A., Inc. v. Natural Resources Defense Council, Inc.*, this means using the Supreme Court to replace the U.S. Constitution with something called "constitutional law"[16] that is made by judges, often in contradiction of both the document itself and the will of the people.

Those are the big cases. But a a rising tide of laws and regulations is also flowing forth from an alphabet soup of unelected state and federal star chambers. Consider the example of recently enacted rules from the Iowa Civil Rights Commission that require churches to provide "transgender" bathrooms and threaten to restrict what is said from the pulpit if it " 'directly or indirectly' make(s) 'persons of any particular . . . gender identity' feel 'unwelcome.' "[17] Having used the Supreme Court to circumvent the people on gay rights, the Left's next target is freedom of religion, which, the ACLU helpfully reminds us, is just a cover for bigotry and discrimination that must be eliminated.[18]

Where is the so-called conservative movement in all of this? Opposed to it, usually. At least until they aren't. A political philosophy known generically as "conservatism" is often a better description of psychology or temperament. Where the Left is ideologically motivated and makes sweeping, if wrong and inconsistent, moral claims, the Right too often just likes things the way they are—the safety and security of the known. Sure, this may be a better starting point than the Left's frenzied nihilistic rush into an unknown future where, they confidently assure us, "all the women are strong, all the men are good looking, and all the children are above average." Just like the Lake Wobegon of Garrison Keillor's imagination.

But that sort of temperamental conservatism is morally and politically insufficient because it is not grounded in reason and can point to no guiding principles. Since the Left wins most—maybe all—of the major political battles, a conservatism that is based mostly on a temperamental defense of the status quo will, over time, accept and eventually defend anything it opposes today. Such a conservatism is based in moral relativism every bit as much as the historicist ideologies of the radical Left is. Its supporters just don't know it. This is how checklist conservatives become defenders not of timeless principles, still less of the American people, but of a political order defined by yesterday's radicals.

We shouldn't be surprised at any of this, because conservatives forgot two big things: the appropriate role of government and the necessity in all things of the American people. This is especially true of the generation that came of age after Reagan, though all the symptoms were there much earlier. The simple truth that the American government is an extension of the American people and exists only for their benefit—to secure their natural rights—has been lost.

So-called movement conservatives fought the culture war and lost. In good faith, they fought bad policies, endowed think tanks, backed candidates, took control of Congress and the majority of statehouses— and still the country continued moving to the Left. Government grew more remote and less accountable, because while the Right was focused on the details of Congressional policy battles—each of them important but not decisive—the Left was seizing control of the courts, the administrative state, and the commanding heights of the culture.

It's hard enough putting together a winning electoral coalition that elects a president who will appoint "conservative" judges and a Senate that will confirm them. But when those judges have been steeped in leftist culture, it is no surprise that legal positivism has found its way even into the Federalist Society or that it was Bush appointee Chief Justice John Roberts who created from whole cloth a way to save Obamacare. When radicals captured the elite universities, it set the stage for a permanent divide between the ruling class and the rest of the country.

After Reagan left office, Republicans exchanged hard-headed, interests-based foreign policy for the naive belief that if we export what R. R. Reno has called the hearth gods of health, wealth, and hedonism—really just stand-ins for a shallow materialism—the world will enter into the millennial peace brought about by the end of history. Instead, it ignores the permanent reality of human nature and conflates cause and effect. Lasting prosperity is the fruit of a healthy culture, not the cause of it.

Meanwhile, a lethal coalition of those guided by hopeless naiveté and cunning design has led America into military conflicts without victory abroad, immigration policies that undermine the interests of American citizens, and trade deals that benefit crony capitalists here and abroad at the expense of the middle class. This cannot last.

Conservatism has been a defensive ideology for too long. Fortunately government of, by, and for the people can be recovered. But only the American people can save themselves, and only then with a politics rooted in commonsense morality, self-evident truths, and everyday virtue. Rote repetition of the conservative checklist won't do.

13

FIRST ADMIT THERE IS
A PROBLEM

CONSERVATIVE SELF-DESTRUCTION

IN SEPTEMBER OF 2016, an initial group of some 125 conservative scholars (the list would expand to 140 over ensuing weeks) issued a call of support for Donald Trump's candidacy and election.[1] The point of disseminating such a call was threefold: to counter the narrative Conservatism Inc. had been promulgating, that all conservative intellectuals were against Trump; that there was not just a conservative intellectual case to be made for Donald Trump's candidacy but a strong conservative case to be made; and to let the base of supporters for Donald Trump know they were not alone. Whether the media would pick up on any of this was irrelevant, for the media were not for Trump and nothing would convince them to be.

The bulk of the scholars may not have had regular syndicated weekly columns or been mainstays of the Fox News/CNN/MSNBC revolving contributors' doors, but they were well known in their fields, to most conservative writers across several generations and to the think tank community. To be sure, some were more familiar names to the public, such as Larry Arnn (the President of Hillsdale), Hadley Arkes (Amherst College and well-published op-ed contributor and author), William Bennett (former Education Secretary), George Gilder (well-respected conservative author), Newt Gingrich (former presidential candidate and Speaker of the House of Representatives), David Horowitz (long-time conservative activist, author, and lecturer), Michael Ledeen (well-published author and frequent cable news commentator on issues relating to military strategy and Radical Islam), Stephen Moore (go-to supply-side economist and veteran of the D.C. think-tank community), and Peter Thiel (co-founder of PayPal and author).[2] They issued two calls to their fellow conservatives and countrymen, the first brief, the second more fully outlining several issues from restoring constitutional government to promoting economic growth to preserving religious liberty and reforming our education system. Their second, longer statement read:

> We are a group of scholars and writers who support Donald Trump, and who in our previous letter wrote that "given our choices in the presidential election, we believe that Donald Trump is the candidate most likely to restore the promise of America."
>
> We continue to believe this, and today urge opponents of the progressive agenda to put aside any differences and to join with us, as a vote for Donald Trump is the only feasible method of defending the principles of freedom, justice and prosperity we hold in common against the most serious threat we have ever faced, a threat that begins to look like the final defeat of republican government, and the permanent decline of the country we love.[3]

While many back in the DC-Manhattan Never Trump, Conservatism Inc. fold were still explaining that Donald Trump could not win and should not win, this group was doing its best to roll up its sleeves to save America as they, as we, saw it.

Donald Trump has changed positions? Fine, so has almost every other candidate. Donald Trump has used vulgar language? Fine, so has almost everyone from time to time. Donald Trump has wandered off the reservation on this or that conservative issue? Fine, Hillary Clinton has never wandered off the liberal-left reservation. Donald Trump cannot be trusted to keep his word? Fine, that is speculative but for damned sure, Hillary Clinton will keep hers. Polls show Donald Trump cannot win? Polls can be wrong and negative polls can also be self-fulfilling prophecies when commentators publicly root for their party's candidate to lose. And since when did conservatives and Republicans give up the ship when the odds were long? Why have magazines and think tanks promoted issues and causes for forty and more years when those causes and issues had still not become the majority consensus, accepted by the public, or formalized as policy?

It is worth considering: If *National Review*'s project, commencing in the 1950s, was to create something more than just a respectful bench-mark of conservative thought, that is, to actually give its thought shape and turn airy abstraction into actual policies—"a habitation and a name," to borrow from Shakespeare—how had it fared? Yes, the long twilight struggle against communism had been won. Yes, tax cuts had become Republican Party catechism. But what of everything else, from the growth of the administrative and regulatory state—socialism at home, if you will—to a whole host of social issues, from the burgeoning twilight struggle of World War IV (radical Islam) to national sovereignty and illegal immigration? What of racial preferences? What of the culture?

It is now a commonplace to point out the obvious challenge to conservative ideas. The political culture in America had become firmly a liberal-Left entrenchment: the media, elementary and secondary education systems, higher education, entertainment, the corporate boardrooms and the policies and statements that flowed outward from those boardrooms. Given those political and ideological headwinds, it's amazing conservatives and Republicans could ever win anything. But while they did get elected from time to time, were those policies making any headway? Government only grows bigger. Abortion and the precedent of *Roe v. Wade* only becomes more settled. Health care got nationalized. Illegal immigration actually became debatable. Race consciousness and policies based on race continue without question. Tax rates move up and down. The national deficit grows.

The liberals and the Left owned and ran the game. Conservatives and Republicans got to play a little, but it was never their game. Or, as Donald Trump put it: "we aren't winning." The "we" being Americans. It was and is easy enough to complain about all this—and those complaints are the meat and potatoes of the think tank and conservative journalistic community. That's what they do best: complain. But what of changing? What of governing?

Recall the reasons the editors of *National Review* outlined as the purpose of their magazine in 1955: the growth of government; "the conflict between the Social Engineers, who seek to adjust mankind to conform with scientific utopias, and the disciples of Truth, who defend the organic moral order"; communism (labeled as "the most blatant form of satanic utopianism" by the editors in 1955); liberal fads in the arts and education; "Fabian operators" . . . "bent on controlling both our major political parties (under the sanction of such fatuous and unreasoned slogans as 'national unity,' 'middle-of-the-road,' 'progressivism,' and 'bipartisanship.')"; "harassed business" and unions; and "world government" and "internationalism."[4]

Aside from the defeat of Communism, for which the election of Ronald Reagan played a large part and, perhaps, declining membership in unions, what item of that list had gotten better? Had it not all gotten worse? And was Communism not replaced by the threat of Radical Islam? And was there still not China? And had not the United States, in Barack Obama's final year of office, normalized relations with Cuba?

Somehow, somewhere, someone needed to admit to a problem—the first step in any necessary recovery. And somehow, somewhere, someone needed to admit that the consensus candidates, the "respectable" candidates, were neither winning (as in John McCain or Mitt Romney) nor getting the job done if they won (as in George W. Bush). Comes now the brash outsider who talks of making America great again, admitting there is a problem. The same outsider who would speak of these very issues, including the one so many Americans wanted a candidate to speak about but that Republican presidential candidates were typically loathe to do: illegal immigration. Comes now the outsider who would not play by the normal rules and deploy the usual language. Conservatism, Inc., hated it. The grassroots loved it.

For all the 2015 and early 2016 talk of another Bush-Clinton election, Jeb Bush won a total of three delegates, spending more than fifty million dollars for each one.[5] It is hard now to recall how much of the establishment was behind Jeb's candidacy, but he was their candidate and the early favorite. The thoughtful, respectable, conservative Marco Rubio was a fallback, especially for the neoconservatives—he came in fourth place.[6] And while Ted Cruz was a conservative by any definition and would likely have run a very conservative administration had he won, his appeal was never more than regional, and something about him made him unattractive to a national audience, in a national election. He was not going to win Michigan or Wisconsin, and he would have had a very hard time in Ohio, Florida, and beyond. He was not a candidate Reagan Democrats would or could cotton to. He did not speak to the Seitzs of the Trumbull counties.

No, what was needed was something else. Someone who truly did not care what the media said about him, or at least was willing to push back against it. Someone who could go over their heads and speak directly to the people—be it via Twitter or strong language. Someone who took on the issue of illegal immigration, and not as an afterthought but as a main theme. Someone who spoke of jobs and employment, not just tax reform. Someone who spoke of the problem of the elites. Someone who spoke of the problem of political correctness. Someone who spoke of crushing Radical Islam. Someone who spoke of America!

Yale Professor David Gelernter put it this way in our nomination for what could be the second most incisive op-ed or essay of the year (after

"The Flight 93 Election"). After running through all of the character deficits of Donald Trump and revealing that they were no worse than any of Hillary Clinton's, Professor Gelernter put it this way:

> Mr. Trump's candidacy is a message from the voters. He is the empty gin bottle they have chosen to toss through the window. The message begins with the fact that voters hear what the leaders and pundits don't: the profound contempt for America and Americans that Mrs. Clinton and President Obama share and their frightening lack of emotional connection to this nation and its people.[7]

His was a bottle through the window, trying to break through, but Professor Gelernter would probably concede to us it had a strong brew in it, and was not necessarily "empty" beyond the proverbial convenience of the image. But he would go on explaining what Donald Trump spoke to, an unarticulated long series of failures ("emasculation") that nobody else addressed:

> Trump voters have noticed that, not just over Mr. Obama's term but in recent decades, their own opinions have grown increasingly irrelevant. It's something you feel, like encroaching numbness. Since when has the American public endorsed affirmative action? Yet it's a major factor in the lives of every student and many workers. Since when did we decide that men and women are interchangeable in hand-to-hand combat on the front lines? Why do we insist on women in combat but not in the NFL? Because we take football seriously. That's no joke; it's the sad truth.
>
> Did we invite the federal bureaucracy to take charge of school bathrooms? I guess I missed that meeting. The schools are corrupt and the universities rotten to the core, and everyone has known it since the 1980s. But the Democrats are owned by the teachers unions, and Republicans have made only small-scale corrections to a system that needs to be ripped out and carefully disposed of, like poison ivy. . . .
>
> The Emasculated Voter to whom no one pays any attention is the story of modern democracy.[8]

That was *it!* The emasculated voter, or, rather the emasculated American. Perhaps even the emasculated America. "I want America's enemies off-balance and guessing. For eight years it's been Humiliate America season—buzz our ships, capture and embarrass our men, murder an American ambassador—a resoundingly successful attempt to spit in our faces and tell each one of us to drop dead."[9]

And then comes the candidate willing to talk about these things in a manner few other candidates would, if they brought these issues up at all. To speak of such things was to be taken seriously about them. To tell an African American audience: "You're living in poverty, your schools are no good, you have no jobs . . ." and to ask—to shout—"What the hell do you have to lose?!"[10] We all thought it, nobody said it. Nobody but Donald Trump. And he was not afraid of the African American grievance industry that would push back against him. After all, Donald Trump had nothing to lose either. Is there a greater definition of a conviction politician who campaigns with such an attitude? Just say it, dammit!

But behind the gin bottle, behind the uncouthness, there was, indeed, an intellectual case, too. And not an insubstantial one. Hadley Arkes, Larry Arnn, William Bennett, Michael Ledeen, and the other "writers and scholars for Trump"—that was a faculty any conservative college or university would be proud of (or any college in the 1970s, before political correctness ruined colleges and universities, and faculties could actually be hired based on merit, academic heft, and prowess). What were they saying?

It went beyond the admission of a problem—that conservatives, or Americans, or America, was not winning anymore. It went beyond Hillary Clinton's potential presidency freezing in amber the liberal progressivism of the Obama administration. It was not just that Donald Trump and his voters were yelling "Stop!" but that they actually had a program of recovery.

To Hadley Arkes of Amherst College, to oppose Trump was to forget what opposing Goldwater had led to: "[T]he regime itself was changed: The Great Society extended and confirmed the reach of the federal authority until it covered hiring and firing in corporations and even small, private colleges. And it extended federal controls over local education. We are faced now with a comparable threat to change the regime yet again."[11]

To Professor Frank Buckley of George Mason Law School: Donald Trump was "someone who could rescue what is living from what is dead in conservatism. And by dead I mean what passes for the higher thinking of today's conservatism, the contempt for the poorest Americans, the indifference to mobility, the compromises with corruption, and mostly the sense of failure, the small-souled man's belief that our best days are behind us."[12]

To James Pierson: "Donald Trump has a plan to re-energize the U.S. economy after more than a decade of slow growth, stagnating incomes, and rising government debt." "Mr. Trump will focus on national security in all of its dimensions by attacking the interlocking problems of terrorism, illegal immigration, and rising crime in the inner cities." "For conservatives and moderates who hope for a stronger and more dynamic America, and a nation of rising incomes, strong communities, and secure borders, the choice could not be clearer."[13]

To William Bennett: "Beyond legal interpretations having to do with everything from religious liberty, the Second Amendment, property rights, illegal immigration, constitutional interpretation, and beyond, a Trump presidency would be staffed by Republicans and conservatives. A Clinton presidency would be staffed by Democrats and liberals—all committed to preserving and building on the last eight years."[14]

To Roger L. Simon: "Donald Trump, for all his rough edges, is the 'bad medicine' necessary to fix an increasingly acute situation. The standard form politician would not be enough to derail a 'progressive' agenda that is leading our country into economic and cultural oblivion. Sometimes an outsider is needed—and this is one of them. The Founders would have approved."[15]

To Bradley C. S. Watson at Saint Vincent College:

Donald Trump shows an intuitive grasp of what most politicians must have explained to them: here in America, the people rule. Popular sovereignty requires borders, and it requires security. . . . The laws as well as the agencies of government must be trimmed and tamed so that they once again serve the people. Donald Trump grasps this too: the Supreme Court is the least republican branch of the federal government, and the people cannot rule if they are subjected to capricious judicial edicts masquerading as constitutional interpretation. Trump has put forth a serious list of judicial nominees who would only go where the text, tradition, logic, and structure of the Constitution—rather than currently fashionable political preferences—point. Beyond this, Trump has wisely called for the resignation of a transparently political Supreme Court justice, thereby reminding us of constitutionally legitimate political checks against an overweening judiciary.[16]

To Michael Ledeen, foreign policy and Radical Islam expert:

I like his sense of humor most of the time. I like his feisty desire to win, not just for himself but for all of us. I like many of the strong and smart people that are working with him. Again, the contrast is luminously clear: he likes Lt. Gen Mike Flynn, with whom I recently wrote a book, while Hillary likes Sidney Blumenthal, a very bad man. I'd rather see General Flynn in the White House than Mr. Blumenthal. By a long shot.[17]

To one of us, Chris Buskirk:

Trump's candidacy has already done the nation a great service by giving voice to the nagging, sometimes urgent, concerns of ordinary people imperiled by ruling class hegemony. . . . Only Trump, of the two candidates running this year—or of any candidate running since 1984—has shown an innate understanding of the challenges the country faces and a willingness to name them publicly and face them head-on. A Trump presidency would not mark the beginning of the end of what promises to be a long struggle to regain constitutional government, but it might mark the end of the beginning.[18]

To the other, Seth Leibsohn:

Donald Trump is the only choice for those that look around the world—and at home—and see something very much wrong going on. What is that wrong? The inversion of common sense. We conservatives have long-lamented the increasing state of political correctness and multiculturalism, the "kick me" sign on our country's back, and the increasing hostility to our allies and appeasement of our enemies. Donald Trump stands athwart the latter and has staked his campaign on reversing all of the former—in a way no other Republican has, in a very long time.[19]

To Ken Masugi: "His rallies revitalized democratic politics in both parties and formed a new 'America First' center, which had hitherto groaned under the yoke of globalist multiculturalism, the new majority faction governing America since Reagan."[20]

On and on the reasons could go. But, still, there was *National Review*, Mitt Romney, George Will, Charles Krauthammer, *The Weekly Standard*, *Commentary*, and so many others. What was the last unanswered complaint of theirs? The uncouthness, the unpreparedness, the unboundness, the questionable business practices—in short: trust. But trust of what? That Donald Trump would not do what he said he would do? Every Republican president suffered that problem, every president suffered that problem. Politics *is* that problem. That he would unleash constitutional crises by his autocratic attitudes and styles?

It, of course, was all possible. But compared to what? As Jonathan Rauch could detail:

[M]any of the worrisome things that an antidemocratic president might do look just like things that other presidents have done. Use presidential power to bully corporations? Truman and Kennedy did that. Distort or exaggerate facts to initiate or escalate a war? Johnson and George W. Bush did that. Lie point-blank to the public? Eisenhower did that. Defy orders from the Supreme Court? Lincoln did that. Suspend habeas corpus? Lincoln did that, too. Spy on

American activists? Kennedy and Johnson did that. Start wars at will, without congressional approval? Truman did that. Censor "disloyal" speech and fire "disloyal" civil servants? Wilson did that. Incarcerate U.S. citizens of foreign extraction? Franklin D. Roosevelt did that. Use shady schemes to circumvent congressional strictures? Reagan did that. Preempt Justice Department prosecutors? Obama did that. Assert sweeping powers to lock people up without trial or judicial review? George W. Bush did that. Declare an open-ended national emergency? Bush did that, and Obama continued it. Use regulatory authority aggressively and, according to the courts, sometimes illegally? Obama did that. Kill a U.S. citizen abroad? Obama did that, too. Grant favors to political friends, and make mischief for political enemies? All presidents do that.[21]

So, to more than sixty million Americans, what Richard Nixon once called "the forgotten Americans; the non-shouters; the non-demonstrators,"[22] the problems were all there to see. But the problems with Donald Trump were the problems of candidates past, candidates who never spoke to the issues Donald Trump did, never spoke with the boldness (or sincerity, or brashness, if you like) that he spoke of them—making him seem all the more serious about them. The problems these sixty-plus million Americans also had were real, and they knew that whether it was the politically correct world they had foisted on them, the threats from Radical Islam they saw growing and unaddressed, or the lack of common sense about illegal immigration, they were not to speak of them, not in polite society.

But Donald Trump could. And he would. He diagnosed the problems that were hitherto ineffable but felt, and he proposed the solutions that were hitherto seen as too simplistic, even maddeningly so. But to fix or tame the Leviathan, was not a little aggressiveness, or a lot, in order?

Conservatives like to go back to Ronald Reagan's 1964 *Time for Choosing* speech. They like to ask why we can't have that again. They like to ask "Who is the next Reagan?" It's a question that comes up every four years. But it is not a fair question. For one, there is a lot of mythology around Ronald Reagan. His greatness was in his building a coalition and articulating a conservative message that could break through to the average voter. His governance was also to be esteemed. But it too had a lot of fits and starts. Just one year into Reagan's first term, Norman Podhoretz was already writing for the *New York Times* that Ronald Reagan was "disappointing" and that he and his fellow foreign policy hawks were "growing daily more anguished over the slipping away of a precious political opportunity that may never come again."[23] Reagan had given us Antonin Scalia on the Supreme Court, but also, of course, Sandra Day O'Connor and Anthony Kennedy. A list of successes and failures could occupy all of this book, as it has others. Suffice to say: (2) Reagan was not perfect and (2) the standard of "Who is the next Reagan?" is unmeetable—nobody is the next anybody.

The question is, or ought to be, who comes closest to doing what Reagan did successfully. As for the *Time for Choosing* speech—were there not echoes and similarities in what Donald Trump campaigned on and spoke about at the Republican convention? Of course there were. Were too many of Conservatism Inc. blind or deaf to those similarities? Of course they were. We had arrived at a point in the 2016 election where Donald Trump could get no credit from Conservatism Inc. for anything. If he said something brash, they pounced and tsk tsked. If he said something off the reservation, they said "See!" If he said anything conservative—which he did more than saying anything brash or off the reservation—they said he could not be believed. It was a hell of a conspiracy: When he says something wrong, that's his essence. When he says something right, we cannot believe him.

But the voting class was not the analytical class. Voters do not scrub histories of policy statements from a decade ago. Voters do not analyze every statement by every candidate. Voters do not project what talking point they think will resonate to their neighbors and larger communities. Voters say what they think. And what they think is based on how they live. They may get five minutes or less of news a day, but they know what they see around them. They know what their bills amount to, they know that their health care premium costs have gone up. And they know what they hear about and read about when terrorists blow up a marathon or a nightclub or an army fort. They also know that drug abuse, if not affecting their family, does affect someone they know or know of. And they know that experts have not helped them with any of this—and in many cases have made their problems worse.

They also know that analysts care about things they do not. It was the second week of February 2017 as we were editing this book. The topic of Donald Trump's tweets came up. The analyst class said he had to stop, that they were distracting to his presidency and his message. They were offending too many people. We had taken a lot of calls on our radio show about this subject. Then called one "Judy," from Glendale, Arizona. She said the tweets were irrelevant to her. That like most Americans, she read about them here and there but was not even on Twitter. We asked: "But what you read, does it offend you when they are offensive?" Her reply: "I just say, 'yeah, whatever' and go on with my day. We have an economy and terrorism and illegal immigration to worry about, not that stuff."

"Yeah, whatever." Those two words explained so much of the campaign and its divide between what a few thousand analysts were worried about and what the voters thought. In those two words, a volume of political science was taught. It was the science that understood the distinction between wheat and tares. It was the science that understood the limits of human perfection. It was the science of serious politics.

14

RESTORING ACCOUNTABILITY

WHO SHOULD THE MEDIA LISTEN TO?

THE HIGHWAY OF POLITICAL JOURNALISTS, pundits, and campaign managers is littered with wrong people. It is one big bowl of wrong. All of them, however, do not think it matters. Nor do the media outlets that continue to go to them for expert analysis. No matter how many elections they get wrong, that they call wrong, they are to be seen and heard everywhere: on Fox News, on CNN, on MSNBC, on NPR. Quoted in *USA Today*, the *New York Times*, the *Wall Street Journal*, the *Washington Post*, and everywhere else. They make high six-figure salaries, receive lucrative five- and six-figure contracts to contribute to the cable shows, and receive hundreds of thousands of dollars more consulting in corporate and nonprofit America.

We Americans are told to listen to them. We Americans then quote them, all the time. We think we are in the know because we think these experts are knowledgeable, that they know something more than we do. "Did you see what Frank Luntz said?" "Karl Rove wrote that . . ." "The panel on CNN agreed that . . ." "Nate Silver has the election at . . ." "A poll of polls is showing . . ." Yet if we were buying stocks based on these analyses, we would all be bankrupt by now. These "experts" have been proven wrong again and again and again. Year in and year out, election in and election out, these "experts," ostensibly on the air and in the press and paid to tell us how Americans vote and what Americans believe, get it wrong. This is their job—and they are much more often wrong than they are ever right.

And yet the news shows and newspapers keep going to them. In any other profession they would be finished, forgotten, or embarrassed out of their fields. If they were doctors with such a record of mistakes, they would lose their licenses. If they were lawyers with such a record of losses, they would lose their businesses. If they were chefs known for their failed meals or food poisoning, they would be fired. If they were coaches with this many losses and bad player picks, they would be out of a job.

But not in politics. Politics does not work that way. Commentary does not work that way. Analysis does not work that way. They have zero accountability. If political science is to the body politic what medical science is to the human body, should we not—by now—have political scientists or analysts who know their country and their countrymen at least somewhat as well as doctors know their patients? Well, one might excuse, there is a difference between social science and physical or hard science. A human organism is predictable whereas the human brain and political psyche are unpredictable, erratic even. Maybe. Or maybe it is that the human brain and human emotions are more susceptible to outside forces and manipulations. Or that there is no accounting for political winds and economic circumstances.

Again, maybe. But if voters, that is, the American people, know their own vicissitudes and political cognitive dissonances, their own fickle natures and changing mindsets, why do the experts not know that about the voters? And why is there zero humility from the experts? Take Frank

Luntz as but one example of many. Throughout the campaign, as almost every campaign, Luntz assembles sample groups or "focus groups" that become mini-townhalls of voters expressing their views on candidate speeches and debate performances. Presumably, from these focus groups we receive a sense of what the larger public is thinking. And presumably, as well, Frank Luntz has some of the most keen insight into the public's mind. To what end? To what purpose? To what accuracy? Come election day 2016, as Americans were watching the state-by-state election returns, Luntz would tweet at four o'clock in the afternoon: "In case I wasn't clear enough from my previous tweets: Hillary Clinton will be the next President of the United States."[1]

This prediction was preceded earlier in the day by such tweets as "Memo to Republicans and Republican pollsters: Tonight will look more like 2012 than 2004," meaning a Republican loss and a Democratic win, and "I'm starting to think Democrats will take the Senate majority tonight."[2] That did not happen either. He also tweeted: "Michigan is going to end up for Hillary tonight."[3] Nope.

Karl Rove, often referred to as "the architect" by fans on Fox News and talk radio, presumably for helping strategize George W. Bush's presidential victories, never seemed much of an architect to us—unless winning the presidency by throwing an election to the United States Supreme Court that favored your candidate in a five-to-four vote was some kind of brilliant mastermind strategy of campaign architecture. But, still, there he was throughout the 2016 election, as he was in the 2012 election, making his predictions.

In late October 2012, Karl Rove wrote: "In addition to the data, the anecdotal and intangible evidence—from crowd sizes to each side's closing arguments—give the sense that the odds favor Mr. Romney. They do. My prediction: Sometime after the cock crows on the morning of Nov. 7, Mitt Romney will be declared America's 45th president."[4] He wasn't. And in 2016, there he was again, in late October, predicting this about Donald Trump's candidacy: "I don't see it happening. Maybe it could, but I doubt that in the just over two weeks that we've got left, conducting the kind of campaign he is conducting, that he's going to be able to swing one out of every, you know, 10 voters . . . in a state, and convert them."[5]

Of course these predictions were preceded by a series of predications that also had Donald Trump losing. For example, in January 2016, Karl Rove wrote, "If the GOP contest narrows to two or three candidates by March 15, Mr. Trump will not be the party's nominee."[6] And again: "If Mr. Trump is its standard-bearer, the GOP will lose the White House and the Senate, and its majority in the House will fall dramatically."[7] The opposite of all that happened.

Rove and Luntz had good company. James Fallows at the *Atlantic* wrote of Donald Trump, "The chance of his winning [the] nomination and election is exactly zero."[8] Ben White of *Politico* and CNBC had this: "Donald Trump is not going to be the next president of the United States. This reporter is already on record pledging to eat a bag of rusty nails if the real estate tycoon with the high hair manages to snag the GOP nomination, much less takes down likely Democratic nominee Hillary Clinton next fall."[9] Joe Scarborough at MSNBC said, "That's a guy who knows he is going to lose."[10] Bret Stephens at the *Wall Street Journal* said, "[A] lot of people have no idea that Trump is headed for a historic defeat."[11] Eugene Robinson at the *Washington Post*: "This election, not only does Florida fall to Hillary Clinton but this election, overall, we could be talking landslide."[12] Mark Halprin, the managing editor at *Bloomberg Politics,* predicted, "Hillary Clinton, today, is more likely to win in a landslide that would not only have an impact on this race, but realign the country politically to some extent than Donald Trump is to win narrowly, or at all."[13] This list goes on and on.

Who were these people? Well, of course, we know who they are—but did the voters? Did the voters care? Did these experts talk to them, or just themselves? Did they know that voters were tired of process talk and actually thought about the merits of what politics is really about, which is how we live our lives and how our country conducts itself? Did these experts have no concept of the difference between the box office and the other critics? Or remember that their club of maybe a few hundred, while well-paid and taken seriously by a club of maybe a dozen television hosts, was outnumbered by a bigger and more important club: the voters?

Very few analysts and strategists ever give a speech without making at least some reference to "the American people." But do they actually know anything about the American people—or, yes, care about them? To say "Make America Great Again" is, to the elites, a version of exceptionalism that has not found succor in any college faculty lounge in America and reeks of a form of jingoism or arrogance about our country that we have been told for decades is not the last best hope of earth but, rather, one place among the nations that needs to respect the multicultural world we live in and not say our country is better than any other country. But that is not what most Americans actually think. Most Americans love their country more than any other, and while it may have been cute or convenient to talk of Donald Trump's ego, as so many did, his campaign was about making America great again and putting America first, and Hillary Clinton's slogan was "I'm with her." What, just what, between those two slogans, reveals the bigger ego trip?

When Donald Trump's 2005 off-mic comments about women were revealed, and the entire universe of pundits said the race was over, did a single pundit speak to a single woman who had been supporting Trump? We did. And to a "T," be they married moms or single entrepreneurs, the women we spoke to who had been supporting Trump said versions of "It's sick," "It's terrible," "Embarrassing!" But they also said "No, it does not change my vote." They cared about something more and had long ago come to terms with one simple fact: character was not on the ballot in 2016. As David Gelernter pointed out, in any comparison between Hillary Clinton's character and Donald Trump's, hers was at least as bad as his. Just remember, beyond her long trail of her own scandals and covering up scandals for her husband, Hillary Clinton called a huge swath of Americans "deplorable," while Donald Trump's arguably ugly statements about classes of people were about (a) illegal immigrants and (b) other celebrities like Rosie O'Donnell. Hard to get angrier about denouncing illegal immigrants than about denouncing half the country.

With character not on the ballot, did anyone stop to remember that few people had greater personal character than Mitt Romney and George H. W. Bush—two candidates who lost a combined three presidential elections? One could add Bob Dole and get four presidential elections. One could add the tremendous and famed heroism of John McCain and get to five elections. Americans called character a wash in 2016 and showed, again and again, that while we all clamor for it, it determines an election between candidates almost not at all.

So, how did these experts cover themselves on November 9, 2016 and beyond? These have been the statements, in proliferation: "We were all wrong!" "The greatest political upset in our lifetime." "None of us saw this coming." These were just a few of the confessions pundits, experts, and anchors expressed once the 2016 presidential election was called for Donald J. Trump. A simple Google search of similar expressions reveals tens of thousands of such comments. But a simpler thing—the truth—is that we were not all wrong. And saying we "all" were is an insult—not to us but, rather, to the nearly 63 million voters who voted for someone they wanted to be president and someone they thought could be president. It is also an insult to intelligence.

It took the *Washington Post* less than a month after the election, less than three weeks, to get the bright idea of sponsoring a forum for the public for readers to write in why they voted for Donald Trump. Where were these questions before the election? Who was asking them? If the foregone conclusion is that "Trump will not win," of course—to the experts—why bother asking voters in the first place? Especially when the narrative is that Trump supporters are either racist or deplorable or dumb or a combination of the three.

But, as Peggy Noonan put it: they knew they were not. Who went to those Trump rallies? Certainly there were some caricatures the media liked to focus on to fit their narrative of the typical Trump supporter. But the rallies were dominated by every group and class of American possible, from truckers to doctors, from real estate agents to nurses. And what did they hear at these rallies? The same thing they heard every time Donald Trump spoke. They heard about issues. Issues of crime, of illegal immigration, of terrorism and Radical Islam, of bad trade deals, of failing infrastructure, of illegal drugs, of burdensome regulations, of bad tax policy. In sum, they heard about policy. And for conservatives, they heard about the policy issues the think tanks and journals had been writing about for years but that candidates had not taken up very often or very much—other than in Q&A forums.

Now, here is a very crude but quick and easy test for everyone reading this book. When you heard Hillary Clinton on the campaign trail, what policy issues did you hear about? What one big thing did you hear her say she wanted to do or change? What thing or things did she focus on? To the first two questions, it is a strain to remember. Because she did not. To the last question—what did she focus on—the answer was clear and obvious: She focused on Donald Trump. She focused on how he was unfit to be president and his proposals were simplistic while his rhetoric was irresponsible. He was talking to Americans about America, but she was talking about him—and his supporters.

But politics is serious business. Sure, it is a hobby to some, and it is fun or natural cocktail chatter and Facebook and Twitter bait to others. But at the end of the day, voters spend millions on the candidates they like because they believe in something and want to solidify or change something. The "something" in 2016 was several things. Let's go to what those *Washington Post* post-election responders who supported Trump said.

There were those who wanted to throw the gin bottle through the window, like Andreas, forty-year-old resident of Washington, D.C.:

> What matters most to me is inclusion. Though we live in a "global village" type of world, the benefits (better education, better information and a better variety of choices in general) are not felt by all. That is because, though many politicians say progress and globalization promise better things, they deliver fewer and fewer of those promises

to all. That was reflected in this election the most. People are tired and want change for everyone. I am not sure a Trump presidency delivers the right type of change, but I am hoping that the politicians who have failed time and time again to deliver on the aforementioned promises got the message.[14]

There was Max, a thirty-year-old resident of New York State who was tired of political correctness and also thought about serious policy issues and exceptionalism:

I am a Cruz/Rubio Republican, and I voted for Donald Trump because, first, he will upset the status quo in government (on both sides of the aisle)—a status quo under which the government keeps getting larger while the rest of America keeps gets [sic] smaller. Second, Trump will expose the cynicism in the media—an industry that thrives off of the appeal to the worst of human impulses. Trump may not pursue constitutional conservatism, but he has an excellent chance to enact policies and to create an environment in which this country's economy can get going again. I am also convinced Trump is well suited to restore American leadership—with all of its values—around the world. The American spirit (the term may need to be defined for some millennials, and the best resource is simply a standard history text), which has driven the successes of our past, is sorely lacking at home and around the world. Trump understands this, and I believe he is genuinely interested in making America great again.[15]

There was Kirsten, a thirty-one-year-old woman from Minnesota who understood politics raw, the difference between box office and critics, and the necessity to vote for someone who actually has a chance of winning:

I was literally undecided until I went into the voting booth. I was a strong advocate for Gary Johnson for most of the race, but I changed my mind after I saw him at a lackluster rally in town. Then Trump came through, and the energy and passion was astounding. He overflowed an airport hangar with twenty-four hours' notice on a Sunday during a Vikings home game. Holy crap. So, in the end, I voted for the economy, against Obamacare and against a corrupt government, just as I was planning to for Johnson. But I also voted for the people, because Trump was the clear choice of the silent majority I eventually became a part of.[16]

There was Nicole, a forty-seven-year-old from Vermont, who was tired of the elites and cared about the vast middle of America rather than the special interests:

Donald Trump came to Burlington, Vt.—Bernie Sanders's home town—in December. I stood in line with a few thousand people and was confronted by a few hundred people protesting Trump's appearance and those supporting him. I was still on the fence, but after that rally I knew without a doubt Trump was going to be our next president. He had tapped into what the everyday Joe—and Jane—were feeling but had become PC-shamed from expressing. As Trump cleared each hurdle during the campaign, and I saw how the media, the establishment and celebrities tried to derail him, my hope began to grow that I would be able to witness their collective heads explode when he was successful. Tuesday night was beyond satisfying to watch unfold. I hope all the aforementioned have learned their lesson. I look forward to watching Trump make good on his plans to make America affordable, make America safe and make America work. I always thought it was great.[17]

There was Deniz, a twenty-two-year-old Muslim immigrant from Florida who knew what Donald Trump was speaking about in the context of Radical Islam versus America because she did not need to be taught about it at a university:

My entire family—five Muslim immigrants from Turkey—voted for Donald Trump in Florida because of the Democratic Party's pandering to Islamism. As people who have actually experienced Islamism in its purest form, back in Turkey, we supported the candidate who promised to help us fight that issue, regardless of any of his other policies. For us, the people of the Middle East, this election was just too important to hand over to someone such as Hillary Clinton.[18]

On and on the responses would go—from people who found the Affordable Care Act unaffordable to people who thought Hillary Clinton was more untrustworthy than Donald Trump. The last thing any of them found decisive were the first things the experts thought determinative: that Donald Trump often spoke harshly and that he would not release his taxes. Americans hate taxes. They did not care that he would not release his. They cared about their culture, their country, and their pocketbooks. And they cared about one other thing, too: the elites of the media and expert class that kept telling them they were wrong when they knew they were not.

How, then, do we get a better set of predictors and analyses for our politics? Let us start by stopping a few things. Stop calling non-experts "experts." Stop listening to those whose records in any other industry would get them fired. Stop listening to those who callously and self-assuredly say "we were all wrong" when the "we"—the American people—are more important than the "we" these experts talk to and try to impress.

Second, listen to the listeners. Talk radio hosts, for example, who emphasize taking a lot of calls and who hear what people are saying.

Third, instead of going to places like Trumbull County *after* the election to listen to those who left the Democratic party for Donald Trump, go before the election. Instead of seeking narratives *after* the election in places like the *Washington Post*, seek them before the election.

Fourth, the media must ask itself about its panelists, its experts, its contributors: what is their track record? Do they actually know what they are talking about? Have they figured out what moves Americans to vote for this or that candidate? It is more important for experts to know what Americans want than what they themselves want. Who, after all, in the light of the post-election day really knows more about the American people: George Will or Salena Zito, who went to bars in places like Youngstown, PA with names like the Tin Lizzy Tavern?[19] The question answers itself.

Fifth, and finally: don't project or cosmologize your opinions or think they matter to more people than they do. Appearing on shows like *Morning Joe* may make you feel important—but it does not even reach one million viewers.[20]

When the think tanks and journals, particularly those of a conservative bent, ask for money—any amount—from direct mail and otherwise, they can raise a lot of it. They raise that money from people who believe in what they say, in the causes they stand for and claim to be pushing, waging, making an effort. When a candidate speaks to those very same things, why wouldn't those same donors (five- and ten- and twenty-five-dollar donors) want to put those policies into effect with a candidate who speaks to them and speaks like them? Who on television understood this? And who thought it was more important that once upon a time the candidate may have believed something else? Doesn't everyone change their mind on things? And who has not said something they regret? Or something inartfully? And who thinks someone's gender really determines their qualifications for anything other than child-making?

For those who love their country and take politics and policy seriously, for those who were waiting to hear a candidate who spoke unapologetically for the causes they believed in, for those who were tired of just getting by or—worse—losing (money, jobs, national credibility, health insurance, anything), this was one of the simplest presidential elections to actually call right. The sad state of affairs we live in is that we throw out platitudes about such things as America and change and common sense—but our experts missed the popularity of the one presidential candidate who spoke to them, got people at his rallies to show up and hear about them, and took those platitudes seriously.

15

RELEARNING THE BASICS

FUNDAMENTAL AMERICAN PRINCIPLES AND POLITICAL PRUDENCE

EVER SINCE RONALD REAGAN'S 1980 VICTORY, it has been Republican Party and conservative catechism to embrace what is often referred to as the three-legged stool of a strong national defense, economic freedom and tax cuts, and conservative social policy.

When Ronald Reagan showed that a conservative taking on these issues could win, he proved something to the American voter and solidified a conservative claim. That claim? Yes, tax cuts could be popular, even though most Republicans did not speak of them in the modern era, hard as it is to believe, until Ronald Reagan. Yes, Americans can be persuaded that social conservatism is not something to hide from. And, yes, Americans still believe in what John Jay wrote in *Federalist 3*: "Among the many objects to which a wise and free people find it necessary to direct their attention, that of providing for their SAFETY seems to be the first."[1]

As for tax cuts, it is difficult to believe today, so entrenched an idea have they become in the Republican Party, that they were not an issue for Dwight Eisenhower or Richard Nixon or Gerald Ford. The idea that lower marginal tax rates would at once be good for economic growth *and* create new revenue was first articulated by John F. Kennedy in the post–World War II era. In his 1962 speech to the Economic Club of New York, Kennedy said:

> It is increasingly clear that no matter what party is in power, so long as our national security needs keep rising, an economy hampered by restrictive tax rates will never produce enough revenues to balance our budget—just as it will never produce enough jobs or enough profits. Surely the lesson of the last decade is that budget deficits are not caused by wild-eyed spenders but by slow economic growth and periodic recessions, and any new recession would break all deficit records.
>
> In short, it is a paradoxical truth that tax rates are too high today and tax revenues are too low and the soundest way to raise the revenues in the long run is to cut the rates now.[2]

Until Ronald Reagan, Republicans did not really advance this line of thought—and Democrats, after Lyndon Baines Johnson, had long since abandoned it, as they had abandoned so much of the John Kennedy model of muscular economic and national-defense policies. A handful of conservatives who worked with Ronald Reagan in the 1970s re-engaged the tax cut theme: social and economic writer Irving Kristol, *Wall Street Journal* editor Robert Bartley, Congressman Jack Kemp, author Jude Wanniski, and economists Arthur Laffer and Robert Mundell.

To provide but one simple illustration as to how revolutionary an idea this was for the Republican Party, the old guard of the party—represented by the wing of East Coast elites and their 1980 candidate for President, George H. W. Bush—fought the idea as crazy and irresponsible. George H. W. Bush, running for president in 1980 against Ronald Reagan, referred to the idea as "voodoo economics."[3] And it is not an exaggeration to say that when then-President George H. W. Bush abandoned his "read my lips," pledge of "no new taxes" in a budget deal with the Democrats in 1990, his conservative base abandoned him. As Bush would later say, abandoning his pledge was one of his greatest mistakes.[4]

Social issues were also a matter of scorn for the establishment of the Republican Party until Ronald Reagan. Although a lot of mainstream historians and commentators speak highly of Ronald Reagan today, many forget or choose to ignore how much he was committed to the right to life and his opposition to abortion. Indeed, even less remembered is a booklet he published, *as president*, entitled *Abortion and the Conscience of the Nation*—though it is still available on Amazon. There, he would write:

> Abraham Lincoln recognized that we could not survive as a free land when some men could decide that others were not fit to be free and should therefore be slaves. Likewise, we cannot survive as a free nation when some men decide that others are not fit to live and should be abandoned to abortion or infanticide. My Administration is dedicated to the preservation of America as a free land, and there is no cause more important for preserving that freedom than affirming the transcendent right to life of all human beings, the right without which no other rights have any meaning.[5]

As for national defense and safety—yes, the way Ronald Reagan approached those issues, too, was revolutionary. To fill out what John Jay meant by "safety" as the first job of government, he defined it thus: "[S]ecurity for the preservation of peace and tranquility, as well as against dangers from FOREIGN ARMS AND INFLUENCE, as from dangers of the LIKE KIND arising from domestic causes."

Until Ronald Reagan, Republican foreign and defense policy was centered around the issue of co-existence with the Soviet Union. This was the Realpolitik school of thinking, best represented by Henry Kissinger and his dominance as the Republican foreign-policy guru for not only Richard Nixon but Gerald Ford and even to this day. Reagan saw the safety of the United States—as much as the safety of the free world—in actually rolling back communism from where it had spread and defeating the Soviet Union.

Thus, Republican candidates paid lip service to the three-legged stool. Yet as the conservative base analyzed candidates, especially since Reagan, it would analyze them through these lenses—how committed were they to each or all of these causes. Did they embrace them, or did they just pacify the base in a speech here and there?

Three things changed after the 2000 election, partly explained by the terrorist attacks of September 11 and partly explained by the changing trajectory of problems and issues facing a more modern era. First, although we didn't have the threat of the Soviet Union anymore, we faced a new threat of terrorism. Second, individual economic issues became more and more important, including everything from health care to retirement to employment security. And a third thing had changed, too: immigration.

As mentioned previously, there can be and has been little argument among conservatives that Radical Islam would replace Communism as the new foreign-defense concern of our time. As would North Korea. As for domestic challenges, Republican candidates—since Reagan—have generally been as uncomfortable talking about illegal immigration as they were abortion. Indeed, one might say illegal immigration, like abortion, became the topic polite conservatives shunned and turned away from in polite company. The phrase "I'm an economic conservative, not a social conservative" or "I'm an economic conservative and a social liberal" easily tripped off Republican tongues in public and private. Of course such an idea wholly misunderstood not only Ronald Reagan but the entire warp and woof of what conservatism meant.

But the economic challenges had changed, too—and talk of cutting taxes was not what it used to be. To have electoral victories, it is imperative for conservative and Republican candidates to understand this. Ramesh Ponnuru, of *National Review*, reminds his readers of this. For example, writing in the *New York Times* in 2013: "Today's Republicans are very good at tending the fire of Ronald Reagan's memory but not nearly as good at learning from his successes. They slavishly adhere to the economic program that Reagan developed to meet the challenges of the late 1970s and early 1980s, ignoring the fact that he largely overcame those challenges, and now we have new ones."[6]

Today, looking back at the failed presidential candidacies of John McCain and Mitt Romney, one has a hard time remembering much of what they offered the American people *where the American people were concerned.* Except one big thing about each: John McCain was known as weak or soft on illegal immigration and Mitt Romney was the architect in his home state of Massachusetts of what would become Obamacare. So on two of the most important new and main issues, the GOP nominated, in the space of four years, two candidates fully incapable not only of reaching the base but of reaching out to independents and disaffected Democrats with an alternative to what the Democratic party had become all about.

Donald Trump had no problem talking of dismantling Obamacare, and he spoke more about illegal immigration and Radical Islam than almost everything else. But there is supposed to be something more, much more, to the policies of the Republican Party and its standard-bearers. If the party is the vehicle for conservative ideas to be put in practice, what was informing conservatism?

As in previous chapters, we have detailed the various patchworks and schisms that came to define the conservative movement generally. Some parts were social and traditionalist, some were dominated by concerns over communism, some were religiously inspired, others were inspired by the application of the social sciences to either fix or improve various aspects of the welfare state. But there was a mindset to a conservative philosophy that had existed with a small heartbeat and brainbeat, but had not yet fully been accepted or taken a preeminent place in the larger movement's intellectual body. Here, we mean a conservatism that was uniquely tied to the notion of American greatness or exceptionalism, a conservatism that was uniquely American in its political philosophy based on the founding, a conservatism that emanated outward from the Claremont Institute in southern California and was philosophically driven by Harry V. Jaffa.

Thus, it was no accident so many of the conservative scholars—outposts in the movement, if you will—who supported Donald Trump, as we did, were fellow students of Jaffa's and affiliated with, if not one-time directors of, the Claremont Institute. This list would include Hadley Arkes, Larry Arnn, Bill Bennett, John Eastman, Doug Jeffrey, Brian Kennedy, Charles Kesler, Ken Masugi, R. J. Pestritto, Julie Ponzi, Dennis Teti, and Thomas West.

Explaining the unique outlook of the Institute's thinking, *Claremont Review of Books* editor, Professor Charles Kesler, would write of the *Review* as much as of the Institute:

> Here we follow the lead of the Claremont Institute itself, which is pledged to restore the principles of the American Founding to their rightful, preeminent authority in our public life. As Harry V. Jaffa has argued wisely and often, a return to the principles of the Constitution and the Gettysburg Address requires something like a revolution not only against modern liberalism but also within modern conservatism.
>
> Some conservatives start, as it were, from Edmund Burke; others from Friedrich Hayek. While we respect both thinkers and their schools of thought, we begin instead from America, the American political tradition in all its genius and profundity, and the relation of our tradition to revealed wisdom and to what the elderly Jefferson once called, rather insouciantly, "the elementary books of public right, as Aristotle, Cicero, Locke, Sidney, etc."
>
> We think conservatism should take its bearings from the founders' statesmanship, our citizens' loyalty to the Declaration and Constitution, and the scenes, both tender and proud, of our national history. This kind of approach clears the air. It concentrates the mind. It engages and informs the ordinary citizen's patriotism. And it introduces a new, sharper view of liberalism as descended not from the French Revolution, the Industrial Revolution, nor (God forbid) Abraham Lincoln, but from that movement which, a century

ago, criticized George Washington's and Lincoln's Constitution as outmoded and, as we'd say today, racist, sexist, and antidemocratic. The Progressives broke with the old Constitution and its postulates, and set out to make a new, living constitution and a new, unlimited state, and the Obama administration's programs are merely the latest, and worst, installment of that purported evolution.[7]

Seeing America and her founding—as much as her history, warts and all—as something more than "solid but low" in the philosophical tradition could be seen in all the works of Harry Jaffa, but, just as importantly, in the hearts, if not minds, of patriotic Americans.

While Donald Trump, unlike Barry Goldwater, probably had never heard of Harry Jaffa, the themes Trump sounded, in taking on the issues that had supplanted the 1980s, were resonant with all Jaffa had dedicated his political writings to. In one of his later writings, Jaffa, in an essay whose title gives some idea of his work, *The American Founding as the Best Regime*, concluded:

> The decline of the West is the paramount reality facing us today. Perhaps our most immediate danger comes from the historical pessimism of those who counsel us that this is inevitable and that nothing can be done by taking thought. But this danger is itself a danger only if we believe it. It is precisely by taking thought that this superstition can be dispelled and, with it, the unreasoning fears that it breeds.[8]

Donald Trump would not and certainly does not speak in those terms, but in all he stood for and spoke about—the decline of America but *the ability to fix it* or Make America Great Again—was the campaign to frontally and directly challenge the decline of the West, including the decline of America. Conservatives believe that theirs is the movement that loves America rather than the movement Jeane Kirkpatrick would famously describe in 1984, as the essence of the Democrats and the left, a movement of "Blame America First."[9] Contrary to the Democrat Left, Jaffe taught an American greatness philiosophy, but it had to emanate from somewhere, somewhere beyond our spacious skies and purple mountains. It emanated in the natural and political right our country was founded upon:

> The end of the Cold War has also brought an end to the remission of the disease of moral relativism that is corroding the life of western civilization. It would certainly seem that the salvation of the West must come, if it is to come, from the United States. The salvation of the United States, if it is to come, must come from the Republican Party. And the salvation of the Republican Party, if it is to come, must come from the conservative movement within it. And the salvation of the conservative movement, if it is to come, must come from the renewal and reaffirmation of the principles of the American Founding, embodied above all in the Declaration of Independence, such a reaffirmation as happened in the events that led to the election of Abraham Lincoln.[10]

We can hear our and Trump's critics right now, saying things such as "Donald Trump is totally unfamiliar and unschooled in these things." He may be unschooled in them, but "unfamiliar"? Might not a conservative talking about making America great again and taking on the new challenges of the day that others feared speaking about—from illegal immigration to internationalism to Radical Islam—have this written on his heart, as it were?

Here's the thing, the elitist thing, the thing that has corroded so much of our politics, the thing Conservatism, Inc., misses: while the Never-Trump movement delighted in saying how unfamiliar or unschooled Donald Trump was in his intellectual curiosity, did they ever say or write that about such candidates as John McCain and Mitt Romney, candidates who evidenced no such schooling either? Candidates who lost but whom they supported and heralded? The difference was Donald Trump spoke retail to what the "crisis" we like to talk about means wholesale. And Conservatism, Inc., certainly could say all these very same things about the voters and the vast American people as well—at least 95 percent of whom have never read any of our journals or essays or know the names of the founding editors of *National Review,* much less the work of the Claremont Institute.

But patriotism is written on Americans' hearts. Republicans like to say they are the party of Lincoln. Do they know what they mean when they say that? Do they understand not only the beautiful patriotism he spoke of or the meaning of the Declaration of Independence and its philosophy he relied on in everything he said and stood for? For the most part, of course not. But they know he stood for something important. They know, even if they do not say it, he was, as Clinton Rossiter put it, the "martyred Christ of democracy's passion play."

And if the conservatism of the 1980s was in need of update, what of the conservatism of the 1860s? It is practically too obvious to say the policies would of necessity be different in any decade, much less century, but the principles? Lincoln understood the founding principles, perhaps better than any national figure since. Reagan captured them and translated them retail in the 1970s and 1980s. And Donald Trump raised them once again by speaking to policies that would return us to greatness in a new era. While those principles are rebuked, as all of American exceptionalism is rebuked, by the left and the elites from the media to academia, millions of Americans still hew to them and thirst to hear about them. They delighted in Donald Trump fighting with just those very institutions that so challenged him and them.

Larry Arnn put it this way:

> Trump ran in utter defiance of the political correctness that enforces this new [progressive] system of government. He did not bend his knee to identity groups. He claimed to represent all "citizens," a favorite term, by which he means citizens who hold that status under the law. He said he would represent their interest and their country, which he will make great again, and not the interest of any others. He did not care that this intention was conflated with racism. He saw that conflation as another sign of corruption, which it certainly is. Unless he is insensate, which he does not seem, Trump is possessed of moral courage as much as assertiveness, and his assertiveness is a sight to behold.[11]

Courage, we know from Aristotle, is the first of the virtues—and Arnn is surely right about Donald Trump's courage. He stood up to and for the things so many Americans had thought but were afraid to talk about when it came to such issues as race and political correctness, when it came to such ideas as a full-throated defense of America—and what he meant by "America." He meant, as his policies and campaign themes spelled out, sovereignty, defeating the enemy, and work. On his way there, he would fight back and hit back the media as good as he would get, a fight and a hit that delighted silenced and cowed Americans.

Conservatism, Inc., would write and speak of these things for years, but Heaven forfend a candidate should sound like he was picked out of the Boston telephone directory and speak of these things, too. But to the degree Donald Trump will govern as he campaigned, he will bring back the basics of conservatism—and there is every reason to believe he will do just that.

A look at his cabinet is one very good indication. Donald Trump did not just pick conservatives for his cabinet—something Conservatism, Inc., assured us he would not do, assuring so many of us Trump was not a real conservative—he picked the most conservative cabinet of any president in the modern era. Yes, that includes a more conservative cabinet than even Ronald Reagan chose for his first term. Again, proving he would govern as he campaigned, among his first orders were to address the refugee crisis and put a temporary stop to visitors from nations representing a terrorist threat.

He would nominate to the Supreme Court Neil Gorsuch, about the best conservative pick one could imagine. Donald Trump's famous mid-February 2017 press conference was another indication. Of the concern he would go native or let his supporters down, nope: he went back and forth with the press, doubling down on referring to CNN as "fake news," saying he would stop calling their network by that phrase and start referring to it as "very fake news."[12]

What is to be learned? First, yes: conviction politicians, candidates who say what they mean and mean what they say, still exist. Second, measure a candidate with a single standard compared to others. Was it offensive or the cause of great doubt that Donald Trump had changed his mind on several issues over the years? With every other candidate we used to call that "conversion" and support it. Third, know the most important of things: the basic symbols and ethics of America—from sovereignty to safety—and know that Americans still believe in them, too. Fourth, know that what CNN or the *New York Times* or the faculty clubs believe is not what the American people believe—know the difference between box office and critics. Fifth, and finally: principles can be tied to prudence because the basics of America still thrive; they just need to be communicated, and more importantly, defended. And sometimes their defense, to borrow a phrase from Flannery O'Connor, requires pushing hard against the age that pushes against you.

Donald Trump pushed and pushed hard. Americans loved it. And the cause required it.

16

THE WAY FORWARD

SAVING THE REVOLUTION

THIS BOOK ENDS AS IT BEGAN, with a question: Where do we go from here? The political class failed and the people we call experts—most poignantly those who call themselves conservatives—did more than just fail to accurately predict the outcome of one of the most significant elections in American history. Through their rhetoric and their response to both Trump the man and the agenda he represents they exposed and delegitimized themselves and their claims to speak for rank-and-file American conservatives. This did not happen *because* they opposed Donald Trump but *how,* and more importantly, *why* they opposed him. Their actions since the election have only further proven that the gap between the DC conservatives and ordinary Americans is wide and growing.

One example among many is when former Bush speechwriter and current *New York Times* columnist Peter Wehner told us more about himself than Donald Trump when he mewled in May 2017 that President Trump is "a transgressive personality and a man of illiberal tendencies who was unlikely to be contained by norms and customs. He would not use power benevolently but unwisely, recklessly, and in ways that would undermine our democratic institutions and faith in our government."[1]

First of all for a self-described conservative like Peter Wehner to use the term *transgressive* while writing or speaking in public makes him likely to forfeit his credibility—at least among conservatives. It is a term of derision used by the radical Left and their fellow travelers with its ideological roots in Marx and Marcuse. It is used to indicate that certain people or ideas are simply unacceptable to address or dignify with any response other than opprobrium. Wehner's accusation that Donald Trump "would undermine our democratic institutions and faith in our government" is based on . . . exactly nothing other than priggish elitism that he doesn't even try to disguise.

But Wehner is emblematic of a large portion of the permanent political class: self-righteous, entitled, out of touch. They wanted conservative Supreme Court justices like Neil Gorsuch but not so much that they would support the man who appointed him. They wanted reinstatement of the Mexico City Policy that ends U.S. government support for international organizations that provide abortion services but not enough to back the man who did just that. They wanted an attorney general who would support police, enforce the law fairly, and end the Obama-era DOJ shakedowns that funneled hundreds of millions of dollars in settlement dollars to far Left groups. But not enough to support the president that appointed Jeff Sessions to the job.

Conservatives have gotten a lot of what they have said that they wanted for years within the first few months of the Trump administration, but they're still not happy. Similarly, the Israelites refused to enter the Promised Land after hearing the report from the spies Moses sent into Canaan. Their hearts melted. They grumbled that the inhabitants of the land were too strong and their cities too well fortified, and they refused to cross over the Jordan and possess the land. As a result they spent forty years in the desert and only Caleb and Joshua were permitted to enter the Promised Land.

The story is instructive for today. To be clear, I make absolutely no theological judgements about people, motives, or character. But the story speaks for itself on its own terms. Conservatism Inc. refused political success when it was offered. I do not mean mere electoral success, but the enactment of policies they claim to support. And as a result they will not enter the Promised Land. A new generation not beholden to the tired catechism behind checklist conservatism will replace them. Interestingly, the new generation is not tied to an age cohort. It is a generation defined by ideas that are both timeless and urgent, and they will—we will—replace the failed and failing institutions that placed their own narrow interests over those of the American people they are supposed to serve and that refused to seek victory or take it when it was offered. Conservatism Inc. didn't really want to win. The American people do.

But America was born in revolution—perhaps that explains our entrepreneurial streak as a people—and a few new, dynamic enterprises have been launched to replace the old. There will be more. The archipelago of journals and institutions that came to be known as Conservatism Inc. was built for another era. They existed to fight the Cold War abroad and oppose collectivism at home. Their record is 1-1. Not bad. But since the end of the Cold War and the few years immediately after it, it has failed to address the core issues important to Trump voters for years. Worse, they failed to understand or recall what, as conservatives, they were meant to conserve. We see the Trump presidency as an opportunity for an intellectual and political realignment that favors a restoration of the Founders' constitutionalism.

It has become abundantly clear that what was the status quo on the American Right cannot last in the Trump era or beyond. But that is the cherished hope of Republican pols and conservative intellectuals—that they can just ride out the storm, wait for Trump to leave Washington, and then things will return to the way they were. In their dreams he will withdraw under a cloud of scandal ending with their return to power—or at least privilege—since it has become clear that Conservatism Inc. didn't want to govern, it just wanted to talk.

But there is no going back. The old model is broken. That doesn't mean incumbent institutions won't continue to exist; they will just become less relevant. Sears hasn't been a dynamic enterprise for at least two generations, but it survives even as it teeters on the edge of bankruptcy. Unless they adapt and improve this will be the fate of many of the legacy institutions that make up Conservatism Inc. The sort of change that is required is hard. And unlikely.

Conservatism Inc. discredited itself during and after the election: its virulent opposition to Donald Trump caused many leading voices to betray fundamental conservative principles. Bill Kristol tweeting that he would rather be ruled by the deep state than by the Trump state is just one example among many.

That was just the outward—and very public—evidence of a deeper rot that had eroded the structure of the American ruling class. In hindsight, winning the Cold War looks like both the pinnacle of the modern American Right and the moment at which it became a spent force. Everything that came afterwards resembled nothing so much as an aging athlete vainly trying to recapture past glory. The Bush years were tragedy, Jeb's campaign was farce. The historicist underpinning of modern American conservative intellectualism made them uniquely unable either to see the Titanomachia developing in front of them or to govern.

However, clarity is a victory of its own. During the 2016 election and the early stages of the Trump presidency we have achieved a level of clarity only known in epochal times. It has been, as Reagan called it, a time for choosing. And the intellectual and political class chose each other. Successive leftist governments have proven again and again that their rule is antithetical to the defense of liberty and justice and destructive of the institutions that make self-government possible and beneficial. At the same time, conservatives have proven themselves incapable and mostly disinterested in governing at all. Basing a political movement on yelling "stop!" turns out not to get you very far. It has been rank-and-file conservative voters who have propelled Republicans to electoral victories over past few decades even as institutional conservatism has yelled, "stop!"

These same forces opposed Ronald Reagan who was also denounced as a populist know-nothing. And very often it was Republicans who undermined the Reagan agenda. Sound familiar? Reagan famously said that "government is not the solution, government is the problem." That notion resonated with voters but appalled establishment Republicans. Reagan wanted to reduce the size and scope of government and return power to the states and to the people. Voters got it. Elected Republicans stopped him cold, especially on his domestic agenda.

In 2016 Donald Trump ran for president promising to drain the swamp and his top political strategist has a stated goal of deconstructing the administrative state. To say the least (the very least!), those employed and enriched by the administrative state and their political enablers on Capitol Hill are less than enthusiastic about the aforementioned deconstruction. Too much of the Republican Party fundamentally believes in the right of the administrative state (of which the welfare state is a part) to run people's lives. The only difference between those people and their counterparts on the Left is the means. Ronald Reagan talked in moral terms. He cut taxes because it is right that people should keep more of what they earn. But even then much of the Party—at least the political class—supported tax cuts because they would lead to economic growth that would fund their out-of-control spending in the ballooning federal budget. This is a fundamental difference.

So what is to be done? There is a temptation to reply with airy platitudes. Trump supporters often ask why more hasn't been done. The simple answer is that, like Reagan, he is opposed not only by Democrats and permanent Washington, but by many members of his own party in Congress. It will take another election—or two or three—to effect significant change. The groundwork has been laid and the importance of Trump's victory should not be minimized. But a lasting political restoration requires an intellectual reformation.

Trump's political strategist Stephen Bannon—a serious intellect and an impressive autodidact—understands not just the battle but the war. In a tantalizing but overlooked comment in an interview

Bannon compared himself to Cromwell—not Oliver but Thomas. That Cromwell was a counsellor to Henry VIII. Trump opponents will want to make snarky jibes comparing Trump to Henry and miss the point entirely. Cromwell was a savvy political operator who helped Henry remake English politics and, significantly, was a key force behind the English Reformation promoting and defending key churchmen like Archbishop of Canterbury Thomas Cranmer and Bishops Nicholas Ridley and Hugh Latimer. (Those three would become known to history as the Oxford Martyrs after they were burned at the stake in 1555 by Queen "Bloody" Mary I.)

The intellectual reformation of the American Right, necessary for a political restoration, is underway, but it is still in its infancy. There are our four goals:

AMERICAN FIRST FOREIGN POLICY. We need a foreign policy that recognizes America's role as the leading economic and military power in the world but always makes the self-evident political, economic, and security interests of American citizens the standard by which all foreign policy is judged. Our earliest presidents showed the way on this—engaged with foreign powers but always with the goal of protecting the American people and their prosperity.

PRO-WORKER ECONOMIC AND TRADE POLICY. Critics will no doubt see this as a call for protectionism or government planning of the economy. It isn't. It is a call for intellectuals, academics, pundits, and policymakers to recognize that the role of the American government is not to promote an idealized notion of free trade. It is to promote the prosperity of the American people. Free trade is a means not an end in itself. They must also recognize that all trade between nations is subject to intergovernmental agreements that are negotiated. In the spirit of Adam Smith, we should aggressively pursue our own self-interest and expect other nations to do the same. We are not, as too many free-trade absolutists seem to believe, above the fray. We are rational (or should be) actors within the international marketplace. And finally, policymakers must pursue policies that will expand and defend the middle class. The health of the middle class is the single metric by which the long-term health of the nation's economy—and to some extent its politics—can be easily judged.

PRO-CITIZEN IMMIGRATION AND BORDER POLICY. A high view of citizenship that includes devotion to protect the value and prerogatives of citizenship is fundamental to the protection and perpetuation of liberty and self-government. This should be uncontroversial, but even with Republican and conservative circles the idea and importance of citizenship—which is exclusionary by nature—is fallen on hard times. Borders must be protected and citizens must come first.

DECONSTRUCTION OF THE ADMINISTRATIVE STATE. Government must be accountable to its citizens upon whom it relies for its legitimacy. The administrative state fails to meet this basic threshold. If Congress wants to enact new laws, it must legislate them not delegate its essential function to unelected functionaries within the executive branch. The growth of the administrative state is a threat to the sovereignty of the American people and, if left unchecked, to the legitimacy of regime. In its present state it is evidence of a federal government that has grown too large and as such infringes daily on the right of its citizens and of other elements of government in particular the states.

What are the elements of a successful reformation of the American Right that can lead to the long sought political restoration?

For the reformation to succeed the Right must recognize that the American people are sovereign and that they—*we*—must save themselves. There will be no *deus ex machina*. Elites have not just failed but have formed a faction of the type the founders warned against. They have blurred the distinction between principle and prudence. Effective politics requires both.

Movement conservatives must remain hopeful but realistic. That was the position of the Founders. They understood the political implications of man being made in the divine image but also recognized that the depravity of fallen man required significant institutional checks to prevent government from becoming abusive. We see those in the Constitution. Instead the modern Right has swallowed the Marxist/Hegelian view of the world and innately believe the leftist conceit that they are on the wrong side of history. Movement conservatives who believe that they are fighting for a lost cause are always looking for ways to preemptively negotiate their surrender.

In a remarkable feat of cognitive dissonance, elite conservatives hold the contradictory view that their ideas about free markets, free trade, and global democracy are on the march while being unwilling to defend their own people or nation. Witness the aggressive neoconservative foreign policy based upon moral imperialism. There is a way to square this circle however: globalism. Elites on the American Right have stopped believing in the primacy of the nation state, which means that they have also given up on America—they just don't know it yet. This country is just a laboratory for their ideas and the promise of American conservatism as preached by many of its public intellectuals has degenerated from a more or less coherent political philosophy—or at least a coalition of compatible political philosophies—into a parlor game, a graduate school seminar disembodied from a real nation and real people. That's why Conservatism Inc. was rejected by voters in 2016 along with its carefully groomed, picked, and financed candidates.

Finally, for the reformation of the American right to work, it must give up on liberal guilt. The Left is wrong. Not just incorrect, but morally wrong. They may wrap themselves in happy talk of compassion and progress but leftist politics have caused more misery for more people than any other political ideology in the modern era. Mark Bauerlein, reformed atheist and professor of English at Emory, nailed it with his analysis of the Left's use of guilt as a political tool:

> In the last 50 years of culture wars in America, there has been no stronger weapon than guilt. It is the Left's great hammer of progress. It figured powerfully in the Civil Rights Movement, the anti-war

movement, women's liberation, and same-sex marriage. Guilt runs
through the teaching of U.S. history from 5th grade through college.
It colors controversies over affirmative action, transgender bathrooms,
and the glass ceiling. The entire careers of Leftist commentators from
the self-righteous Bill Moyers to the self-regarding Ta-Nehisi Coates
rest upon it. If we add up the successes guilt has brought to progressive causes and identity politics, we realize just how important guilt
is to the Left agenda. Without it, in fact, the Left fails. . . .

Because [Donald Trump] won't accept this appointed condition,
he has no white guilt. He doesn't feel any male guilt either or American
guilt or Christian guilt. He talks about the United States with uncritical
approval—"America First"—and that's a thought crime in the eyes
of liberals. It ignores slavery, Jim Crow, the Indian wars, Manzana.
Donald Trump would never refer to America as beset by the original
sin of racism, as Barack Obama did frequently, and that makes him
worse than a conservative. President Trump is a bigot. And he wouldn't
say, "Black Lives Matter," either, a slogan that implies whites don't care
about black lives, but insisted, "All lives matter."

Finally, while Christians, especially Catholics and Evangelicals,
are supposed to feel guilty for their doctrine on gender roles and
abortion, President Trump quickly dropped gender identity from
Title IX and nominated a religious conservative to the Supreme Court.

That's what happens when a political leader doesn't share the
guilt, and progressives know it. For decades they have pushed a campaign of guilt in classrooms, museums, movies, books, and newsrooms
precisely to forestall those moves. If you can persuade an opponent
that he's wrong about a political issue, you can win the day's debate.
But if you can make him feel guilty about his opinion, you've got
him on the defensive forever.

Guilt isn't political, it's psychological. . . .

Donald Trump's success, then, amounts to a calamitous disarma-
ment of the Left. Not his occupation of the White House, but his
termination of the game of guilt—for now, at least."[2]

Once Americans get past the leftist guilt game—and most of Middle America is well past it—there are a few principles to bear in mind.

- Understand the requirement of successful coalition government. This means coalitions within the Republican Party of the kind that Buckley and Reagan successfully formed. We have to be able to work together towards common ends.

- Recognize the different elements of the conservative coalition and their political and philosophical distinctives. What binds them together? Where are the differences? How can they work together to govern?

- We must recommit to first principles and distinguish between principles and prudence Every political dispute does not rise to the level of character-defining debate.

- We must break up the self-centered and self-serving DC institutional power base and decentralize the power. This has already happened in part. Conservatives like to talk about economist Joseph Schumpeter's theory that entrepreneurship and innovation can unleash gales of creative destruction but the American Right need just such a storm. New institutions must rise to reinvigorate the conservative and American politics.

- We must reject the fatalism of the post-Cold War Right. The battle isn't lost. There is no right or wrong side of history only right and wrong. The fight goes on and today it's our responsibility to take it up. There are victories yet to be won if only we will heed the call.

Paul wrote "For if the trumpet give an uncertain sound, who shall prepare himself to the battle?" (1 Cor. 14:8, KJV). We hope this book has made a distinct sound.

Lasting political change must be bottom up not top down. Conservatives like to talk about the virtues of decentralization but, as the Left would say, they don't live their values.

Trump supporters want the president to be successful but even more important in the long run is the need for a political movement that builds upon the agenda described by Trump in the campaign that energized millions. Donald Trump is the tribune of the people. But it is up to the people to govern themselves.

Voters looking for salvation from on high will be disappointed. Self-government is about empowering the people to rule themselves: It's the constitutional order that is important and the people who run it. On the final day of the Constitutional Convention in 1787 Benjamin Franklin was approached by a lady as he left the hall. The exchange was recorded for history by fellow delegate Dr. James McHenry of Maryland: The lady asked, "Well Doctor, what have we got a republic or a monarchy?" Franklin famously replied, "A republic. If you can keep it."

That's just as true now as it was then—it is the American people who are the rightful keepers of this republic not a distant ruling class. The question is whether we will reassert those rights or allow the slow erosion that has brought us to this point to continue and thereby kill the promise of the American experiment in free government.

THE FLIGHT 93 ELECTION

BY PUBLIUS DECIUS MUS
SEPTEMBER 5, 2016

TWO THOUSAND SIXTEEN IS THE FLIGHT 93 ELECTION: charge the cockpit or you die. You may die anyway. You—or the leader of your party—may make it into the cockpit and not know how to fly or land the plane. There are no guarantees.

Except one: if you don't try, death is certain. To compound the metaphor: a Hillary Clinton presidency is Russian Roulette with a semi-auto. With Trump, at least you can spin the cylinder and take your chances.

To ordinary conservative ears, this sounds histrionic. The stakes can't be that high because they are never that high—except perhaps in the pages of Gibbon. Conservative intellectuals will insist that there has been no "end of history" and that all human outcomes are still possible. They will even—as Charles Kesler does—admit that America is in "crisis." But how great is the crisis? Can things really be so bad if eight years of Obama can be followed by eight more of Hillary, and yet Constitutionalist conservatives can still reasonably hope for a restoration of our cherished ideals? Cruz in 2024!

Not to pick (too much) on Kesler, who is less unwarrantedly optimistic than most conservatives. And who, at least, poses the right question: Trump or Hillary? Though his answer—"even if [Trump] had chosen his policies at random, they would be sounder than Hillary's"— is unwarrantedly ungenerous. The truth is that Trump articulated, if incompletely and inconsistently, the right stances on the right issues— immigration, trade, and war—right from the beginning.

But let us back up. One of the paradoxes—there are so many—of conservative thought over the last decade at least is the unwillingness even to entertain the possibility that America and the West are on a trajectory toward something very bad. On the one hand, conservatives routinely present a litany of ills plaguing the body politic. Illegitimacy. Crime. Massive, expensive, intrusive, out-of-control government. Politically correct McCarthyism. Ever-higher taxes and ever-deteriorating services and infrastructure. Inability to win wars against tribal, sub-Third-World foes. A disastrously awful educational system that churns out kids who don't know anything and, at the primary and secondary levels, can't (or won't) discipline disruptive punks, and at the higher levels saddles students with six-figure debts for the privilege. And so on and drearily on. Like that portion of the mass where the priest asks for your private intentions, fill in any dismal fact about American decline that you want and I'll stipulate it.

Conservatives spend at least several hundred million dollars a year on think-tanks, magazines, conferences, fellowships, and such, complaining about this, that, the other, and everything. And yet these same conservatives are, at root, keepers of the status quo. Oh, sure, they want some things to change. They want their pet ideas adopted—tax deductions for having more babies and the like. Many of them are even good ideas. But are any of them truly fundamental? Do they get to the heart of our problems?

If conservatives are right about the importance of virtue, morality, religious faith, stability, character and so on in the individual; if they are right about sexual morality or what came to be termed "family values"; if they are right about the importance of education to inculcate good character and to teach the fundamentals that have defined knowledge in the West for millennia; if they are right about societal norms and public order; if they are right about the centrality of initiative, enterprise, industry, and thrift to a sound economy and a healthy society; if they are right about the soul-sapping effects of paternalistic Big Government and its cannibalization of civil society and religious institutions; if they are right about the necessity of a strong defense and prudent statesmanship in the international sphere—if they are right about the importance of all this to national health and even survival, then they must believe— mustn't they?—*that we are headed off a cliff.*

But it's quite obvious that conservatives don't believe any such thing, that they feel no such sense of urgency, of an immediate necessity to change course and avoid the cliff. A recent article by Matthew Continetti may be taken as representative—indeed, almost written for the purpose of illustrating the point. Continetti inquires into the "condition of America" and finds it wanting. What does Continetti propose to do about it? The usual litany of "conservative" "solutions," with the obligatory references to decentralization, federalization, "civic renewal," and—of course!—Burke. Which is to say, conservatism's typical combination of the useless and inapt with the utopian and unrealizable. Decentralization and federalism are all well and good, and as a conservative, I endorse them both without reservation. But how are they going to save, or even meaningfully improve, the America that Continetti describes? What can they do against a tidal wave of dysfunction, immorality, and corruption? "Civic renewal" would do a lot of course, but that's like saying health will save a cancer patient. A step has been skipped in there somewhere. How are we going to achieve "civic renewal"? Wishing for a tautology to enact itself is not a strategy.

Continetti trips over a more promising approach when he writes of "stress[ing] the 'national interest abroad and national solidarity at home' through foreign-policy retrenchment, 'support to workers buffeted by globalization,' and setting 'tax rates and immigration levels' to foster social cohesion." That sounds a lot like Trumpism. But the phrases that Continetti quotes are taken from Ross Douthat and Reihan Salam, both of whom, like Continetti, are vociferously—one might even say fanatically—anti-Trump. At least they, unlike Kesler, give Trump credit for having identified the right stance on today's most salient issues. Yet, paradoxically, they won't vote for Trump whereas Kesler hints that he will. It's reasonable, then, to read into Kesler's esoteric endorsement of Trump an implicit acknowledgment that the crisis is, indeed, pretty dire. I expect a Claremont scholar to be wiser than most other conservative intellectuals, and I am relieved not to be disappointed in this instance.

Yet we may also reasonably ask: What explains the Pollyanna-ish declinism of so many others? That is, the stance that things are really bad—but not so bad that we have to consider anything really different! The obvious answer is that they don't really believe the first half of that formulation. If so, like Chicken Little, they should stick a sock in it. Pecuniary reasons also suggest themselves, but let us foreswear recourse to this explanation until we have disproved all the others.

Whatever the reason for the contradiction, there can be no doubt that there is a contradiction. To simultaneously hold conservative cultural, economic, and political beliefs—to insist that our liberal-left present reality and future direction is incompatible with human nature and must undermine society—and yet also believe that things can go on more or less the way they are going, ideally but not necessarily with some conservative tinkering here and there, is logically impossible.

Let's be very blunt here: if you genuinely think things can go on with no fundamental change needed, then you have implicitly admitted that *conservatism is wrong*. Wrong philosophically, wrong on human nature, wrong on the nature of politics, and wrong in its policy prescriptions. Because, first, few of those prescriptions are in force today. Second, of the ones that are, the left is busy undoing them, often with conservative assistance. And, third, the whole trend of the West is ever-leftward, ever further away from what we all understand as conservatism.

If your answer—Continetti's, Douthat's, Salam's, and so many others'—is for conservatism to keep doing what it's been doing— another policy journal, another article about welfare reform, another half-day seminar on limited government, another tax credit proposal— even though we've been losing ground for at least a century, then you've implicitly accepted that your supposed political philosophy doesn't matter and that civilization will carry on just fine under leftist tenets. Indeed, that leftism is *truer* than conservatism and superior to it.

They will say, in words reminiscent of dorm-room Marxism—but our proposals have *not* been tried! Here our ideas sit, waiting to be implemented! To which I reply: eh, not really. Many conservative solutions—above all welfare reform and crime control—have been tried, and proved effective, but have nonetheless failed to stem the tide. Crime, for instance, is down from its mid-'70s and early '90s peak—but way, way up from the historic American norm that ended when liberals took over criminal justice in the mid-'60s. And it's rising fast today, in the teeth of ineffectual conservative complaints. And what has this temporary crime (or welfare, for that matter) decline done to stem the greater tide? The tsunami of leftism that still engulfs our every—literal and figurative—shore has receded not a bit but indeed has grown. All your (our) victories are short lived.

More to the point, what has conservatism achieved lately? In the last twenty years? The answer—which appears to be "nothing"—might seem to lend credence to the plea that "our ideas haven't been tried." Except that the same conservatives who generate those ideas are in charge of selling them to the broader public. If their ideas "haven't been tried," who is ultimately at fault? The whole enterprise of Conservatism Inc. reeks of failure. Its sole recent and ongoing success is its own self-preservation. Conservative intellectuals never tire of praising "entrepreneurs" and "creative destruction." Dare to fail! they exhort businessmen. Let the market decide! Except, um, not with respect to us. Or is their true market not the political arena, but the fundraising circuit?

Only three questions matter. First, how bad are things really? Second, what do we do right now? Third, what should we do for the long term?

Conservatism Inc.'s "answer" to the first may, at this point, simply be dismissed. If the conservatives wish to have a serious debate, I for one am game—more than game; eager. The problem of "subjective certainty" can only be overcome by going into the agora. But my attempt to do so—the blog that Kesler mentions—was met largely with incredulity. How can they say that?! How can anyone apparently of our caste (conservative intellectuals) not merely support Trump (however lukewarmly) but offer reasons for doing do?

One of the *Journal of American Greatness*'s deeper arguments was that only in a corrupt republic, in corrupt times, could a Trump rise. It is therefore puzzling that those most horrified by Trump are the least willing to consider the possibility that the republic is dying. That possibility, apparently, seems to them so preposterous that no refutation is necessary.

As does, presumably, the argument that the stakes in 2016 are—everything. I should here note that I am a good deal gloomier than my (former) JAG colleagues, and that while we frequently used the royal "we" when discussing things on which we all agreed, I here speak only for myself.

How have the last two decades worked out for you, personally? If you're a member or fellow-traveler of the Davos class, chances are: pretty well. If you're among the subspecies conservative intellectual or politician, you've accepted—perhaps not consciously, but unmistakably—your status on the roster of the Washington Generals of American politics. Your job is to show up and lose, but you are a necessary part of the show and you do get paid. To the extent that you are ever on the winning side of anything, it's as sophists who help the Davoisie oligarchy rationalize open borders, lower wages, outsourcing, de-industrialization, trade giveaways, and endless, pointless, winless war.

All of Trump's sixteen Republican competitors would have ensured more of the same—as will the election of Hillary Clinton. That would be bad enough. But at least Republicans are merely reactive when it comes to wholesale cultural and political change. Their "opposition" may be in all cases ineffectual and often indistinguishable from support. But they don't dream up inanities like thirty-two "genders," elective bathrooms, single-payer, Iran sycophancy, "Islamophobia," and Black Lives Matter. They merely help ratify them.

A Hillary presidency will be pedal-to-the-metal on the entire Progressive-left agenda, plus items few of us have yet imagined in our darkest moments. Nor is even that the worst. It will be coupled with a level of vindictive persecution against resistance and dissent hitherto seen in the supposedly liberal West only in the most "advanced" Scandinavian countries and the most leftist corners of Germany and England. We see this already in the censorship practiced by the Davoisie's social media enablers; in the shameless propaganda tidal wave of the mainstream media; and in the personal destruction campaigns—operated through the former and aided by the latter—of the Social Justice Warriors. We see it in Obama's flagrant use of the IRS to torment political opponents, the gaslighting denial by the media, and the collective shrug by everyone else.

It's absurd to assume that any of this would stop or slow—would do anything other than massively intensify—in a Hillary administration. It's even more ridiculous to expect that hitherto useless conservative opposition would suddenly become effective. For two generations at least, the Left has been calling everyone to their right Nazis. This trend has accelerated exponentially in the last few years, helped along by some on the Right who really do seem to merit—and even relish—the label. There is nothing the modern conservative fears more than being called "racist," so alt-right pocket Nazis are manna from heaven for the Left. But also wholly unnecessary: sauce for the goose. The Left was calling us Nazis long before any pro-Trumpers tweeted Holocaust denial memes. And how does one deal with a Nazi—that is, with an enemy one is convinced intends your destruction? You don't compromise with him or leave him alone. You crush him.

So what do we have to lose by fighting back? Only our Washington Generals jerseys—and paychecks. But those are going away anyway. Among the many things the "Right" still doesn't understand is that the Left has concluded that this particular show need no longer go on. They don't think they need a foil anymore and would rather dispense with the whole bother of staging these phony contests in which each side ostensibly has a shot.

If you haven't noticed, our side has been losing consistently since 1988. We can win midterms, but we do nothing with them. Call ours Hannibalic victories. After the Carthaginian's famous slaughter of a Roman army at Cannae, he failed to march on an undefended Rome, prompting his cavalry commander to complain: "you know how to win a victory, but not how to use one." And, aside from 2004's lackluster 50.7 percent, we can't win the big ones at all.

Because the deck is stacked overwhelmingly against us. I will mention but three ways. First, the opinion-making elements—the universities and the media above all—are wholly corrupt and wholly opposed to everything we want, and increasingly even to our existence. (What else are the wars on "cis-genderism"—formerly known as "nature"—and on the supposed "white privilege" of broke hillbillies really about?) If it hadn't been abundantly clear for the last fifty years, the campaign of 2015–2016 must surely have made it evident to even the meanest capacities that the intelligentsia—including all the organs through which it broadcasts its propaganda—is overwhelmingly partisan and biased. Against this onslaught, "conservative" media is a nullity, barely a whisper. It cannot be heard above the blaring of what has been aptly called "The Megaphone."

Second, our Washington Generals self-handicap and self-censor to an absurd degree. Lenin is supposed to have said that "the best way to control the opposition is to lead it ourselves." But with an opposition like ours, why bother? Our "leaders" and "dissenters" bend over backward to play by the self-sabotaging rules the Left sets for them. Fearful, beaten dogs have more *thymos*.

Third and most important, the ceaseless importation of Third World foreigners with no tradition of, taste for, or experience in liberty means that the electorate grows more left, more Democratic, less Republican, less republican, and less traditionally American with every cycle. As does, of course, the U.S. population, which only serves to reinforce the two other causes outlined above. This is the core reason why the Left, the Democrats, and the bipartisan junta (categories distinct but very much overlapping) think they are on the cusp of a permanent victory that will forever obviate the need to pretend to respect democratic and constitutional niceties. Because they are.

It's also why they treat open borders as the "absolute value," the one "principle" that—when their "principles" collide—they prioritize above all the others. If *that* fact is insufficiently clear, consider this. Trump is the most liberal Republican nominee since Thomas Dewey. He departs from conservative orthodoxy in so many ways that *National Review* still hasn't stopped counting. But let's stick to just the core issues animating his campaign. On trade, globalization, and war, Trump is to the left (conventionally understood) not only of his own party, but of his Democratic opponent. And yet the Left and the junta are at one with the house-broken conservatives in their determination—desperation—not merely to defeat Trump but to destroy him. What gives?

Oh, right—there's that *other* issue. The sacredness of mass immigration is the mystic chord that unites America's ruling and intellectual classes. Their reasons vary somewhat. The Left and the Democrats seek ringers to form a permanent electoral majority. They, or many of them, also believe the academic-intellectual lie that America's inherently racist and evil nature can be expiated only through ever greater "diversity." The junta of course craves cheaper and more docile labor. It also seeks to legitimize, and deflect unwanted attention from, its wealth and power by pretending that its open borders stance is a form of *noblesse oblige*. The Republicans and the "conservatives"? Both of course desperately want absolution from the charge of "racism." For the latter, this at least makes some sense. No Washington General can take the court—much less cash his check—with that epithet dancing over his head like some Satanic Spirit. But for the former, this priestly grace comes at the direct expense of their worldly interests. Do they honestly believe that the right enterprise zone or charter school policy will arouse 50.01 percent of our newer voters to finally reveal their "natural conservatism" at the ballot box? It hasn't happened anywhere yet and shows no signs that it ever will. But that doesn't stop the Republican refrain: more, more, more! No matter how many elections they lose, how many districts tip forever blue, how rarely (if ever) their immigrant vote cracks 40 percent, the answer is always the same. Just like Angela Merkel after yet another rape, shooting, bombing, or machete attack. More, more, more!

This is insane. This is the mark of a party, a society, a country, a people, a civilization that wants to die. Trump, alone among candidates for high office in this or in the last seven (at least) cycles, has stood up to say: I want to live. I want my party to live. I want my country to live. I want my people to live. I want to end the insanity.

Yes, Trump is worse than imperfect. So what? We can lament until we choke the lack of a great statesman to address the fundamental issues of our time—or, more importantly, to connect them. Since Pat Buchanan's three failures, occasionally a candidate arose who saw one piece: Dick Gephardt on trade, Ron Paul on war, Tom Tancredo on immigration. Yet, among recent political figures—great statesmen, dangerous demagogues, and mewling gnats alike—only Trump-the-alleged-buffoon not merely saw all three and their essential connectivity, but was able to win on them. The alleged buffoon is thus more prudent—more practically wise—than all of our wise-and-good who so bitterly oppose him. This should embarrass them. That their failures instead embolden them is only further proof of their foolishness and hubris.

Which they self-laud as "consistency"—adherence to "conservative principle," defined by the 1980 campaign and the household gods of reigning conservative think-tanks. A higher consistency in the service of the national interest apparently eludes them. When America possessed a vast, empty continent and explosively growing industry, high immigration was arguably good policy. (*Arguably*: Ben Franklin would disagree.) It hasn't made sense since World War I. Free trade was unquestionably a great boon to the American worker in the decades after World War II. We long ago passed the point of diminishing returns. The Gulf War of 1991 was a strategic victory for American interests. No conflict since then has been. Conservatives either can't see this—or, worse, those who can nonetheless treat the only political leader to mount a serious challenge to the status quo (more immigration, more trade, more war) as a unique evil.

Trump's vulgarity is in fact a godsend to the conservatives. It allows them to hang their public opposition on his obvious shortcomings and to ignore or downplay his far greater strengths, which should be even more obvious but in corrupt times can be deliberately obscured by constant references to his faults. That the Left would make the campaign all about the latter is to be expected. Why would the Right? Some—a few—are no doubt sincere in their belief that the man is simply unfit for high office. David Frum, who has always been an immigration skeptic and is a convert to the less-war position, is sincere when he says that, even though he agrees with much of Trump's agenda, he cannot stomach Trump. But for most of the other Never Trumpers, is it just a coincidence that they also happen to favor Invade the World, Invite the World?

Another question JAG raised without provoking any serious attempt at refutation was whether, in corrupt times, it took a . . . let's say . . . "loudmouth" to rise above the din of The Megaphone. We, or I, speculated: "yes." Suppose there had arisen some statesman of high character—dignified, articulate, experienced, knowledgeable—the exact opposite of everything the conservatives claim to hate about Trump. Could this hypothetical paragon have won on Trump's same issues? Would the conservatives have supported him? I would have—even had he been a Democrat.

Back on planet earth, that flight of fancy at least addresses what to do now. The answer to the subsidiary question—will it work?—is much less clear. By "it" I mean Trumpism, broadly defined as secure borders, economic nationalism, and America-first foreign policy. We Americans have chosen, in our foolishness, to disunite the country through stupid immigration, economic, and foreign policies. The level of unity America enjoyed before the bipartisan junta took over can never be restored.

But we can probably do better than we are doing now. First, stop digging. No more importing poverty, crime, and alien cultures. We have made institutions, by leftist design, not merely abysmal at assimilation but abhorrent of the concept. We should try to fix that, but given the Left's iron grip on every school and cultural center, that's like trying to bring democracy to Russia. A worthy goal, perhaps, but temper your hopes—and don't invest time and resources unrealistically.

By contrast, simply building a wall and enforcing immigration law will help enormously, by cutting off the flood of newcomers that perpetuates ethnic separatism and by incentivizing the English language and American norms in the workplace. These policies will have the added benefit of aligning the economic interests of, and (we may hope) fostering solidarity among, the working, lower middle, and middle classes of all races and ethnicities. The same can be said for Trumpian trade policies and anti-globalization instincts. Who cares if productivity numbers tick down, or if our already somnambulant GDP sinks a bit further into its pillow? Nearly all the gains of the last twenty years have accrued to the junta anyway. It would, at this point, be better for the nation to divide up more equitably a slightly smaller pie than to add one extra slice—only to ensure that it and eight of the other nine go first to the government and its rentiers, and the rest to the same four industries and two hundred families.

Will this work? Ask a pessimist, get a pessimistic answer. So don't ask. Ask instead: is it worth trying? Is it better than the alternative? If you can't say, forthrightly, "yes," you are either part of the junta, a fool, or a conservative intellectual.

And if it doesn't work, what then? We've established that most "conservative" anti-Trumpites are in the Orwellian sense objectively pro-Hillary. What about the rest of you? If you recognize the threat she poses, but somehow can't stomach him, have you thought about the longer term? The possibilities would seem to be: Caesarism, secession/crack-up, collapse, or managerial Davoisie liberalism as far as the eye can see . . . which, since nothing human lasts forever, at some point will give way to one of the other three. Oh, and, I suppose, for those who like to pour a tall one and dream big, a second American Revolution that restores Constitutionalism, limited government, and a 28 percent top marginal rate.

But for those of you who are sober: can you sketch a more plausible long-term future than the prior four following a Trump defeat? I can't either.

The election of 2016 is a test—in my view, the final test—of whether there is any *virtù* left in what used to be the core of the American nation. If they cannot rouse themselves simply to vote for the first candidate in a generation who pledges to advance their interests, and to vote against the one who openly boasts that she will do the opposite (a million more Syrians, anyone?), then they are doomed. They may not deserve the fate that will befall them, but they will suffer it regardless.

SOURCE: © Claremont Institute, http://www.claremont.org/crb/basicpage/the-flight-93-election/. Reprinted by permission.

Notes

FOREWORD

1. George F. Will, "The Wisdom of Pat Moynihan," *Washington Post,* October 3, 2010, http://www. washingtonpost.com/wp-dyn/content/article/2010/10/01/AR2010100105262.html.

CHAPTER 1: THE AGONY OF VICTORY

1. Seth Stevenson, "Two Crap Sandwiches," *Slate,* September 30, 2016, http://www.slate.com/articles/ news_and_politics/politics/2016/09/jonah_goldberg_on_why_he_won_t_vote_for_hillary_or_ trump.html.

2. Publius Decius Mus, "The Case Against 'the Conservative Case . . . ,'" *American Greatness,* October 3, 2016, https://amgreatness.com/2016/10/03/case-conservative-case/.

3. "Open Letter on Donald Trump from GOP National Security Leaders," March 2, 2016, https:// warontherocks.com/2016/03/open-letter-on-donald-trump-from-gop-national-security-leaders/.

4. Ibid.

5. Louis Nelson, "Paul Wolfowitz: 'I might have to vote for Hillary Clinton,'" *Politico,* August, 26, 2016, http://www.politico.com/story/2016/08/paul-wolfowitz-may-vote-clinton-227452.

6. Ibid.

7. Jonah Goldberg, "Evan McMullin—the Last Best Hope for the Never Clinton and Never Trump Masses," *LA Times,* October 25, 2016, http://www.latimes.com/opinion/op-ed/la-oe-goldberg-evan-mcmullin-write-in-20161025-snap-story.html.

8. David Harsanyi, "Why President Trump Would Be a Bigger Disaster Than President Clinton," *National Review,* February 26, 2016, http://www.nationalreview.com/article/431962/donald-trump-hillary-clinton-choose-wisely

9. Stephen F. Hayes, "Donald Trump Is Crazy, and So Is the GOP for Embracing Him," *Weekly Standard,* July 22, 2016, http://www.weeklystandard.com/donald-trump-is-crazy-and-so-is-the-gop-for-embracing-him/article/2003466.

10. Jonah Goldberg, "'New Nationalism' Amounts to Generic White-Identity Politics," *National Review,* August 17, 2016, http://www.nationalreview.com/article/439048/trumps-nationalism-white-identity-politics-brand-name.

11. Pema Levy, "The White Nationalist Propagandist Who Will Advise President Trump," Mother Jones, November 14, 2016, http://www.motherjones.com/politics/2016/11/white-nationalist-who-will-advise-donald-trump-white-house.

12. Ben Shapiro, "The End Is Nigh: Donald Trump, Horseman Of The Republican Apocalypse," *Daily Wire*, October 10, 2016, http://www.dailywire.com/news/9836/end-nigh-donald-trump-horseman-republican-ben-shapiro.

13. Ben Shapiro, "Here's Why Trump's Long Con Works So Well," *Daily Wire*, April 18, 2016, http://www.dailywire.com/news/5026/heres-why-trumps-con-man-act-works-ben-shapiro.

14. Ronald L. Rubin, "The Art of the Con," *Weekly Standard*, March 18, 2016, http://www.weeklystandard.com/the-art-of-the-con/article/2001643.

15. Kevin D. Williamson, "Thank Goodness Trump Is a Compulsive Liar," *National Review*, August 10, 2016, http://www.nationalreview.com/article/438829/donald-trump-social-security-lies-lies-lies.

16. Amanda Carpenter, "Blackballing Those Who Endorse Trump," *Conservative Review*, March 18, 2016, https://www.conservativereview.com/commentary/2016/03/blackballing-those-who-endorse-trump.

17. Eugene Scott, "Glenn Beck Covers His Face in Cheetos Dust to Mimic Donald Trump," April 29, 2016, http://www.cnn.com/2016/04/29/politics/glenn-beck-donald-trump-cheetos/.

18. NR Symposium, "Conservatives against Trump," *National Review*, January 21, 2016, http://www.nationalreview.com/article/430126/donald-trump-conservatives-oppose-nomination.

19. https://twitter.com/realDonaldTrump/status/690382619213742082.

20. Jonah Goldberg, "No Movement That Embraces Trump Can Call Itself Conservative," *National Review*, September 5, 2015, http://www.nationalreview.com/g-file/423607/no-movement-embraces-trump-can-call-itself-conservative-jonah-goldberg.

21. Jonah Goldberg, "If Candidate Trump Can't Be Managed, What Makes You Think President Trump Could Be?" *National Review*, October 1, 2016, http://www.nationalreview.com/g-file/440609/if-candidate-trump-cant-be-managed-what-makes-you-think-president-trump-could-be.

22. George Will, "Donald Trump's Rise Reflects America's Decay," *National Review*, September 28, 2016, http://www.nationalreview.com/article/440459/donald-trump-2016-republicans-conservatives-might-part-ways-if-he-wins.

23. David French, "As Nominee, Donald Trump Would Do Incalculable Damage to the Pro-Life Cause," *National Review*, March 30, 2016, http://www.nationalreview.com/corner/433476/nominee-donald-trump-would-do-incalculable-damage-pro-life-cause.

24. https://twitter.com/BillKristol/status/727819046025089024.

25. Russell Moore, "Have Evangelicals Who Support Trump Lost Their Values?" *New York Times*, September 17, 2015, https://www.nytimes.com/2015/09/17/opinion/have-evangelicals-who-support-trump-lost-their-values.html.

26. Erick Erickson, "You Hurt Your Witness Now and You Should Be Ashamed," *Resurgent*, October 7, 2016, http://theresurgent.com/you-hurt-your-witness-now-and-you-should-be-ashamed/.

CHAPTER 2: WHAT WENT WRONG

1. Zach Carter, "Karl Rove: Donald Trump Can't Win," *Huffington Post*, October 23, 2016, http://www.huffingtonpost.com/entry/karl-rove-donald-trump-cant-win_us_580cb4c1e4b000d0b15727dc.

2. Meghashyam Mali, "Rove Predicts Romney Victory with at Least 279 Electoral College Votes," *the Hill* (blog), November 1, 2012, http://thehill.com/blogs/blog-briefing-room/news/265227-rove-predicts-romney-victory-with-at-least-279-electoral-college-votes.

3. "Karl Rove's Election Night Melt-down over Ohio Results on Fox News," Fox News, November 7, 2012, https://www.youtube.com/watch?v=9TwuR0jCavk.

4. Michael Tanner, "Neither Trump nor His Message Is Built to Win a National Election," *National Review,* October 12, 2016, http://www.nationalreview.com/article/440985/we-already-have-one-party-committed-big-government.

5. Kevin D. Williamson, "So Much (for) Winning," *National Review,* October 27, 2016, http://www.nationalreview.com/article/441442/republican-congress-conservative-majority-restrain-hillary.

6. William Kristol, "The Loser," *Weekly Standard,* October 31, 2016, http://www.weeklystandard.com/the-loser/article/2004996.

7. David Brooks, "No, Donald Trump Won't Win," *New York Times,* December 4, 2015, https://www.nytimes.com/2015/12/04/opinion/no-donald-trump-wont-win.html.

8. Jon Wiener, " Relax, Donald Trump Can't Win," *Nation,* June 21, 2016, https://www.thenation.com/article/trump-cant-win/.

9. Chris Cillizza and Aaron Blake, "Donald Trump's Chances of Winning Are Approaching Zero," *Washington Post,* October 24, 2016, https://www.washingtonpost.com/news/the-fix/wp/2016/10/24/donald-trumps-chances-of-winning-are-approaching-zero/?utm_term=.615d00941cf8.

10. Reena Flores, "In a Stunner, Donald Trump Wins the Presidency," CBS News, November 9, 2016, http://www.cbsnews.com/news/in-a-surpising-upset-donald-trump-wins-the-presidency/.

11. Karen Tumulty, Philip Rucker, and Anne Gearan, "Donald Trump Wins the Presidency in Stunning Upset over Clinton," November 9, 2016, https://www.washingtonpost.com/politics/election-day-an-acrimonious-race-reaches-its-end-point/2016/11/08/32b96c72-a557-11e6-ba59-a7d93165c6d4_story.html?utm_term=.653488f7b461.

12. Matt Flegenheimer and Michael Barbaro, "Donald Trump Is Elected President in Stunning Repudiation of the Establishment," *New York Times*, November 9, 2016, https://www.nytimes.com/2016/11/09/us/politics/hillary-clinton-donald-trump-president.html.

13. Kurt Wagner, "With Donald Trump's Surprising Victory, Silicon Valley Is Having a Meltdown," *Recode,* November 9, 2016, http://www.recode.net/2016/11/9/13574396/donald-trump-victory-silicon-valley-meltdown.

14. Alex Griswold, "Email: Hillary Clinton Met Off-the-Record With 'Sympathetic' NY Times Reporter," *Mediate,* October 11, 2016, http://www.mediaite.com/print/email-hillary-clinton-met-off-the-record-with-sympathetic-ny-times-reporter/.

15. Alex Griswold, "We Shouldn't Cheer When Journalists Abandon Neutrality to Attack Trump," *Mediate,* August 8, 2016, http://www.mediaite.com/online/we-shouldnt-cheer-when-journalists-abandon-neutrality-to-attack-trump/.

16. Alexis Levinson and Tim Alberta, "Trump Bulldozes Blue Wall, Wins White House," *National Review,* November 9, 2016, http://www.nationalreview.com/article/442015/2016-election-donald-trump-wins-white-house-historic-upset.

17. Kevin D. Williamson, "In Dallas, Scenes from a GOP Funeral," *National Review,* May 15, 2016, http://www.nationalreview.com/article/435401/donald-trump-texas-republicans-his-candidacy-hurts-hispanic-outreach.

18. David French, "Working-Class Whites Have Moral Responsibilities—In Defense of Kevin Williamson," *National Review,* March 14, 2016, http://www.nationalreview.com/corner/432796/working-class-whites-have-moral-responsibilities-defense-kevin-williamson.

19. Victor Davis Hanson, "The Democrat Patient," *National Review,* January 31, 2017, http://www.nationalreview.com/article/444419/democratic-party-illness-correct-diagnosis-treatment-ignored.

NOTES

20. James Rainey, "New York Times Editor Dean Baquet on if the Press Has Been 'Too Timid' in Political Coverage," *Variety,* January 17, 2017, http://variety.com/2017/biz/news/dean-baquet-new-york-times-donald-trump-election-1201961137/.

21. Dan Gillmor, "Trump, Free Speech, and Why Journalists Must Be Activists," *Talking Points Memo,* December 4, 2016, http://talkingpointsmemo.com/cafe/trump-free-speech-and-why-journalists-must-be-activists.

22. Stephen J. A. Ward, "Three Duties in a Time of Trump," Center for Journalism Ethics, December 5, 2016, https://ethics.journalism.wisc.edu/2016/12/05/three-duties-in-a-time-of-trump/.

23. Scott Adams, "Be Careful What You Wish For (Especially if It Is Hitler)," *Scott Adams' Blog,* January 29, 2017, http://blog.dilbert.com/post/156540315831/be-careful-what-you-wish-for-especially-if-it-is.

CHAPTER 3: DON'T SHOOT FIRST

1. Patrick J. Buchanan, Address to the Republican National Convention, delivered 17 August 1992, Houston, Texas, http://www.americanrhetoric.com/speeches/patrickbuchanan1992rnc.htm.

2. Ibid.

3. The American Presidency Project, http://www.presidency.ucsb.edu/ws/?pid=25968.

4. Joel Siegel, "Bush Curries N.Y. Favor Blasts GOP Right Wing Again on Social Issues," *New York Daily News,* October 6, 1999, http://www.nydailynews.com/archives/news/bush-curries-n-y-favor-blasts-gop-wing-social-issues-article-1.856056.

5. Robert H. Bork, "Slouching Toward Bush Won't Save Us From Gomorrah," *Wall Street Journal,* October 11, 1999, http://www.wsj.com/articles/SB93957468882618348.

6. Tobin Harshaw, "Kennedy, Bork and the Politics of Judicial Destruction," *New York Times* Opinionator, August 28, 2009, https://opinionator.blogs.nytimes.com/2009/08/28/weekend-opinionator-kennedy-bork-and-the-politics-of-judicial-destruction/?_r=0.

7. William F. Buckley, "Presidential Candidates Drone On, Saying Nothing, So Nobody Pays Attention," UPI, reprinted in the *Sun Sentinel,* May 13, 1992, http://articles.sun-sentinel.com/1992-05-13/news/9202080155_1_candidates-los-angeles-money.

8. Ballotpedia, "California Affirmative Action, Proposition 209 (1996)," https://ballotpedia.org/California_Affirmative_Action,_Proposition_209_(1996).

9. Ballotpedia, "California Proposition 187, Illegal Aliens Ineligible for Public Benefits (1994)," https://ballotpedia.org/California_Proposition_187,_Illegal_Aliens_Ineligible_for_Public_Benefits_(1994).

10. Ballotpedia, "California Proposition 227, the 'English in Public Schools' Initiative (1998)," https://ballotpedia.org/California_Proposition_227,_the_%22English_in_Public_Schools%22_Initiative_(1998).

11. "Remarks by the President upon Arrival," The White House, Office of the Press Secretary, September 16, 2001, https://georgewbush-whitehouse.archives.gov/news/releases/2001/09/20010916-2.html.

12. Joe Meacham, "FDR's D-Day Prayer," *Time,* June 5, 2014, http://time.com/2826476/fdr-d-day-prayer/.

13. Toby Harden, "Bin Laden Is Wanted: Dead or Alive, Says Bush," *Telegraph,* September 18, 2001, http://www.telegraph.co.uk/news/worldnews/asia/afghanistan/1340895/Bin-Laden-is-wanted-dead-or-alive-says-Bush.html.

14. Alexander Mooney, "Bush: 'I Regret Saying Some Things I Shouldn't Have Said,'" CNN, November 11, 2008, http://www.cnn.com/2008/POLITICS/11/11/bush.post.presidency/.

223

15. "Backgrounder: The President's Quotes on Islam," The White House, https://georgewbush-whitehouse.archives.gov/infocus/ramadan/islam.html.

16. Ibid.

17. Ibid.

18. NRO, "Enforcement First," *National Review,* June 19, 2006, http://www.nationalreview.com/article/217972/enforcement-first-nro-primary-document.

19. Michelle Malkin, *Invasion: How America Still Welcomes Terrorists, Criminals, and Other Foreign Menaces to Our Shores* (Washington, DC: Regnery, 2002).

20. Tim Harris, "Trump to Megyn Kelly: I Don't Have Time For Political Correctness and Neither Does This Country," *RealClear Politics,* August 6, 2015, http://www.realclearpolitics.com/video/2015/08/06/trump_to_megyn_kelly_i_dont_have_time_for_political_correctness_and_neither_does_this_country.html.

21. Adam Edelman, "A look at Trump's most outrageous comments about Mexicans as he attempts damage control by visiting with country's president," *New York Daily News*, August 31, 2016, http://www.nydailynews.com/news/politics/trump-outrageous-comments-mexicans-article-1.2773214.

22. Larry O'Connor, "Bennett: #NeverTrump-ers put vanity above country; 'Terrible case of moral superiority'," Hot Air, August 19, 2016, http://hotair.com/archives/2016/08/19/bennett-nevertrump-ers-put-vanity-above-country-terrible-case-of-moral-superiority/.

23. https://twitter.com/charlesmurray/status/766451904528445440.

CHAPTER 4: CONSERVATIVE STOCKHOLM SYNDROME

1. Laura Lambert, "Stockholm syndrome," *Encyclopaedia Brittanica,* November 27, 2016, https://www.britannica.com/topic/Stockholm-syndrome.

2. Rafael Romo, "What Nevada Showed about Trump's Hispanic Support—and What It Didn't," CNN, February 25, 2016, http://www.cnn.com/2016/02/25/politics/donald-trump-hispanic-latino-voters/.

3. William Buckley during ABC's coverage of the 1968 Democratic convention in Chicago, https://www.youtube.com/watch?time_continue=1&v=nYymnxoQnf8.

4. Dereh Gregorian, "Not One 'Buck'ley for You!" *New York Post,* October 2, 2008, http://nypost.com/2008/10/02/not-one-buckley-for-you/.

5. Chuck Raasch and Christine Byers, "Michael Brown's Mother Appears at Democratic National Convention, Prompting Police Ire," *St. Louis Post-Dispatch,* July 27, 2016, http://www.stltoday.com/news/local/metro/michael-brown-s-mother-appears-at-democratic-national-convention-prompting/article_4b4e6e1a-55c7-5267-828a-e74472b0a7ee.html.

6. Peggy Noonan, "The Year of the Reticent Voter," *Wall Street Journal,* September 22, 2016, https://www.wsj.com/articles/the-year-of-the-reticent-voter-1474586866.

7. Miriam Wasser, "Arizona Republican Debate Viewers Agree on One Thing: Hillary Should Be Worried," *Phoenix New Times,* September 17, 2015, http://www.phoenixnewtimes.com/news/arizona-republican-debate-viewers-agree-on-one-thing-hillary-should-be-worried-7666968.

8. Will Drabold, "Watch Donald Trump Jr. Speak at the Republican Convention," *Time,* July 19, 2016, http://time.com/4414200/republican-convention-donald-trump-jr-speech-transcript-video/.

9. Jacob Weisberg, "The Road to Reagandom," *Slate,* January 8, 2016, http://www.slate.com/articles/news_and_politics/politics/2016/01/ronald_reagan_s_conservative_conversion_as_spokesman_for_general_electric.html.

CHAPTER 5: THE RISE AND FALL OF THE SUBTEXT

1. Whit Stillman, Barcelona, Barcelona Films and Castlerock Entertainment, 1994, http://www.imdb.com/title/tt0109219/quotes.

2. Leo Strauss, "How to Study Medieval Philosophy," Lecture to be delivered on May 16, 1944, at the Fourth Institute of Biblical and Post-Biblical Studies, http://wyclif.wz.cz/text/Strauss.Leo..How%20to%20Study%20Medieval%20Philosophy.pdf.

3. Leo Strauss, *What Is Political Philosophy* (Chicago: University of Chicago Press, 1959), 67.

4. Chris Buskirk, "Scholars & Writers for Trump," September 28, 2016, https://amgreatness.com/2016/09/28/writes-scholars-for-trump/.

5. Brad Todd, "Dear Journalists: Stop Taking Trump Literally," CNN, November 28, 2016, http://www.cnn.com/2016/11/28/opinions/journalists-stop-taking-trump-seriously-todd/.

6. Tim Hains, "CNN's Van Jones Speaks with Obama Voters Who Switched to Trump," *RealClear Politics,* December 7, 2016, http://www.realclearpolitics.com/video/2016/12/07/van_jones_speaks_with_obama_voters_who_switched_to_trump.html.

7. Ibid.

8. Ibid.

9. Ibid.

10. Ibid.

11. Barton Swaim, "A Trump Achievement That Everyone Can Cheer," *Wall Street Journal,* January 13, 2017, http://www.wsj.com/articles/a-trump-achievement-that-everyone-can-cheer-1484348389.

12. Rod Dreher, "Trump: Tribune of Poor White People," *American Conservative,* July 22, 2016, http://www.theamericanconservative.com/dreher/trump-us-politics-poor-whites/.

13. Ibid.

14. Nico Pitney, "Obama's Nomination Victory Speech in St. Paul," *Huffington Post,* November 5, 2008, http://www.huffingtonpost.com/2008/06/03/obamas-nomination-victory_n_105028.html.

15. https://twitter.com/KariLakeFox10/status/825952941391564800.

16. Dan Riehl, "After Getting Everything Wrong in 2016, Stephen Hayes Elevated to Editor-in-Chief at the Weekly Standard," *Breitbart,* December 18, 2016, http://www.breitbart.com/big-journalism/2016/12/18/after-getting-everything-wrong-in-2016-stephen-hayes-elevated-to-editor-in-chief-at-the-weekly-standard/.

17. https://twitter.com/EliotACohen/status/765738531784273920.

CHAPTER 6: IDENTITY GROUP POLITICS

1. Angelo M. Codevilla, The Ruling Class: How They Corrupted America & What We Can Do About It (New York: Beaufort Books, 2010).

2. Publius Decius Mus, "The Flight 93 Election," *American Greatness,* September 5, 2016, https://amgreatness.com/2016/09/05/flight-93-election/.

3. Michael Warren, "Kristol: Trump Is 'Discrediting Conservatism,'" *Weekly Standard,* August 12, 2016, http://www.weeklystandard.com/kristol-trump-is-discrediting-conservatism/article/2003815.

4. Blake Neff, "HuffPo Announces Plans To Bash Trump In EVERY Article About Him," *Daily Caller,* January 28, 2016, http://dailycaller.com/2016/01/28/huffpo-announces-plans-to-bash-trump-in-every-article-about-him/#ixzz4XaMiUvYL.

5. Bret Stephens, "The Donald and the Demagogues," *Wall Street Journal,* August 31, 2015, https://www.wsj.com/articles/the-donald-and-the-demagogues-1441064072.

6. "Donald Trump Is a Scam. Evangelical Voters Should Back Away," *Christian Post,* February 29, 2016, http://www.christianpost.com/news/donald-trump-scam-evangelical-voters-back-away-cp-editorial-158813/.

7. Tocqueville, *Democracy in America*—Volume I, Part II, Chapter 7.

8. Victor Davis Hanson, "The Democrat Patient," *National Review,* January 31, 2017, http://www.nationalreview.com/article/444419/democratic-party-illness-correct-diagnosis-treatment-ignored.

9. Craig Mills, "Here's Why Democrats Must Not Abandon Identity Politics," *Daily Beast,* December 21, 2016, www.thedailybeast.com/articles/2016/12/21/here-s-why-democrats-must-not-abandon-identity-politics.html.

10. Chris Buskirk, "How Checklist Conservatism Failed America," *American Greatness,* October 4, 2016, https://amgreatness.com/2016/10/04/checklist-conservatism-failed-america/.

11. Larry P. Arnn, "A More American Conservatism," *Imprimis,* December 2016, Vol. 45, No. 12, https://imprimis.hillsdale.edu/a-more-american-conservatism/3/.

CHAPTER 7: UTOPIANISM

1. Ben Johnson, "58,586,256 abortions since Roe v. Wade: New National Right to Life Report," *Life Site News,* January 14, 2016, https://www.lifesitenews.com/news/58586256-abortions-since-roe-v.-wade-new-national-right-to-life-report.

2. Gregory Dart, *Rousseau, Robespierre and English Romanticism* (New York: Cambridge University Press, 1999), 68.

3. Jean-Jacques Rousseau (1754), "Discourse on the Origin of Inequality, part two," *The Basic Political Writings* (Indianapolis: Hackett Publishing, 2012), 64.

4. Ibid.

5. This can be seen as beginning with the Noahic covenant in Genesis 8:20 - 9:17.An enlightening exploration of the subject can be found in theologian Dr. David VanDrunen's book *Natural Law and the Two Kingdoms.*

6. Ron Kampeas, "Neoconservative Norman Podhoretz Backs Donald Trump," *Forward,* September 9, 2016, http://forward.com/news/breaking-news/349547/neoconservative-norman-podhoretz-backs-donald-trump/.

7. Obituary of Jeane Kirkpatrick, *Economist,* December 19, 2006, http://www.economist.com/node/8447241.

8. Bret Stephens, "The GOP's Mexico Derangement," *Wall Street Journal,* June 6, 2016, https://www.wsj.com/articles/the-gops-mexico-derangement-1465254607.

9. Obituary of Jeane Kirkpatrick, *Economist,* December 19, 2006, http://www.economist.com/node/8447241.

10. http://archive.frontpagemag.com/readArticle.aspx?ARTID=1096.

11. Dave Burke, "92% of Left-Wing Activists Live with Their Parents and One in Three Is Unemployed, Study of Berlin Protesters Finds," *Daily Mail,* February 7, 2017, http://www.dailymail.co.uk/news/article-4200272/92-Berlin-left-wing-activists-live-parents.html.

12. TK

CHAPTER 8: AMERICA FIRST?

1. David E. Sanger, "With Echoes of the '30s, Trump Resurrects a Hard-Line Vision of 'America First,'" *New York Times,* January 20, 2017, https://www.nytimes.com/2017/01/20/us/politics/trump-resurrects-dark-definition-of-america-first-vision.html.

2. Bill Kristol interviewing Charles Murray, American Enterprise Institute, "It Came Apart: What's Next for a Fractured Culture?" https://www.youtube.com/watch?v=bs0h9ieLPyw.

3. Alexander Hamilton (Lucius Crassus), "Examination of Jefferson's Message to Congress of December 7, 1801," viii, January 7, 1802, in Henry Cabot Lodge, ed., *The Works of Alexander Hamilton*, Vol. 8 (New York: Putnam's, 1904).

4. Jonah Goldberg, "What Trump Means When He Says, 'America First,'" *National Review,* January 25, 2017, http://www.nationalreview.com/article/444211/donald-trump-america-first-slogan-stands-nationalist-identity.

5. Abraham Lincoln, "Electric Cord Speech, Chicago, Illinois," July 10, 1858, *Vindicating the Founders,* http://www.vindicatingthefounders.com/library/electric-cord-speech.html.

6. https://twitter.com/BillKristol/status/822496003391705089.

7. "Decius Out of the Darkness: A Q&A with Michael Anton," *American Greatness*, February 12, 2017, https://amgreatness.com/2017/02/12/decius-darkness-qa-michael-anton/.

CHAPTER 9: WISE FOREIGN POLICY

1. Krishnadev Calamur, "A Short History of 'America First,'" *Atlantic,* January 21, 2017, https://www.theatlantic.com/politics/archive/2017/01/trump-america-first/514037/.

2. Susan Dunn, "Trump's 'America First' Has Ugly Echoes from U.S. History," CNN, April 28, 2016, http://www.cnn.com/2016/04/27/opinions/trump-america-first-ugly-echoes-dunn/.

3. http://www.pbs.org/wgbh/amex/lindbergh/sfeature/fallen.html.

4. Krishnadev Calamur, "A Short History of 'America First,'" *Atlantic,* January 21, 2017, https://www.theatlantic.com/politics/archive/2017/01/trump-america-first/514037/.

5. Interview with Presidential Candidate Donald Trump, CNN Transcript, February 28, 2016, http://www.cnn.com/TRANSCRIPTS/1602/28/sotu.01.html.

6. Aaron Morrison, "David Duke's Donald Trump Endorsement Never Happened, Former KKK Grand Wizard Says," *International Business Times*, March 2, 2016, http://www.ibtimes.com/david-dukes-donald-trump-endorsement-never-happened-former-kkk-grand-wizard-says-2329067.

7. Stephanie Butnick, "Another Jewish Trump Wedding for the Books," *Tablet,* November 10, 2014, http://www.tabletmag.com/scroll/186935/another-jewish-trump-wedding-for-the-books.

8. Maya Shwayder, "Donald Trump, Big In Israel, Endorses Prime Minister Benjamin Netanyahu," *International Business Times,* January 1, 2015, http://www.ibtimes.com/donald-trump-big-israel-endorses-prime-minister-benjamin-netanyahu-1017172.

9. D'Angelo Gore, "What's Trump's Position on NATO?" FactCheck.org, May 11, 2016, http://www.factcheck.org/2016/05/whats-trumps-position-on-nato/.

10. Ibid.

11. Robert C. O'Brien, "Trump Just Keeps Winning: America's Allies Are Boosting Defense Spending," *National Interest,* December 8, 2016, http://nationalinterest.org/blog/the-buzz/trump-just-keeps-winning-americas-allies-are-boosting-18665.

12. Karl Rove, "The President's Apology Tour," *Wall Street Journal,* April 23, 2009, https://www.wsj.com/articles/SB124044156269345357.

13. Toby Harnden, "Barack Obama: 'Arrogant US Has Been Dismissive' to Allies," *Telegraph,* April 3, 2009, http://www.telegraph.co.uk/news/worldnews/barackobama/5100338/Barack-Obama-arrogant-US-has-been-dismissive-to-allies.html.

14. Ibid.

15. Barack Obama, "The President's News Conference in Strasbourg," *American Presidency Project,* April 4, 2009, http://www.presidency.ucsb.edu/ws/?pid=85959.

16. Sarah Begley, "Garrison Keillor to Say So Long to Lake Wobegon," *Time,* July 20, 2015, http://time.com/3965277/garrison-keillor-retiring/.

17. Joselyn King, "During Speech in St. Clairsville, Donald Trump Says America Has to Win Again," *Intelligencer,* June 29, 2016, http://www.theintelligencer.net/news/top-headlines/2016/06/during-speech-in-st-clairsville-donald-trump-says-america-has-to-win-again/.

18. "Ronald Reagan and the United Nations: Diplomacy Without Apology," Reagan Foundation, http://home.reaganfoundation.org/site/DocServer/ReaganMomentsEssay-Diplomacy-Without-Apology.pdf?docID=1824.

19. Ryan Lizza, "Leading from Behind," *New Yorker*, April 26, 2011, http://www.newyorker.com/news/news-desk/leading-from-behind.

CHAPTER 10: THE END OF HISTORY

1. Bill Chappell, "President Obama Slams 'Yapping' Over 'Radical Islam' and Terrorism," NPR's the Two-Way, June 14, 2016, http://www.npr.org/sections/thetwo-way/2016/06/14/482041137/president-obama-slams-yapping-over-radical-islam-and-terrorism.

2. Larisa Epatko, "Obama Explains Why He Doesn't Use 'Radical Islam,'" PBS Newshour, June 14, 2016, http://www.pbs.org/newshour/rundown/watch-live-obama-statement-on-countering-violent-extremism/.

3. "Full Speech: Donald Trump Addresses Radical Islamic Terrorism," *The Hill* (blog), August 15, 2016, http://thehill.com/blogs/pundits-blog/presidential-campaign/291498-full-transcript-donald-trump-addresses-radical.

4. Ibid.

5. Ibid.

6. "Inaugural Address: Trump's Full Speech," CNN, January 21, 2017, http://www.cnn.com/2017/01/20/politics/trump-inaugural-address/.

7. See Berman's book *Terrorism and Liberalism* (New York: W. W. Norton & Company, 2003). Berman intellectually and historically details the intellectual roots of Islamism as originating in twentieth century fascism.

8. Christopher Hitchens, "Defending Islamofascism," *Slate,* October 22, 2017, http://www.slate.com/articles/news_and_politics/fighting_words/2007/10/defending_islamofascism.html.

9. Ibid.

10. Norman Podhoretz, *World War IV: The Long Struggle Against Islamofascism* (New York: Vintage Books, 2007).

11. Ibid.

12. C. S. Lewis, *Mere Christianity,* Revised and Expanded Edition (New York: HarperOne, 2015), 28.

13. Francis Fukuyama, "The End of History?" *National Interest,* 1989, https://ps321.community.uaf.edu/files/2012/10/Fukuyama-End-of-history-article.pdf.

14. Francis Fukuyama, *The End of History and the Last Man* (New York: Avon Books, 1992), 46.

15. "Transcript: Obama's Speech Against the Iraq War," NPR, January 20, 2009, http://www.npr.org/templates/story/story.php?storyId=99591469.

16. Zane Albayati, "Hillary Clinton's Iraq War Vote Still Matters," *National Interest,* January 19, 2014, http://nationalinterest.org/commentary/hillary-clintons-iraq-war-vote-still-matters-9737.

17. David Rose, "Neo Culpa," *Vanity Fair,* November 3, 2006, http://www.vanityfair.com/news/2006/12/neocons200612.

18. Rowan Scarborough, "President Obama Ignored General's Pleas to Keep American Military forces in Iraq," June 15, 2014, http://www.washingtontimes.com/news/2014/jun/15/obama-ignored-generals-pleas-to-keep-american-forc/.

19. David Blair, "Video: Barack Obama 'Deeply Troubled' by Violence in Iran," *Telegraph,* June 17, 2009, http://www.telegraph.co.uk/news/worldnews/middleeast/iran/5556155/Iran-election-Barack-Obama-refuses-to-meddle-over-protests.html.

20. "Analysis: Obama Telling Mubarak: Time to Go," CBS News, February 5, 2011, http://www.cbsnews.com/news/analysis-obama-telling-mubarak-time-to-go/.

21. "Full Transcript of Obama's Middle East Speech," *Haaretz,* May 20, 2011, http://www.haaretz.com/middle-east-news/full-transcript-of-obama-s-middle-east-speech-1.363035.

22. Ben Wedeman, "Iraqis say Trump's Travel Ban Ignores Their Service to the US," CNN, February 2, 2017, http://www.cnn.com/2017/02/02/middleeast/iraq-trump-travel-ban/.

23. Andrew C. McCarthy, "The Senators Sway," *National Review,* April 2, 2011, http://www.nationalreview.com/node/263694/void(0)/*295*.

24. Tim Mak, "Leak: McCain Pushed to Arm Qadhafi," *Politico,* August 26, 2011, http://www.politico.com/story/2011/08/leak-mccain-pushed-to-arm-qadhafi-062114.

25. Ryan Lizza, "The Consequentialist," *New Yorker,* May 2, 2011, http://www.newyorker.com/magazine/2011/05/02/the-consequentialist.

26. Dominic Tierney, "The Legacy of Obama's 'Worst Mistake,'" *Atlantic,* April 15, 2016, https://www.theatlantic.com/international/archive/2016/04/obamas-worst-mistake-libya/478461/.

27. Barbara Starr, "First on CNN: US Bombs ISIS Camps in Libya, Dozens Killed," CNN, January 19, 2017, http://www.cnn.com/2017/01/19/politics/us-airstrikes-libya-isis/.

28. Azad Essa, "US Government Admits Deploying Troops in Yemen," *Al Jazeera*, May 7, 2016, http://www.aljazeera.com/news/2016/05/government-admits-deploying-troops-yemen-160507095524640.html.

29. "Obama Warns Syria not to Cross 'Red Line,'" CNN, August 21, 2012, http://www.cnn.com/2012/08/20/world/meast/syria-unrest/.

30. Salma Abdelaziz, Hala Gorani, and Ana Brickford, "U.N. Confirms Use of Chemical Weapons in Syria," CNN, December 12, 2013, http://www.cnn.com/2013/12/12/world/meast/syria-civil-war/.

31. Cristina Silva, "Syrian Civilian Death Toll 2016: ISIS, Assad Regime Fuel Refugee Crisis with Growing War," *International Business Times,* September 13, 2016, http://www.ibtimes.com/syrian-civilian-death-toll-2016-isis-assad-regime-fuel-refugee-crisis-growing-war-2415265.

32. Charles de Secondat, Baron de las Brede et de Montesquieu, "Selections from Considerations on the Causes of the Greatness of the Romans and Their Decline (1734)," http://www.rschindler.com/montesquieu.htm. http://www.rschindler.com/montesquieu.htm.

33. Plato, *The Republic,* Translated by Benjamin Jowett, http://classics.mit.edu/Plato/republic.2.i.html.

34. "Washington's Farewell Address 1796," The Avalon Project, Yale Law School, http://avalon.law.yale.edu/18th_century/washing.asp.

35. Patrick J. Garrity, "She Goes Not Abroad, in Search of Monsters to Destroy," Miller Center of Public Affairs, University of Virginia, March 2009, http://www.classicsofstrategy.com/She%20Goes%20Not%20Abroad.pdf.

36. Barack Obama in a private conversation, but "stuff" was not the word he used; reported in Jeffrey Goldberg, "The Obama Doctrine," *Atlantic,* April 2016, http://www.theatlantic.com/magazine/archive/2016/04/the-obama-doctrine/471525/.

37. "From Alexander Hamilton to James McHenry, 18 March 1799," National Archives, Founders Online, https://founders.archives.gov/documents/Hamilton/01-22-02-0344.

38. Glenn Kessler, "Spinning Obama's Reference to Islamic State as a 'JV' Team," *Washington Post,* September 3, 2014, https://www.washingtonpost.com/news/fact-checker/wp/2014/09/03/spinning-obamas-reference-to-isis-as-a-jv-team/?utm_term=.88a5c582ccae.

39. "Transcript: Donald Trump Expounds on His Foreign Policy Views," *New York Times,* March 26, 2016, https://www.nytimes.com/2016/03/27/us/politics/donald-trump-transcript.html.

40. Marisa Schultz and Bob Fredericks, "Donald Trump Explains How He'd Rule the World," *New York Post,* April 27, 2016, http://nypost.com/2016/04/27/trump-vows-to-put-america-first-in-foreign-policy-speech/.

41. "Full Speech: Donald Trump Addresses Radical Islamic Terrorism," *The Hill,* August 15, 2016, http://thehill.com/blogs/pundits-blog/presidential-campaign/291498-full-transcript-donald-trump-addresses-radical.

42. "Full Text: 2017 Donald Trump Inauguration Speech Transcript," *Politico,* January 20, 2017, http://www.politico.com/story/2017/01/full-text-donald-trump-inauguration-speech-transcript-233907.

CHAPTER 11: THE PURITY RITES

1. Clinton Rossiter, *Conservatism in America: The Thankless Persuasion* (New York: Vintage Books, 1962), vii.

2. William F. Buckley Jr., "Our Mission Statement," *National Review,* November 19, 1955, http://www.nationalreview.com/article/223549/our-mission-statement-william-f-buckley-jr.

3. Ibid.

4. Ibid.

5. Ibid.

6. Ibid.

7. George F. Will, "George Will: How Republicans Win by Losing," *St. Louis Post-Dispatch,* March 9, 2012, http://www.stltoday.com/news/opinion/columns/george-will/george-will-how-republicans-win-by-losing/article_f3d2508b-ff68-5fa6-9144-bc4a8e9ae99d.html.

8. "Goldwater's 1964 Acceptance Speech," *Washington Post,* http://www.washingtonpost.com/wp-srv/politics/daily/may98/goldwaterspeech.htm.

9. Ronald Reagan, "A Time for Choosing (aka 'The Speech')" aired October 27, 1964, http://www.americanrhetoric.com/speeches/ronaldreaganatimeforchoosing.htm.

10. Ibid.

11. Ibid.

12. Ibid.

13. Ibid.

14. Donald J. Trump, "Trump: Nevada, US Need a President Who Obeys Rule of Law," *Reno Gazette-Journal,* January 7, 2016, http://www.rgj.com/story/opinion/voices/2016/01/07/trump-nevada-us-need-president-who-obeys-rule-law/78422530/.

15. "Against Trump," *National Review,* January 21, 2016, http://www.nationalreview.com/article/430137/donald-trump-conservative-movement-menace.

16. "Conservatives against Trump," *National Review,* January 21, 2016, http://www.nationalreview.com/article/430126/donald-trump-conservatives-oppose-nomination.

17. "Against Trump," *National Review.*

18. Ibid.

19. Steve Krakauer, "Glenn Beck Gives To 'Hippie' Charities, and Other Things You'll Learn This Weekend," *Mediaite,* February 19, 2010, http://www.mediaite.com/online/glenn-beck-gives-to-hippie-charities-and-other-things-youll-learn-this-weekend/.

20. Nicholas Schmidle, "Glenn Beck Tries Out Decency," *New Yorker,* November 14, 2016, http://www.newyorker.com/magazine/2016/11/14/glenn-beck-tries-out-decency.

21. "Conservatives against Trump."

22. Ibid.

23. https://twitter.com/jpodhoretz/status/750477796703629312.

CHAPTER 12: FOLLOWING, NOT LEADING

1. Historical Federal Workforce Tables (1962–2014), U.S. Office of Personnel Management, https://www.opm.gov/policy-data-oversight/data-analysis-documentation/federal-employment-reports/historical-tables/total-government-employment-since-1962/.

2. Lionel Trilling, *New World Encyclopedia*, http://www.newworldencyclopedia.org/entry/Lionel_Trilling.

3. Michael Kranish, "Romney Followed Rapid Evolution as He Aimed Toward Presidency," *Boston Globe,* August 26, 2012, https://www.bostonglobe.com/news/nation/2012/08/25/views-political-evolution-mitt-romney-day-that-george-romney-declared-his-candidacy-for-governor-mitt-was-there-absorbing-his-father/A9eYm7uWdzyeyawGLBu3LL/story.html.

4. https://twitter.com/MittRomney/status/705434937336451072.

5. Alex Pfeiffer, "Bill Kristol Says 'Lazy' White Working Class Should Be Replaced By 'New Americans,'" *Daily Caller,* February 8, 2017, http://dailycaller.com/2017/02/08/bill-kristol-says-lazy-white-working-class-should-be-replaced-by-new-americans/.

6. Keith Boag, "Runaway Trump Train Divides Republican Party," CBS News, October 11, 2016, http://www.cbc.ca/m/touch/world/story/1.3798759.

7. Julia Hahn, "Paul Ryan Tells Sean Hannity He Will Not Support Any Cuts to Muslim Immigration: 'That's Not Who We Are,'" *Breitbart,* November 19, 2015, http://www.breitbart.com/big-government/2015/11/19/paul-ryan-tells-sean-hannity-will-not-support-cuts-muslim-immigration-thats-not/.

8. Andrew C. McCarthy, "The Republican Embrace of the Welfare State," *National Review,* October 26, 2013, http://www.nationalreview.com/article/362259/republican-embrace-welfare-state-andrew-c-mccarthy.

9. Kellan Howell, "EPA, FDA Stocking up on Body Armor During President Obama's Watch," *Washington Times,* January 7, 2016, http://www.washingtontimes.com/news/2016/jan/7/golden-hammer-feds-spending-millions-to-arm-agenci/.

10. "Armed EPA Raid in Alaska Sheds Light on 70 Fed Agencies with Armed Divisions," Fox News, September 14, 2013, http://www.foxnews.com/politics/2013/09/14/armed-epa-agents-in-alaska-shed-light-on-70-fed-agencies-with-armed-divisions.html.

11. Maura Reynolds, "Bush Says U.S. Must Spread Democracy," *Baltimore Sun,* November 7, 2003, http://www.baltimoresun.com/news/bal-te.bush07nov07-story.html.

12. Joel Kotkin, "In the Future We'll All Be Renters: America's Disappearing Middle Class," *Daily Beast,* August 10, 2014, http://www.thedailybeast.com/articles/2014/08/10/in-the-future-we-ll-all-be-renters-america-s-disappearing-middle-class.html.

13. Julie Segal, "5 Years After Dodd-Frank, U.S. Banks Dominate More than Ever," *Institutional Investor,* June 2, 2015, http://www.institutionalinvestor.com/article/3458500/asset-management-regulation/5-years-after-dodd-frank-us-banks-dominate-more-than-ever.html.

14. Andy Selepak, "Compassionate Conservatism for Illegal Immigrants," *Accuracy in Media,* March 25, 2007, http://www.aim.org/special-report/compassionate-conservatism-for-illegal-immigrants/.

15.	Jessica Taylor, "Mitt Romney Finally Takes Credit for Obamacare," *It's All Politics,* October 23, 2015, http://www.npr.org/sections/itsallpolitics/2015/10/23/451200436/mitt-romney-finally-takes-credit-for-obamacare.

16.	Angelo M. Codevilla, "After the Republic," *CRB Digital,* September 27, 2016, http://www.claremont.org/crb/basicpage/after-the-republic/.

17.	Joy Pullmann, "Iowa Bureaucrats Force Trans Bathrooms On Churches, Forbid Non-PC Preaching," *Federalist,* July 6, 2016, http://thefederalist.com/2016/07/06/iowa-bureaucrats-force-trans-bathrooms-on-churches-forbid-non-pc-preaching/.

18.	"End the Use of Religion to Discriminate," ACLU, https://www.aclu.org/feature/end-use-religion-discriminate.

CHAPTER 13: FIRST, ADMIT THERE IS A PROBLEM

1.	"Conservatives for Trump: A Symposium Featuring Scholars & Writers for Trump," *American Greatness,* September 28, 2016, https://amgreatness.com/2016/09/28/conservatives-for-trump-a-symposium-featuring-writers-and-scholars-for-trump/.

2.	Bruce Abramson, Ph.D., J.D., et al., "Statement of Unity, Scholars & Writers for America," October 30, 2016, http://scholarsandwritersforamerica.org.

3.	Ibid.

4.	William F. Buckley Jr., "Our Mission Statement," *National Review,* November 19, 1955, http://www.nationalreview.com/article/223549/our-mission-statement-william-f-buckley-jr.

5.	Phillip Bump, "For What He Spent per Delegate, Jeb Bush Could Have Bought 24 Trump Tower Apartments," *Washington Post,* July 20, 2016, https://www.washingtonpost.com/news/the-fix/wp/2016/07/20/how-much-each-republican-candidate-raised-for-every-vote-won/?utm_term=.7a0ceb24788a.

6.	Ibid.

7.	David Gelerneter, "Trump and the Emasculated Voter," *Wall Street Journal,* October 14, 2016, https://www.wsj.com/articles/trump-and-the-emasculated-voter-1476484865.

8.	Ibid.

9.	Ibid.

10.	Tom LoBiano and Ashley Killough, "Trump Pitches Black Voters: 'What the Hell Do You Have to Lose?'" August 19, 2016, http://www.cnn.com/2016/08/19/politics/donald-trump-african-american-voters/.

11.	"Conservatives for Trump: A Symposium Featuring Scholars & Writers for Trump," *American Greatness,* September 28, 2016, https://amgreatness.com/2016/09/28/conservatives-for-trump-a-symposium-featuring-writers-and-scholars-for-trump/.

12.	Ibid.

13.	Ibid.

14.	Ibid.

15.	Ibid.

16.	Ibid.

17.	Ibid.

18.	Ibid.

19.	Ibid.

20.	Ibid.

21. Jonathan Rauch, "Containing Trump," *Atlantic,* March 2007, https://www.theatlantic.com/magazine/archive/2017/03/containing-trump/513854/.

22. Richard Nixon, "Address Accepting the Presidential Nomination at the Republican National Convention in Miami Beach, Florida," *The American Presidency Project,* August 8, 1968, http://www.presidency.ucsb.edu/ws/?pid=25968.

23. "The Neo-Conservative Anguish Over Reagan's Foreign Policy," *New York Times* magazine, May 2, 1982, http://www.nytimes.com/1982/05/02/magazine/the-neo-conservative-anguish-over-reagan-s-foreign-policy.html?pagewanted=all.

CHAPTER 14: RESTORING ACCOUNTABILITY

1. https://twitter.com/FrankLuntz/status/796136199706574848?ref_src=twsrc%5Etfw.

2. "Read This Epic Timeline of Frank Luntz's Election Night Tweets . . . then Laugh!" http://ilovemyfreedom.org/read-epic-timeline-frank-luntzs-election-night-tweets-laugh/.

3. Ibid.

4. Karl Rove, "Rove: Sifting the Numbers for a Winner," *Wall Street Journal,* October 31, 2012, https://www.wsj.com/articles/SB10001424052970204846304578090820229096046.

5. Jessica Chia, "'I don't see it happening': Republican Strategist Karl Rove Says Trump is BOUND to Lose the Election as His Own Campaign Admits 'We are behind,'" *Daily Mail,* October 24, 2016, http://www.dailymail.co.uk/news/article-3865300/Republican-strategist-Karl-Rove-says-Trump-bound-lose-election.html#ixzz4YlToCCEg.

6. Karl Rove, "My Crystal-Ball Score—Plus 2016 Predictions," *Wall Street Journal,* January 6, 2016, https://www.wsj.com/articles/my-crystal-ball-scoreplus-2016-predictions-1452124623.

7. Ibid.

8. Callum Borchers, "The Wrongest Media Predictions about Donald Trump," *Washington Post,* November 9, 2016, https://www.washingtonpost.com/news/the-fix/wp/2016/11/09/the-wrongest-media-predictions-about-donald-trump/?utm_term=.6d759b030fde.

9. Ibid.

10. Ibid.

11. Ian Schwartz, "WSJ's Bret Stephens: 'Echo Chamber' in Republican Party 'Increasingly Divorced from Reality,'" *RealClear Politics,* August 8, 2016, http://www.realclearpolitics.com/video/2016/08/08/bret_stephens_echo_chamber_republican_party_increasingly_divorced_from_reality.html.

12. Stacey Dash, "9 times liberal pundits were WAY TOO confident in declaring a Hillary Clinton landslide," *Patheos,* November 16, 2016, http://www.patheos.com/blogs/staceydash/2016/11/9-times-liberal-pundits-were-way-too-confident-in-declaring-a-hillary-clinton-landslide/2/.

13. Ibid.

14. "Why I Voted for Trump," *Washington Post Opinion,* https://www.washingtonpost.com/graphics/opinions/trump-supporters-why-vote/.

15. Ibid.

16. Ibid.

17. Ibid.

18. Ibid.

19. Salena Zico, "How Trump won over a bar full of undecideds and Democrats," *New York Post,* September 26, 2016, http://nypost.com/2016/09/26/the-best-debate-takes-come-from-inside-the-bar/.

20. "MSNBC Surges to All-Time Highs in October 2016; Beats CNN in Weekday Prime for Third Straight Month," MSNBC Info, November 1, 2016, http://info.msnbc.com/_news/2016/11/01/36294039-msnbc-surges-to-all-time-highs-in-october-2016-beats-cnn-in-weekday-prime-for-third-straight-month.

CHAPTER 15: RELEARNING THE BASICS

1. John Jay, *The Federalist Papers,* No. 3, http://avalon.law.yale.edu/18th_century/fed03.asp.
2. John F. Kennedy, address to the Economic Club of New York, delivered 14 December 1962, Waldorf Astoria Hotel, New York, *American Rhetoric Online Speech Bank,* http://www.americanrhetoric.com/speeches/jfkeconomicclubaddress.html.
3. Louis Uchitelle, "Bush, Like Reagan in 1980, Seeks Tax Cuts to Stimulate the Economy," *New York Times,* September 22, 1988, http://www.nytimes.com/1988/09/22/us/bush-like-reagan-in-1980-seeks-tax-cuts-to-stimulate-the-economy.html?pagewanted=all.
4. Andrew Rosenthal, "The 1992 Campaign: White House; Bush Says Raising Taxes Was Biggest Blunder of His Presidency," March 4, 1992, http://www.nytimes.com/1992/03/04/us/1992-campaign-white-house-bush-says-raising-taxes-was-biggest-blunder-his.html?pagewanted=all.
5. Ronald Reagan, "Abortion and the Conscience of the Nation," *Human Life Review,* February 3, 1983, http://www.humanlifereview.com/abortion-and-the-conscience-of-the-nation-ronald-reagan-the-10th-anniversary-of-the-supreme-court-decision-in-roe-v-wade-is-a-good-time-for-us-to-pause-and-reflect-our-nationwide-policy-of-abortion-o/.
6. Ramesh Ponnuru, "Reaganism after Reagan," *New York Times,* February 17, 2013, http://www.nytimes.com/2013/02/18/opinion/updating-reaganomics.html.
7. "A Decade of CRB," The Claremont Institute, Winter/Spring 2010/11, https://web.archive.org/web/20110808083312/http://www.claremont.org/publications/crb/id.1795/article_detail.asp.
8. Harry V. Jaffa, "The American Founding as the Best Regime," The Claremont Institute, May 15, 2002.
9. Jeane Kirkpatrick, speech at 1984 Republican National Convention, Dallas, August 20, 1984, http://www.cnn.com/ALLPOLITICS/1996/conventions/san.diego/facts/GOP.speeches.past/84.kirkpatrick.shtml.
10. Harry V. Jaffe, *The False Prophets of American Conservatism: Rehnquist and Scalia* (Washington, DC: Claremont Institute, 2005).
11. Larry P. Arnn, "A More American Conservatism," *Imprimis,* December 2016, https://imprimis.hillsdale.edu/wp-content/uploads/2016/12/Imprimis-Arnn-Dec-2016.pdf.
12. Full transcript: President Donald Trump's news conference, February 17, 2017, http://www.cnn.com/2017/02/16/politics/donald-trump-news-conference-transcript/.

CHAPTER 16: THE WAY FORWARD

1. Peter Wehner, "Don't Be Complicit, Republicans," *New York Times* Op-Ed, May 10, 2017, https://www.nytimes.com/2017/05/10/opinion/james-comey-fired-fbi.html?_r=0.
2. Mark Bauerlein, "No Guilt This Time," *American Greatness*, May 9, 2017, https://amgreatness.com/2017/05/09/no-guilt-time/.

Index